QGIS Python Programming Cookbook

Second Edition

Master over 170 recipes that will help you turn QGIS from a desktop GIS tool into a powerful automated geospatial framework

Joel Lawhead

BIRMINGHAM - MUMBAI

QGIS Python Programming Cookbook

Second Edition

Copyright © 2017 Packt Publishing

All rights reserved. No part of this book may be reproduced, stored in a retrieval system, or transmitted in any form or by any means, without the prior written permission of the publisher, except in the case of brief quotations embedded in critical articles or reviews.

Every effort has been made in the preparation of this book to ensure the accuracy of the information presented. However, the information contained in this book is sold without warranty, either express or implied. Neither the author, nor Packt Publishing, and its dealers and distributors will be held liable for any damages caused or alleged to be caused directly or indirectly by this book.

Packt Publishing has endeavored to provide trademark information about all of the companies and products mentioned in this book by the appropriate use of capitals. However, Packt Publishing cannot guarantee the accuracy of this information.

First published: March 2015

Second edition: March 2017

Production reference: 1030317

Published by Packt Publishing Ltd.
Livery Place
35 Livery Street
Birmingham
B3 2PB, UK.
ISBN 978-1-78712-483-7

www.packtpub.com

Credits

Author

Joel Lawhead

Reviewer

Joshua Arnott

Commissioning Editor

Kunal Parikh

Acquisition Editor

Chaitanya Nair

Content Development Editor

Vikas Tiwari

Technical Editor

Subhalaxmi Nadar

Copy Editor

Muktikant Garimella

Project Coordinator

Sheejal Shah

Proofreader

Safis Editing

Indexer

Francy Puthiry

Graphics

Abhinash Sahu

Production Coordinator

Deepika Naik

About the Author

Joel Lawhead is a PMI-certified Project Management Professional (PMP), a certified Geographic Information Systems Professional, and the Chief Information Officer (CIO) for http://www.nvisionsolutions.com/, an award-winning firm specializing in geospatial technology integration and harsh-environment engineering. Joel builds geospatial systems for US government agencies, including NASA, NOAA, the US Department of Homeland Security, and the military. He also works with private organizations, including the National Oceans and Applications Research Center (NOARC) and The Ocean Cleanup. He has authored other books with Packt Publishing, including *Learning Geospatial Analysis with Python*, *QGIS Python Programming Cookbook*, and *Learning Geospatial Analysis with Python, Second Edition*. His cookbook recipes have been featured in two editions of the O'Reilly *Python Cookbook*. Joel began using Python in 1997 and combined it with geospatial software development in 2000. He is also the developer of the widely used open source Python Shapefile Library (PyShp) and maintains the geospatial technical blog, http://geospatial python.com/, and Twitter feed, @SpatialPython, discussing the use of Python within the geospatial industry. In 2011, Joel reverse-engineered and published the undocumented shapefile spatial indexing format and assisted fellow geospatial Python developer, Marc Pfister, in reversing the compression algorithm, allowing developers around the world to create better integrated and more robust geospatial applications involving shapefiles. In 2002, Joel received the international *Esri Special Achievement in GIS* award for his work on the Real-Time Emergency Action Coordination Tool (REACT) for emergency management using geospatial analysis.

This book would not be possible without the support of my beautiful family, including my wife, Julie, and four children, Lauren, Will, Lillie, and Lainie, who inspire everything I do. I would also like to acknowledge my employers and coworkers at http://www.nvisionsolutions.com/, *a bright, dynamic team of people dedicated to working together at the exciting bleeding-edge of geospatial technology. And finally, thank you to the excellent reviewers for this and my other books, especially Joshua Arnott, who patiently and faithfully burned clumsy sentences to the ground so that a more technically-correct phoenix could rise up the ranks of the Amazon category Top 100 list.*

About the Reviewer

Joshua Arnott is an environmental scientist with over five years of experience working in water management consultancy. His expertise lies in environmental modeling, with a focus on hydrology, water resources, and geoinformatics. He has contributed to several GIS-related open source projects, including QGIS and Shapely. He maintains a blog about programming and GIS at `https://snorfalorpagus.net/`, and he likes cats just as much as everyone else on the Internet.

www.PacktPub.com

For support files and downloads related to your book, please visit www.PacktPub.com.

Did you know that Packt offers eBook versions of every book published, with PDF and ePub files available? You can upgrade to the eBook version at www.PacktPub.com and as a print book customer, you are entitled to a discount on the eBook copy. Get in touch with us at service@packtpub.com for more details.

At www.PacktPub.com, you can also read a collection of free technical articles, sign up for a range of free newsletters and receive exclusive discounts and offers on Packt books and eBooks.

https://www.packtpub.com/mapt

Get the most in-demand software skills with Mapt. Mapt gives you full access to all Packt books and video courses, as well as industry-leading tools to help you plan your personal development and advance your career.

Why subscribe?

- Fully searchable across every book published by Packt
- Copy and paste, print, and bookmark content
- On demand and accessible via a web browser

Customer Feedback

Thanks for purchasing this Packt book. At Packt, quality is at the heart of our editorial process. To help us improve, please leave us an honest review on this book's Amazon page at https://www.amazon.com/dp/1787124835.

If you'd like to join our team of regular reviewers, you can e-mail us at customerreviews@packtpub.com. We award our regular reviewers with free eBooks and videos in exchange for their valuable feedback. Help us be relentless in improving our products!

Table of Contents

Preface

The open source geographic information system QGIS at version 2 now rivals even the most expensive commercial GIS software in both functionality and usability. It is also a showcase of the best geospatial open source technology available. It is not just a project in itself but the marriage of dozens of open source projects in a single, clean interface.

Geospatial technology is not just the application of technology to geography. It is a symphony of geography, mathematics, computer science, statistics, physics, and other fields. The underlying algorithms implemented by QGIS are so complex that only a handful of people in the world understand them all. Yet QGIS packages all of this complexity so well that school children, city managers, disease researchers, geologists, and many other professionals wield this powerful software with ease to make decisions that improve life on Earth.

But this book is about another feature of QGIS that makes it the best choice for geospatial work. QGIS has one of the most deeply integrated and well-designed Python interfaces of any software period. In the latest version, there is virtually no aspect of the program that is off-limits to Python, making it the largest geospatial Python library available. Almost without exception, the Python API, called PyQGIS, is consistent and predictable.

This book exploits the best features of QGIS to demonstrate over 170 reusable recipes that you can use to automate workflows in QGIS or build standalone GIS applications. Most recipes are very compact and have less than 20 lines of code. Even if you can't find the exact solution you are looking for, you should be able to get very close. This book covers a lot of ground and pulls together fragmented ideas and documentation scattered throughout the Internet as well as the results of many hours of experimenting at the edges of the PyQGIS API.

What this book covers

Chapter 1, *Automating QGIS*, provides a brief overview of the different ways of using Python with QGIS, including the QGIS Python Console, standalone applications, plugins, and the Script Runner plugin. This chapter also covers setting and retrieving application settings and a few other Python-specific features.

Chapter 2, *Querying Vector Data*, covers extracting information from vector data without changing the data using Python. Topics include measuring, loading data from a database, filtering data, and other related processes.

Chapter 3, *Editing Vector Data*, introduces creating and updating data to add new information. It also teaches you how to break datasets apart based on spatial or database attributes as well as combine datasets. This chapter also teaches you how to convert data into different formats, change projections, simplify data, and more.

Chapter 4, *Using Raster Data*, demonstrates recipes for using and transforming raster data to create derivative products. This chapter highlights the capability of QGIS as a raster-processing engine and not just a vector GIS.

Chapter 5, *Creating Dynamic Maps*, transitions into recipes for controlling QGIS as a whole to control map, project, and application-level settings. It includes recipes for accessing external web services and building custom map tools.

Chapter 6, *Composing Static Maps*, shows you how to create printed maps using the QGIS Map Composer. You will learn to place reference elements on a map as well as design elements such as logos.

Chapter 7, *Interacting with the User*, teaches you to control QGIS GUI elements created by the underlying Qt framework to create interactive input widgets for scripts, plugins, or standalone applications.

Chapter 8, *QGIS Workflows*, contains more advanced recipes that result in a finished product or an extended capability. These recipes target actual tasks that geospatial analysts or programmers encounter on the job.

Chapter 9, *Other Tips and Tricks*, contains interesting recipes that fall outside the scope of previous chapters. Many of these recipes demonstrate multiple concepts within a single recipe that you may find useful for a variety of tasks.

What you need for this book

You will need the following software to complete all of the recipes in this book. If a specific version is not available, use the most recent version.

- QGIS 2.18
- Python 2.7.6 (should be included with QGIS itself)
- IBM Java 8 JDK
- IBM Eclipse Neon 4.6.0 or higher
- Eclipse PyDev 5.5.0
- Google Earth 7.1.7.2602 or higher

Who this book is for

This book is for geospatial analysts or programmers at any experience level who would like to learn more about controlling QGIS using Python. A basic knowledge of Python is essential and some experience with QGIS is helpful but not required.

Sections

In this book, you will find several headings that appear frequently (Getting ready, How to do it, How it works, There's more, and See also).

To give clear instructions on how to complete a recipe, we use these sections as follows:

Getting ready

This section tells you what to expect in the recipe, and describes how to set up any software or any preliminary settings required for the recipe.

How to do it...

This section contains the steps required to follow the recipe.

How it works...

This section usually consists of a detailed explanation of what happened in the previous section.

There's more...

This section consists of additional information about the recipe in order to make the reader more knowledgeable about the recipe.

See also

This section provides helpful links to other useful information for the recipe.

Conventions

In this book, you will find a number of text styles that distinguish between different kinds of information. Here are some examples of these styles and an explanation of their meaning.

Code words in text, database table names, folder names, filenames, file extensions, pathnames, dummy URLs, user input, and Twitter handles are shown as follows: "Open the `startup.py` file you created."

A block of code is set as follows:

```
import os
os.getcwd()
```

Any command-line input or output is written as follows:

```
sudo apt-get update
```

New terms and **important words** are shown in bold. Words that you see on the screen, for example, in menus or dialog boxes, appear in the text like this: "From the **Window** menu, select **Preferences**."

 Warnings or important notes appear in a box like this.

 Tips and tricks appear like this.

Reader feedback

Feedback from our readers is always welcome. Let us know what you think about this book-what you liked or disliked. Reader feedback is important for us as it helps us develop titles that you will really get the most out of.

To send us general feedback, simply e-mail feedback@packtpub.com, and mention the book's title in the subject of your message.

If there is a topic that you have expertise in and you are interested in either writing or contributing to a book, see our author guide at www.packtpub.com/authors .

Customer support

Now that you are the proud owner of a Packt book, we have a number of things to help you to get the most from your purchase.

Downloading the example code

You can download the example code files for this book from your account at http://www.packtpub.com. If you purchased this book elsewhere, you can visit http://www.packtpub.com/support and register to have the files e-mailed directly to you.

You can download the code files by following these steps:

1. Log in or register to our website using your e-mail address and password.
2. Hover the mouse pointer on the **SUPPORT** tab at the top.
3. Click on **Code Downloads & Errata**.
4. Enter the name of the book in the **Search** box.
5. Select the book for which you're looking to download the code files.
6. Choose from the drop-down menu where you purchased this book from.
7. Click on **Code Download**.

You can also download the code files by clicking on the **Code Files** button on the book's webpage at the Packt Publishing website. This page can be accessed by entering the book's name in the **Search** box. Please note that you need to be logged in to your Packt account.

Once the file is downloaded, please make sure that you unzip or extract the folder using the latest version of:

- WinRAR / 7-Zip for Windows
- Zipeg / iZip / UnRarX for Mac
- 7-Zip / PeaZip for Linux

The code bundle for the book is also hosted on GitHub at
`https://github.com/PacktPublishing/QGIS-Python-Programming-Cookbook-Second-Edit`
`ion`. We also have other code bundles from our rich catalog of books and videos available at
`https://github.com/PacktPublishing/`. Check them out!

Downloading the color images of this book

We also provide you with a PDF file that has color images of the screenshots/diagrams used
in this book. The color images will help you better understand the changes in the output.
You can download this file from
`http://www.packtpub.com/sites/default/files/downloads/QGISPythonProgrammingCook`
`bookSecondEdition_ColorImages.pdf`.

Errata

Although we have taken every care to ensure the accuracy of our content, mistakes do
happen. If you find a mistake in one of our books-maybe a mistake in the text or the code-
we would be grateful if you could report this to us. By doing so, you can save other readers
from frustration and help us improve subsequent versions of this book. If you find any
errata, please report them by visiting `http://www.packtpub.com/submit-errata`, selecting
your book, clicking on the **Errata Submission Form** link, and entering the details of your
errata. Once your errata are verified, your submission will be accepted and the errata will
be uploaded to our website or added to any list of existing errata under the Errata section of
that title.

To view the previously submitted errata, go to `https://www.packtpub.com/books/conten`
`t/support`and enter the name of the book in the search field. The required information will
appear under the **Errata** section.

Piracy

Piracy of copyrighted material on the Internet is an ongoing problem across all media. At
Packt, we take the protection of our copyright and licenses very seriously. If you come
across any illegal copies of our works in any form on the Internet, please provide us with
the location address or website name immediately so that we can pursue a remedy.

Please contact us at `copyright@packtpub.com` with a link to the suspected pirated material.

We appreciate your help in protecting our authors and our ability to bring you valuable content.

Questions

If you have a problem with any aspect of this book, you can contact us at `questions@packtpub.com`, and we will do our best to address the problem.

1
Automating QGIS

In this chapter, we will focus on the tools needed to write Python scripts for the PyQGIS framework. We will cover the following recipes:

- Installing QGIS 2.18 for development
- Using the QGIS Python console for interactive control
- Automatically starting the Python console
- Using Python's Script Runner plugin
- Setting up your QGIS IDE
- Debugging QGIS Python scripts
- Navigating the PyQGIS API
- Creating a traditional QGIS plugin
- Creating a Processing Toolbox plugin
- Distributing a plugin
- Building a standalone application
- Storing and reading global preferences
- Storing and reading project preferences
- Accessing the script path from within your script

Introduction

This chapter explains how to automate QGIS using Python. In addition to setting this up, we will also configure the free Eclipse **Integrated Development Environment** (**IDE**) along with the **PyDev** plugin to make writing, editing, and debugging scripts easier. We will also learn the basics of different types of QGIS Python scripts through the PyQGIS API. Finally, we'll examine some core QGIS plugins that significantly extend its capability.

Installing QGIS 2.18 for development

QGIS has a set of Python modules and libraries that can be accessed from the Python console within it. However, they can also be accessed from outside QGIS to write standalone applications. First, you must make sure that PyQGIS is installed on your platform, then set up some required environment variables.

In this recipe, we will walk you through the additional steps required beyond the normal installation process to prepare your system for development. The steps for each platform are provided, which also include the different styles of Linux package managers. The version of QGIS in your Linux package manager may be older. You can find additional detailed installation instructions at `https://www.qgis.org/en/site/forusers/alldownlo ads.html`.

Getting ready

QGIS uses different installation methods for Windows, GNU/Linux, and Mac OS X. The Windows installer installs everything you need for Python development, including Python itself.

However, on both Linux distributions and Mac OS X, you may need to manually install the Python modules to complete the installation process. On Mac OS X, you can download installers for some commonly used Python modules with QGIS; refer to `http://www.kyngchaos.com/software/python`.

How to do it...

On Linux, you have an option to either compile from the source or just specify the Python interface to be installed through your package manager.

Installing PyQGIS using the Debian package manager

1. For Linux distributions based on the Debian Linux package manager, which includes Ubuntu and Debian, use the following command in a shell:

```
sudo apt-get update
```

2. Next, install the QGIS, PyQGIS, and QGIS GRASS plugins:

```
sudo apt-get install qgis python-qgis qgis-plugin-grass
```

Installing PyQGIS using the RPM package manager

1. For Linux distributions based on the **Red Hat Package Manager** (**RPM**), first updatethe package manager as follows:

```
sudo yum update
```

2. Then, install the packages for the QGIS, PyQGIS, and QGIS GRASS plugins:

```
sudo yum install qgis qgis-python qgis-grass
```

Setting the environment variables

Now we need to set PYTHONPATH to the PyQGIS directory. At the same time, append the path to this directory to the PATH variable so that you can use the PyQGIS modules with an external IDE.

Setting the environment variables on Windows

1. Set the PYTHONPATH variable in a command prompt to the bin directory of the QGIS installation:

```
set PYTHONPATH="C:\Program Files\QGIS 2.18\bin"
```

2. Next, append QGIS's bin directories to the system's PATH variable:

```
set PATH="C:\Program Files\QGIS 2.18\bin";"C:\Program Files\QGIS
2.18";%PATH%
```

Setting environment variables on Linux

1. Set the `PYTHONPATH` variable in a command prompt to the `bin` directory of the QGIS installation:

   ```
   export PYTHONPATH=/usr/share/qgis/python
   ```

2. Now append the QGIS shared library directory to a runtime search path. Note that this location can vary depending on your system configuration:

   ```
   export LD_LIBRARY_PATH=/usr/share/qgis/python
   ```

How it works...

The QGIS installation process and package managers set up the Python module's configuration in a way that it becomes internal to QGIS. When you use the Python console inside QGIS, it knows where all the PyQGIS modules are. However, if you want to use the PyQGIS API outside it by using a system Python installation on either Windows or Linux, it would be necessary for you set some system variables so that Python could find the required PyQGIS modules.

There's more...

This recipe uses the default QGIS paths on each platform. If you aren't sure which PyQGIS path is for your system, you can figure this out from the Python console in QGIS.

Finding the PyQGIS path on Windows

The libraries on Windows, as opposed to other platforms, are stored in a different location. To locate the path, you need to check the current working directory of the Python console:

1. Start QGIS.
2. Select **Python Console** from the **Plugins** menu, which will appear in the lower-right corner of the QGIS application window, as shown in the following screenshot. You can also use the keyboard shortcut *Control+Alt+P* to do this:

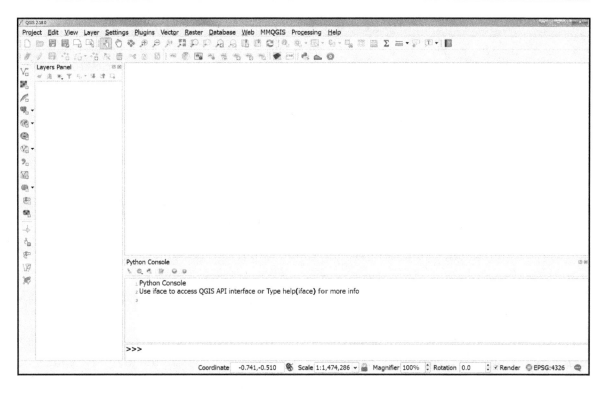

3. Use the `os` module to get the current working directory:

```
import os
os.getcwd()
```

4. Verify that the current working directory of the Python console is returned.

Finding the location of the QGIS Python installation on other platforms

Perform the following steps to find the path needed for this recipe on all the other platforms:

1. Start QGIS.
2. Start the QGIS Python console.

3. Use the `sys` module to locate the PyQGIS path

```
import sys
sys.path
```

4. Python will return a list of paths.
5. Find the path that ends in `/python`, which is the location of the Python installation used by QGIS.

Using the QGIS Python console for interactive control

The Python console allows you to interactively control QGIS; you can test out ideas or just do some quick automation. The console is the simplest way to use the API.

How to do it...

In the following steps, we'll open the console, create a vector layer in the memory, and display it on the map:

1. Start QGIS.
2. From the **Plugins** menu, select **Python Console**.
3. The following code will create a point on the map canvas:

```
layer =  QgsVectorLayer('Point?crs=epsg:4326','MyPoint',"memory")
pr = layer.dataProvider()
pt = QgsFeature()
point1 = QgsPoint(20,20)
pt.setGeometry(QgsGeometry.fromPoint(point1))
pr.addFeatures([pt])
layer.updateExtents()
QgsMapLayerRegistry.instance().addMapLayers([layer])
```

How it works...

This example uses a memory layer to avoid interacting with any data on either a disk or a network so as to keep things simple. Notice that when we declare the layer type, we add the parameter for the **coordinate reference system** (**CRS**) as EPSG:4326. Without this declaration, QGIS will prompt you to choose one. There are three parts, or levels, of abstraction even to create a single point on the map canvas, as shown here:

1. First, create a layer that is of the type geometry. Next, reference a data provider to accept the data source.
2. Then, create a generic feature object, followed by the point geometry.
3. Next, we add the feature to the layer via the underlying data provider, then add the layer to the map canvas.

The layer type is memory, meaning that you can define the geometry and attributes in the code itself rather than an external data source. In this recipe, we just define the geometry and skip defining any attributes.

Automatically starting the Python console

As you become familiar with programming QGIS using Python, you'll want the Python console to always be available in QGIS. So, in this recipe, we'll add a Python startup script to QGIS to make sure the console starts when QGIS does.

Getting ready

First, you need the `startup.py` file, which QGIS will read at startup. You'll be able to use this file to customize different aspects of QGIS:

1. In your user directory, locate the hidden `.qgis2` folder.
2. Your user folder is typically located in `~/.qgis2` on Linux and OSX and `C:\Users\<username>\.qgis2` on Windows, which you can also access the `%USERPROFILE%` environment variable.
3. Create a Python file named `startup.py`.

How to do it...

1. Open the `startup.py` file you created.
2. Add the following lines to it:

```
from console import console
console.console_show()
```

How it works...

When QGIS starts, it looks for a Python script named `startup.py` in the user's folder and executes any code it finds there. If you have an error in the file, QGIS will display an error dialog and disable Python within QGIS.

Using the Python's Script Runner plugin

The QGIS Python Script Runner plugin provides a middle ground for QGIS automation, between the interactive console and the overhead of plugins. It provides a script management dialog that allows you to easily load, create, edit, and run scripts for large-scale QGIS automation.

Getting ready

Install the **Script Runner** plugin using the QGIS plugin manager. Then, run the plugin from the **Plugin** menu to open the **Script Runner** dialog. Configure a default editor to edit the scripts using the following steps:

1. Find the gear icon that represents the **Script Runner Preferences** settings dialog box and click on it.
2. In the **General Options** section, check the **Edit scripts using:** checkbox.
3. Click on the **...** button to navigate to the location of a text editor on your system.
4. Click on the **Open** button.
5. Click on the **OK** button in the **Preferences** dialog.

How to do it...

1. In the **Script Runner** dialog, click on the New Script icon, as shown in the following screenshot:

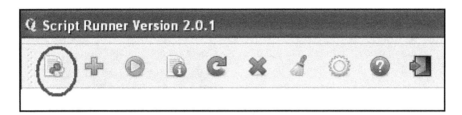

2. Navigate to the directory where you wish to save and name your script.
3. Verify that the new script is loaded in **Script Runner**.
4. Right-click (or control-click on a Mac) on the script name in **Script Runner** and select **Edit script in external editor**.
5. In the editor, replace the template code with the following code:

```
from PyQt4.QtCore import *
from PyQt4.QtGui import *
from qgis.core import *
from qgis.gui import *

def run_script(iface):
    layer =  QgsVectorLayer('Polygon?crs=epsg:4326', 'Mississippi',
                            "memory")
    pr = layer.dataProvider()
    poly = QgsFeature()
    geom = QgsGeometry.fromWkt("""POLYGON ((-88.82 34.99,
                                            -88.09 34.89,
                                            -88.39 30.34,
                                            -89.57 30.18,
                                            -89.73 31,
                                            -91.63 30.99,
                                            -90.87 32.37,
                                            -91.23 33.44,
                                            -90.93 34.23,
                                            -90.30 34.99,
                                            -88.82 34.99))""")
    poly.setGeometry(geom)
    pr.addFeatures([poly])
    layer.updateExtents()
    QgsMapLayerRegistry.instance().addMapLayers([layer])
```

6. Click on the Run Script icon, which is represented by a green-colored arrow.
7. Close the **Script Runner** plugin.
8. Verify that the memory layer polygon is added to the QGIS map, as shown in the following screenshot:

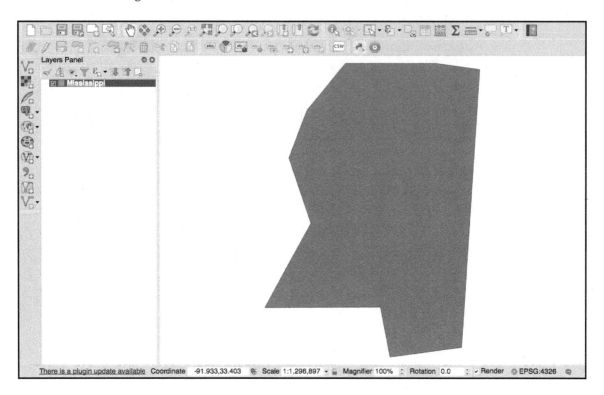

How it works...

Script Runner is a simple but powerful idea. It allows you to build a library of automation scripts and use them from within QGIS without the overhead of building a plugin or a standalone application. All the Python and system path variables are set correctly and inherited from QGIS; however, you must still import the QGIS and Qt libraries.

There's more...

The Script Runner plugin makes managing lots of scripts easier. But there is also a script editor built into the PyQGIS console. This editor is a panel in the QGIS interface that you can use to create, edit, and run scripts. You can trigger the editor using the fourth icon from the left on the PyQGIS console toolbar.

Setting up your QGIS IDE

The Eclipse IDE and the PyDev plugin are cross-platform and free, and they possess advanced debugging tools.

 You can refer to `http://pydev.org/manual_101_install.html` in order to install PyDev correctly.

This tool makes an excellent PyQGIS IDE. Eclipse allows you to have multiple Python interpreters configured for different Python environments. When you install PyDev, it automatically finds the Python installations. On Windows, you also need to add the Python interpreter, installed with PyQGIS. On all platforms, you must tell PyDev where the PyQGIS libraries are.

Getting ready

This recipe uses Eclipse and PyDev. You can use the latest version of both the packages supported by your operating system. All platforms, except for Windows, rely on the Python interpreter. This means that there is an extra step in Windows to add the Python interpreter.

How to do it...

The following steps will walk you through the process of adding the QGIS-specific Python interpreter to Eclipse in order to support the running standalone QGIS applications or the debugging of QGIS plugins.

Adding the Python interpreter to Windows

The process used to add a Python interpreter to Eclipse on Windows is different from the process used on Linux. The following steps describe how to set up the interpreter on the Windows version of Eclipse:

1. Open Eclipse.
2. From the **Window** menu, select **Preferences**.
3. In the pane on the left-hand side of the **Preferences** window, click on the arrow icon next to **PyDev**.
4. From the list of PyDev preferences, select **Interpreters**.
5. In the pane labeled **Python Interpreters**, click on the **New** button.
6. In the **Select interpreter** dialog, name the interpreter `PyQGIS`.
7. Navigate to the location of the Python interpreter called `python.exe`, placed within the `bin` folder of the QGIS program folder. On OS X and Linux, you use the system's Python installation. On Windows, Python is included with QGIS. The default location on Windows is `C:\Program Files\QGIS2.18\bin\python.exe`, as shown in the following screenshot:

8. When you click on the **OK** button, Eclipse will attempt to automatically add every Python library it finds to the Python path to configure this interpreter. We need to control which libraries are added to prevent conflicts. Click on the **Deselect All** button and then click on **OK**:

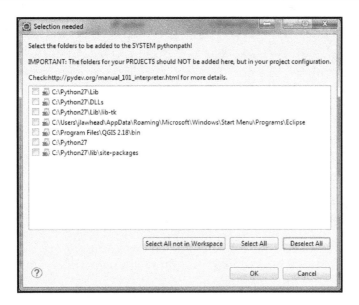

9. Eclipse will issue a warning dialog because you haven't selected any core libraries. Click on the **Proceed anyways** button, as shown here:

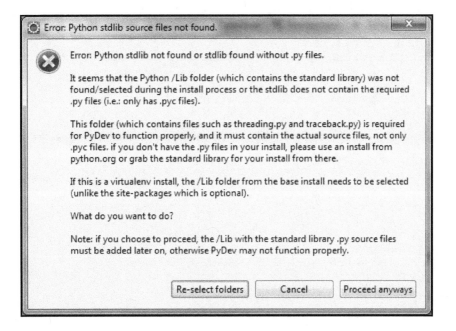

Adding the PyQGIS module paths to the interpreter

Apart from adding the Python interpreter, you also need to add the module paths needed by PyQGIS, using the following steps. These steps will require you to switch back and forth between QGIS and Eclipse.

1. Start QGIS.
2. Select **Python Console** from the **Plugins** menu.
3. Use the `sys` module to locate the PyQGIS Python path, as described in the previous recipe, *Setting the environment variables*:

   ```
   import sys
   sys.path
   ```

4. We also want to add the PyQGIS API so the script has access to all of the QGIS functions within Eclipse. Next, find that path using the QGIS **Python Console** by typing the following command:

   ```
   qgis
   ```

5. For each path in the returned list, click on the **New Folder** button in Eclipse's **Libraries** pane for your QGIS interpreter and browse to that folder until all the paths have been added. If a given folder does not exist on your system, simply ignore it, as shown here:

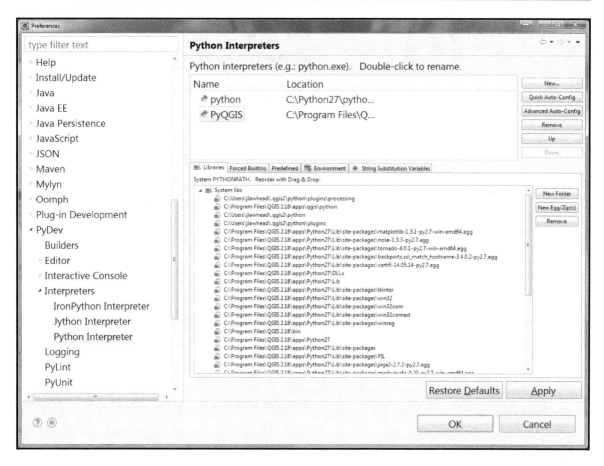

6. Click on the **OK** button in the **Preferences** dialog.

Adding the PyQGIS API to the IDE

To take full advantage of Eclipse's features, including code completion, we will add the QGIS and Qt4 modules to the PyQGIS Eclipse interpreter preferences. The following steps will allow Eclipse to suggest the possible methods and properties of QGIS objects as you type; this feature is known as **autocomplete**:

1. In the PyDev preferences for the PyQGIS interpreter, select the **Forced Builtins** tab, as shown in the following screenshot:

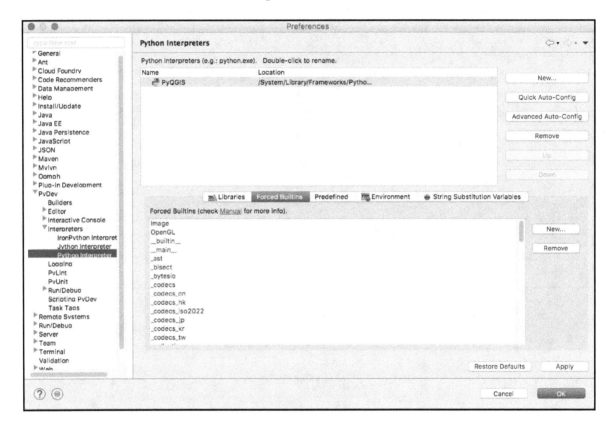

2. Click on the **New** button.
3. In the **Builtin to add** dialog, type `qgis`:

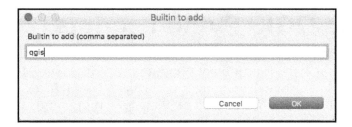

4. Click on the **OK** button.

Adding environment variables

You will also need to create a PATH variable that points to the QGIS binary libraries, DLLs on Windows, and other libraries needed by QGIS at runtime. And you'll need to create this on all platforms in the following way:

1. In the **PyDev preferences** dialog, ensure that the **PyQGIS interpreter** is selected from the list of interpreters.
2. Select the **Environment** tab.
3. Click on the **New** button.
4. In the **Name** field, enter PATH.
5. For the **Value** field, add the path to the QGIS program directory and to any QGIS directories that contain binaries separated by a semicolon. The following is an example from a Windows machine:

```
C:\Program Files\QGIS 2.18;C:\Program Files\QGIS 2.18\bin;
C:\Program Files\QGIS 2.18\apps\qgis\bin;C:\Program Files\QGIS
2.18\apps\Python27\DLLs
```

How it works...

Eclipse and PyDev use only the information you provide to run a script in the Eclipse workspace. This approach is very similar to the popular Python tool **virtualenv**, which provides a clean environment when writing and debugging code to ensure that you don't waste time troubleshooting issues caused by the environment.

Debugging QGIS Python scripts

In this recipe, we will configure Eclipse to debug QGIS Python scripts. This setup will allow you to interactively watch the execution of programs as well as pause the execution as needed. This kind of interactive debugging is particularly useful in a GUI program such as QGIS because in addition to the user interface, there are program functions happening behind the scenes. Debugging programs that have processes in the foreground and background can be extremely difficult. This interactive debugging approach makes the development of complex applications such as these much more efficient by stepping through each part of the program as it is executed. You can see what is happening in real time and troubleshoot more easily.

How to do it...

Both QGIS and Eclipse must be configured for debugging so that the two pieces of software can communicate. Eclipse attaches itself to QGIS in order to give you insights into the Python scripts running in QGIS. This approach allows you to run scripts in a controlled way that can pause the execution while you monitor the program to catch bugs as they occur.

Configuring QGIS

The following steps will add two plugins to QGIS; this will allow Eclipse to communicate with QGIS. The first plugin, **Plugin Reloader**, allows you to reload a QGIS plugin into the memory without restarting QGIS for faster testing. The second plugin, **Remote Debug**, connects QGIS to Eclipse. Remote Debug is an experimental plugin, so we must ensure that experimental plugins are visible to the QGIS plugin manager in the list of the available plugins. This can be done in the following way:

1. Start QGIS.
2. Under the **Plugins** menu, select **Manage and Install Plugins...**
3. In the left pane of the **Plugins** dialog, select the **Settings** tab.

4. Scroll down the **Settings** window and ensure that the **Show also experimental plugins** checkbox is checked, as shown in the following screenshot:

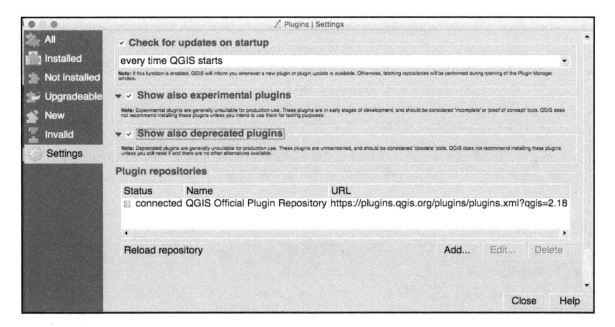

5. Click on the **OK** button.
6. Select the tab labeled **All** in the pane on the left-hand side of the **Plugins** window.
7. In the **Search** dialog at the top of the window, search for **Plugin Reloader**.
8. Select **Plugin Reloader** from the search results and then click on the **Install Plugin** button.
9. Next, search for the **Remote Debug** plugin and install it as well.
10. Finally, install the **HelloWorld** plugin too.

Configuring Eclipse

Now that QGIS is configured for debugging in Eclipse, we will configure Eclipse to complete the debugging communication loop, as shown in the following steps:

1. Start Eclipse.
2. In the **File** menu, select **New** and then click on **Project**.
3. Select **General** and then click on **Project** from the **New Project** dialog.

4. Click on the **Next>** button.

5. Give the project the name `HelloWorld Plugin`.

6. Click on the **Finish** button.

7. Select the new **HelloWorld** plugin project in the project explorer window and select **New**. Then, click on **Folder** from the **File** menu.

8. In the **New Folder** dialog, click on the **Advanced>>** button.

9. Choose the **Link to alternate location (Linked Folder)** radio button.

10. Click on the **Browse** button and browse to the location of the **HelloWorld** plugin folder.

You can find the location of the **HelloWorld** plugin from within the QGIS plugin manager, as shown in the following screenshot:

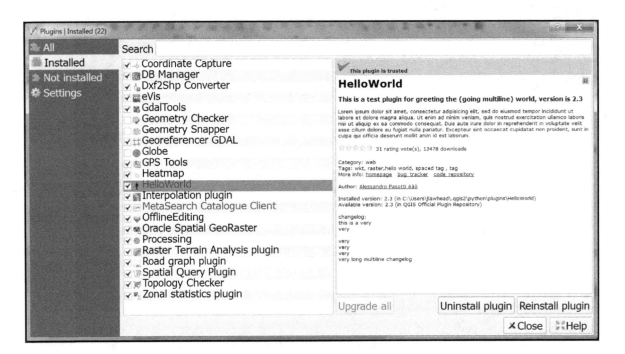

11. Click on the **Finish** button.

Testing the debugger

In the previous parts of this recipe, we configured Eclipse and QGIS so they could work together to debug QGIS plugins. In this section, we will test the configuration using the simplest possible plugin, **HelloWorld**, to run Eclipse using the **Debug Perspective**. We will set up a breakpoint in the plugin to pause the execution and then monitor the plugins execution from within Eclipse, as follows:

1. Under the `HelloWorld` folder, open the `HelloWorld.py` file.
2. From the Eclipse **Window** menu, select **Open Perspective** and then click on **Other...**.
3. From the **Open Perspective** dialog, select **Debug**.
4. Click on the **OK** button.
5. Scroll to the first line of the `hello_world()` function and double-click on the left-hand side of the line number to set a breakpoint, which is displayed as a green-colored icon:

6. From the **Pydev** menu, select **Start Debug Server**.
7. Verify that the server is running by looking for a message in the `Debug` console at the bottom of the window, similar to the following:

```
Debug Server at port: 5678
```

8. Switch over to QGIS.
9. From the QGIS **Plugins** menu, select **Remote Debug** and then select the **Remote Debug** command.
10. Verify that the QGIS status bar in the lower-left corner of the window displays the following message:

```
Python Debugging Active
```

11. Now select **HelloWorld** from the QGIS **Plugins** menu and then select **HelloWorld**.
12. Switch back to Eclipse.
13. Verify that the `hello_world()` function is highlighted at the breakpoint.
14. From the **Run** menu, select **Resume**.
15. Switch back to QGIS.
16. Verify that the **HelloWorld** dialog box has appeared.

How it works...

The **Remote Debug** plugin acts as a client to the PyDev debug server in order to send the Python script's execution status from QGIS to Eclipse. While it has been around for several versions of QGIS now, it is still considered experimental.

The **Plugin Reloader** plugin can reset plugins that maintain the state as they run. The **HelloWorld** plugin is so simple that reloading is not needed to test it repeatedly. However, as you debug more complex plugins, you will need to run it in order to reset it before each test. This method is far more efficient and easier to use than closing QGIS, editing the plugin code, and then restarting it.

 You can find out more about debugging QGIS, including using other IDEs, at
`http://docs.qgis.org/testing/en/docs/pyqgis_developer_cookbook/i`
`de_debugging.html`.

Navigating the PyQGIS API

The QGIS Python API, also known as PyQGIS, allows you to control virtually every aspect of QGIS. The ability to find the PyQGIS object you need in order to access a particular feature of QGIS is critical to automation.

Getting ready

The PyQGIS API is based on the QGIS C++ API. The C++ API is kept up to date online and is well documented.

The QGIS API's web page is located at
`https://qgis.org/api/modules.html`.

The PyQGIS API documentation is not updated frequently because it is nearly identical to the structure of the C++ API. A tool named SWIG, which creates wrappers for multiple languages for C++ libraries, is used to create the PyQGIS API, making the documentation for the C++ API highly applicable for argument types and order. However, the QGIS project on `https://github.com/` maintains a list of all the PyQGIS classes for the latest version. The PyQGIS APIs for different versions are located at `https://github.com/qgis/QGIS/blob/master/python/qsci_apis/`.

You can locate the documented class in the main C++ API and read about it. Then, look up the corresponding Python module and class using the PyQGIS API listing. In most cases, the C++ API name for a class is identical to that in Python. You should note that the PyQGIS versions are tracked separately from the QGIS version and have different version numbers.

In this recipe, we'll locate the PyQGIS class that controls labels in QGIS.

How to do it...

We will perform the following steps to see in which PyQGIS module the QGIS Label object and Qgs Label are located:

1. Go to the QGIS API page at `http://qgis.org/api/index.html`.
2. Click on the **Modules** tab.
3. Click on the link QGIS **core library**.
4. Scroll down the list of modules in alphabetical order until you see **QgsPoint**.
5. Click on the **QgsPoint** link to access the label object documentation.
6. Now go to the PyQGIS API listing at `https://github.com/qgis/QGIS/blob/master/python/qsci_apis/PyQGIS-2.2.api`.
7. Scroll down the alphabetical class listing until you see **qgis.core.QgsPoint?1()**.

How it works...

The QGIS API is divided into five distinct categories, as follows:

- Core
- GUI
- Network analysis
- Server
- Plugins

Most of the time, it's easy to find the class that targets the functionality you need, with most of QGIS being contained in the catch-all core module. The more you use the API, the quicker you'll be able to locate the objects you need for your scripts. You'll also notice that the API file contains the methods for each class with the type of parameters the class accepts.

There's more...

If you're having trouble locating a class containing the keyword you need, you can use the search engine on the QGIS API website.

 Beware, however, that the results returned by this search engine may contain items you don't need and can even send you in the wrong direction because of the use of similar keywords in different modules.

Creating a traditional QGIS plugin

Plugins are the best way to extend QGIS, as they can be easily updated and reused by other people. And as we'll see throughout this book, you can use Python to create plugins. When you create a Python-based plugin, you can usually access that plugin's functionality through the PyQGIS API.

Getting ready

The easiest approach to creating a plugin is to use the **Plugin Builder** plugin to jump-start development. You can find it in the main QGIS plugin repository and install it.

How to do it...

Perform the following steps to create a simple plugin that displays a dialog box with a custom message:

1. Start QGIS.
2. From the **Plugins** menu, select **Plugin Builder** and then click on **Plugin Builder** in the submenu.
3. In the QGIS **Plugin Builder** dialog, name the class `MyPlugin`.
4. Name the plugin `MyPlugin`.
5. Type a short description, such as `A demonstration Plugin`.
6. Enter `myplugin` as the **Module** name.
7. Leave the default version numbers as they are.
8. Enter your name and e-mail address for author information.
9. Click **Next**.
10. Enter a description of the plugin in the **About** field.
11. Click **Next**.
12. In the **Text for menu item** field, enter `My Plugin`.
13. Click **Next** and then on the next dialog click **Next** again.
14. For the **Bug Tracker** field, enter `https://github.com/GeospatialPython/Learn/issues`.
15. For the **Repository** field, `https://github.com/GeospatialPython/Learn/`.
16. Ensure that the checkbox labeled **Flag the plugin as experimental** is checked.
17. Click on the **OK** button.
18. A file browser dialog will appear. You can choose a folder in which you want to create your plugin. Select one of the folders called `plugins` within the `python` folder in either the main user directory or the QGIS program directory. The following examples are from a Windows machine. You should use the folder in your user directory, which is the preferred place for third-party plugins. QGIS standard plugins go to the main program directory:

```
C:\Users\<username>\.qgis2\python\plugins or the %USERPROFILE%
environment variable
```

```
C:\Program Files\QGIS2.18\apps\qgis\python\plugins
```

On OS X or Linux machines, the .qgis2 directory will be in your home directory.

19. Close the **Plugin Builder** information dialog by clicking on the **OK** button.
20. Using Command Prompt, navigate to your new plugin template folder.
21. Use the pyrcc4 command to compile the resource file:

```
pyrcc4 -o resources_rc.py resources.qrc
```

If you are on Windows, it is easier to use the **OSGEO4W** shell, which is installed along with QGIS for the Qt compilation tools to work properly.

22. In a text editor, such as Windows Notepad or vi on Linux, open the user interface XML file named myplugin_dialog_base.ui.
23. Insert the following XML for a custom label near line 31, just before the last </widget> tag. Save the file after this edit:

```xml
<widget class="QLabel" name="label">
  <property name="geometry">
    <rect>
      <x>120</x>
      <y>80</y>
      <width>201</width>
      <height>20</height>
    </rect>
  </property>
  <property name="font">
    <font>
      <pointsize>14</pointsize>
    </font>
  </property>
  <property name="text">
    <string>Geospatial Python Rocks!</string>
  </property>
</widget>
```

24. Now compile the ui file using the pyuic4 tool:

```
pyuic4 -o ui_myplugin.py ui_myplugin.ui
```

25. Your plugin is now ready. Restart QGIS.

26. Select **My Plugin** from the **Plugins** menu and then select **My Plugin** from the submenu to see the dialog you created within QGIS, as shown here:

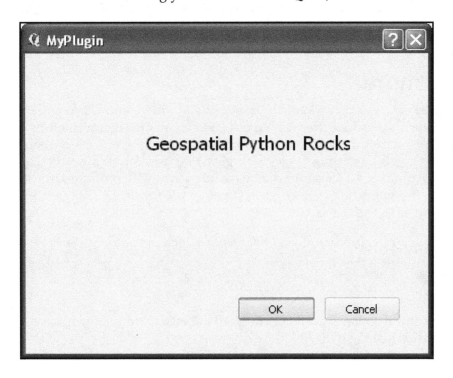

How it works...

This recipe shows you the bare bones needed to make a working plugin. Although we haven't altered it, the code for the plugin's behavior is contained in `myplugin.py`. You can change the icon and the GUI and just recompile any time you want. Note that we must compile the `Qt4` portion of the plugin, which creates the dialog box. The entire QGIS GUI is built on the `Qt4` library, so the `pyrrc4` compiler and `pyuic4` is included to compile the GUI widgets.

You can download the completed plugin with both the source and compiled UI and resource files at
`https://github.com/GeospatialPython/Learn/raw/master/MyPlugin.zip`.

You can find out more about QGIS plugins, including the purpose of the other files in the directory, from the QGIS documentation at `http://docs.qgis.org/testing/en/docs/pyqgis_developer_cookbook/plugins.html`.

There's more...

We have edited the `myplugin_dialog_base.ui` XML file manually to make a small change. However, there is a better way to use Qt Creator. Qt Creator is a fully fledged open source GUI designer for the Qt framework. It is an easy what-you-see-is-what-you-get editor for Qt Widgets, including PyQGIS plugins, that uses the included Qt Designer interface. On Windows, Qt Designer can be found in the QGIS program directory within the `bin` directory. It is named `designer.exe`. On other platforms, Qt Designer is included as part of the `qt4-devel` package.

 You can also download Qt Creator, which includes Qt Designer, from `https://www.qt.io/download/`.

When you run the installer, you can uncheck all the installation options, except the **Tools** category, to install just the IDE.

Creating a Processing Toolbox plugin

The QGIS Processing Toolbox provides a powerful set of algorithms for QGIS Python programming, which we'll see throughout this book. You add your own scripts to the toolbox, and with the latest version of QGIS, you can now turn those scripts into plugins. You can install these plugins like any other QGIS plugin using Plugin Manager and then have those scripts appear in Processing Toolbox. This process is significantly easier than writing a traditional plugin from scratch.

Getting ready

First you need a script to package as a plugin. You can package multiple scripts into a single plugin, but to keep things simple, use one. This sample script will save the current map view as an image. Create the script using the following steps:

1. In **Processing Toolbox**, expand the **Scripts** tree.
2. Double-click on the **Create new script** tool.
3. In the script editor, add the following code, specifying an output directory for your map images:

   ```
   from qgis.utils import iface
   import datetime
   c = iface.mapCanvas()
   t = '{:%Y%m%d%H%M%S}'.format(datetime.datetime.now())
   img_path = '<output directory>/map{}.png'
   c.saveAsImage(img_path.format(t), None, 'PNG')
   ```

4. Click on the **Save As** icon to save the image in your scripts directory as MapImage.py.
5. The script will then appear in the **User Scripts** tree under **Scripts** in **Processing Toolbox**.
6. Set up a map view and then double-click on the script to verify that an image has been created in the output directory.

How to do it...

Now you are ready to create the plugin from your sample script:

1. Under the script tools section in **Processing Toolbox**, double-click on **Create script collection plugin**.
2. Fill out the metadata fields in the dialog.
3. Ensure the **MapImage** script is checked in the **Script selector** dialog.

2. When you navigate to the output folder, create a new folder called `MapImage`:

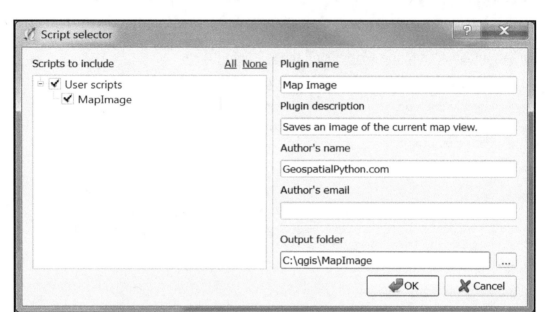

5. Click on the **OK** button
6. Navigate to the output folder and verify the plugin files were created.

How it works...

From a functional perspective, all the script does is copy the files to your user scripts directory. But the plugin packaging allows you to distribute your work to other users using the QGIS plugin framework.

There's more...

The **Processing Toolbox** has a script manager similar to the QGIS plugin manager, in which you can download scripts written by other users for processing, or as examples to write your own scripts. To access this script manager, expand the **Scripts** menu in the Processing Toolbox, then expand the **Tools** menu, and finally double-click **Get scripts from on-line scripts collection**. From there, you can browse a list of downloadable scripts.

Distributing a plugin

Distributing a QGIS plugin means placing a collection of files on a server as a ZIP file, with a special configuration file, in order to allow the QGIS plugin manager to locate and install the plugin. The QGIS project has an official repository, but third-party repositories are also permitted. The official repository is very strict regarding how the plugin is uploaded, so, for this recipe, we'll set up a simple third-party repository for a sample plugin and test it with the QGIS plugin manager to avoid polluting the main QGIS repository with a test project. You should note that QGIS is released under the GNU **General Public License** (**GPL**), so presumably all other plugins fall under the GPL as well, based on the terms of the license.

Getting ready

In order to complete this recipe, you'll need a sample plugin and a web-accessible directory. You'll also need a ZIP tool, such as the free 7-zip program (`http://www.7-zip.org/download.html`). Both OSX and Windows can compress and decompress zip files natively. On Linux, you may need to download a ZIP tool from your package manager. You can use the *MyPlugin* example from the *Creating a QGIS plugin* recipe as the plugin to distribute. For a web directory, you can use a Google Code repository, GitHub repository, or other online directories you can access. Code repositories work well because they are a good place to store a plugin that you are developing.

How to do it...

In the following steps, we will package our plugin, create a server configuration file for it, and place it on a server to create a QGIS plugin repository:

1. First, zip up the plugin directory to create a `.zip` file.
2. Rename the `.zip` file to contain the plugin's version number:

   `Myplugin.0.1.0.zip`

3. Upload this file to a publicly accessible web directory.
4. Upload the `icon.png` file from your plugin directory to the web directory.

5. Next, customize a `plugins.xml` metadata file for your plugin. Most of the data you need can be found in the `metatdata.txt` file in your plugin directory. The following example provides some guidance:

```xml
<?xml version = '1.0' encoding = 'UTF-8'?>
<?xml-stylesheet type="text/xsl"href="" ?>
<plugins>
  <pyqgis_plugin name="My Plugin" version="0.1.0" plugin_id="227">
    <description>
      <![CDATA[Demonstration of a QGIS Plugin]]>
    </description>
    <about></about>
    <version>0.1.0</version>
    <qgis_minimum_version>1.8.0</qgis_minimum_version>
    <qgis_maximum_version>2.9.9</qgis_maximum_version>
    <homepage>
      <![CDATA[https://github.com/GeospatialPython/Learn]]>
    </homepage>
    <file_name>MyPlugin.0.1.0.zip</file_name>
    <icon>https://github.com/GeospatialPython/
    Learn/raw/master/icon_227.png</icon>
    <author_name><![CDATA[Joel Lawhead]]></author_name>
    <download_url>https://github.com/GeospatialPython/
    Learn/raw/master/MyPlugin.0.1.0.zip</download_url>
    <uploaded_by><![CDATA[jll]]></uploaded_by>
    <create_date>2016-11-19T15:31:19.824333</create_date>
    <update_date>2016-11-19T15:31:19.824333</update_date>
    <experimental>True</experimental>
    <deprecated>False</deprecated>
    <tracker>
      <![CDATA[https://github.com/GeospatialPython/Learn/issues]]>
    </tracker>
    <repository>
      <![CDATA[https://github.com/GeospatialPython/Learn/]]>
    </repository>
    <tags><![CDATA[development,debugging,tools]]></tags>
    <downloads>0</downloads>
    <average_vote>0</average_vote>
    <rating_votes>0</rating_votes>
  </pyqgis_plugin>
</plugins>
```

6. Upload the `plugins.xml` file to your web directory.

7. Now start QGIS and launch the plugins manager by going to the **Plugins** menu and selecting **Manage and Install Plugins...**.

8. In the **Settings** tab of the **Plugins | Settings** dialog, scroll down and click on the **Add...** button.
9. Give the plugin a name and then add the complete URL to `plugins.xml` in the URL field.
10. Click on the **OK** button.

11. To make things easier, disable the other repositories by selecting the repository name, clicking on the **Edit** button, and unchecking the **Enabled** checkbox.
12. Click on the **OK** button
13. Click on the **Not installed** tab.
14. Your test plugin should be the only plugin listed, so select it from the list.
15. Click on the **Install plugin** button in the bottom-right corner of the window.
16. Click on the **Close** button.
17. Go to the **Plugins** menu and select your plugin to ensure that it works.

How it works...

The QGIS repository concept is simple and effective. The `plugins.xml` file contains a `<download_url>` tag that points to a ZIP file plugin on the same server or on a different server. The `name` attribute of the `<pyqgis_plugin>` tag is what appears in the QGIS plugin manager.

Building a standalone application

QGIS is a complete desktop GIS application. However, with PyQGIS, it can also be a comprehensive geospatial Python library to build standalone applications. In this recipe, we will build a simple standalone script that will create a map with a line on it.

Getting ready

All you need to do to get ready is ensure that you have configured Eclipse and PyDev for PyQGIS development, as described in the *Setting up your QGIS IDE* recipe of this chapter.

How to do it...

In PyDev, create a new project called MyMap with a Python script called MyMap.py, as follows:

1. In the Eclipse **File** menu, select **New** and then click on **PyDev Project**.
2. In the PyDev project's **Name** field, enter MyMap.

3. Next, select the **Python** radio button from the **Project Type** list.
4. From the **Interpreter** pull-down menu, select **PyQGIS**.
5. Leave the radio button checked for **Add project directory to the PYTHONPATH**.
6. Click on the **Finish** button.
7. Now select the project in the PyDev package explorer.
8. From the **File** menu, select **New** and then click on **File**.
9. Name the file myMap.py.
10. Click on the **Finish** button.
11. Add the following code to the file that is open in the editor:

```
from qgis.core import *
from qgis.gui import *
from qgis.utils import *
from PyQt4.QtCore import *
from PyQt4.QtGui import *

app = QgsApplication([], True)
path = "C:/Program Files/QGIS2.18/apps/qgis"
app.setPrefixPath(path, True)
app.initQgis()
canvas = QgsMapCanvas()
title = "PyQGIS Standalone Application Example"
canvas.setWindowTitle(title)
canvas.setCanvasColor(Qt.white)
layer_info = 'LineString?crs=epsg:4326'
layer = QgsVectorLayer(layer_info, 'MyLine' , "memory")
pr = layer.dataProvider()
linstr = QgsFeature()
wkt = "LINESTRING (1 1, 10 15, 40 35)"
geom = QgsGeometry.fromWkt(wkt)
linstr.setGeometry(geom)
pr.addFeatures([linstr])
layer.updateExtents()
QgsMapLayerRegistry.instance().addMapLayer(layer)
canvas.setExtent(layer.extent())
canvas.setLayerSet([QgsMapCanvasLayer(layer)])
```

```
canvas.zoomToFullExtent()
canvas.show()
exitcode = app.exec_()
QgsApplication.exitQgis()
sys.exit(exitcode)
```

12. From the **Run** menu, select **Run**.
13. Verify that the standalone QGIS map appears in a new window, as shown here:

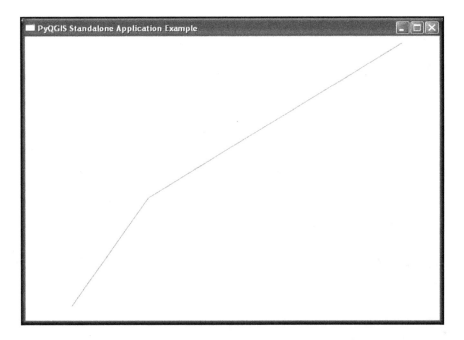

How it works...

This recipe uses as little code as possible to create a map canvas and draw a line to demonstrate the skeleton of a standalone application, which you can build up further to add more functionality, as we will see in later recipes.

To create line geometry, we use **Well-Known Text** (**WKT**), which provides a simple way to define the line vertices without creating a bunch of objects. The map does not appear until you call the `canvas.show()` method. This allows you to set up the map behind the scenes and then display it when it is complete.

There's more...

The standalone application can be compiled into an executable that can be distributed without installing QGIS using either py2exe or PyInstaller.

You can find out more about py2exe at `http://www.py2exe.org`.

You can learn more about PyInstaller at `https://github.com/pyinstaller/pyinstaller/wiki`.

Storing and reading global preferences

PyQGIS allows you to store application-level preferences and retrieve them. QGIS also has project-level preferences, which can override the application-level preferences in some cases. In this recipe, we'll focus on reading and writing the global preferences that serve as the application defaults. QGIS actually takes advantage of Qt's built-in preferences management.

Getting ready

This code can be run in any type of PyQGIS application. In this example, we'll run it in the QGIS Python console for an easy demonstration. We'll also change the default CRS for new projects and then read the value back from the global settings.

How to do it...

In this recipe, we will set the default projection used by QGIS for new projects. We'll do this using the Python console:

1. Start QGIS.
2. From the Plugins menu, select **Python Console**.

3. We will need to import the Qt core library, as follows:

```
from PyQt4.QtCore import *
```

4. In the Python console, run the following code:

```
settings = QSettings(QSettings.NativeFormat,
                     QSettings.UserScope,'QuantumGIS', 'QGis')
settings.setValue('/Projections/projectDefaultCrs', 'EPSG:2278')
settings.value('/Projections/projectDefaultCrs')
settings.sync()
```

How it works...

This API is actually the Qt API that QGIS relies on for settings. In the QSettings object, we specify the native format for storage, which is the default format for the platform. On Windows, the format is the registry; on OS X, it's the plist files, and on Unix, it's the text files. The other QSettings parameters are the **organization** and the **application**, often used as a hierarchy to store information. Note that when you change the settings, you must call the sync() method at the end to save them and let them take effect. Note that when you are writing a standalone QGIS application, you should use your own organization and application name for settings and not QGIS.

There's more...

If you want to see all the options that you can change, call the allKeys() method of QSettings; this will return a list of all the setting names.

Storing and reading project preferences

The QGIS application settings are stored using the Qt API. However, QGIS project settings have their own object. In this recipe, we'll set and read the project title, and then set and read a custom preference for a plugin.

Getting ready

We are going to set a plugin preference using the sample plugin created in an earlier recipe, *Creating a QGIS plugin*, of this chapter. You can substitute the name of any plugin you want, however. We will also run this recipe in the QGIS Python console for quick testing, but this code will normally be used in a plugin.

How to do it...

In this recipe, we will first write and then read the title of the current project. Then, we will create a custom value for a plugin called **splash**, which can be used for the plugin startup splash screen if desired. Here are the steps to store and read project preferences:

1. Start QGIS.
2. From the **Plugins** menu, select **Python Console**.
3. In the console, run the following code:

```
proj = QgsProject.instance()
proj.title("My QGIS Project")
proj.title()
msg = "Geospatial Python Rocks!"
proj.writeEntry("MyPlugin", "splash", msg)
proj.readEntry("MyPlugin", "splash", "Welcome!")[0]
```

How it works...

In the first two lines, we change the title of the current active project and then echo it back. In the next set of two lines, we set up and read the custom settings for a plugin. Notice that the readEntry() method returns a tuple with the desired text and a boolean, acknowledging that the value is set, so we extract the first index to get the text. The read method also allows the default text in case that property is not set (rather than throw an exception, which must be handled), as well as the boolean value False to inform you that the default text was used because the property was not set. The values you set using this method are stored in the project's XML file when you save it.

There's more...

The Qgs Project object has a number of methods and properties that may be useful. The QGIS API documentation details all of them at `http://qgis.org/api/classQgsProject.html`.

Accessing the script path from within your script

Sometimes, you need to know exactly where the current working directory is so that you can access external resources.

Getting ready

This code uses the Python built-in library, and can be used in any context. We will run this recipe in the QGIS Python console.

How to do it...

In this recipe, we will get the current working directory of the Python console, which can change with the configuration:

1. Start QGIS.
2. From the **Plugins** menu, select **Python Console**.
3. In the Python console, run the following code:

```
import os
os.getcwd()
```

How it works...

QGIS relies heavily on file system paths to run the application and manage external data. When writing cross-platform QGIS code, you cannot assume the working directory of your script.

There's more...

You can also use Python's __file__ variable, which tells you the path of the script currently being executed. For example, path = os.path.dirname(__file__)

On his blog, one of the QGIS developers, Gary Sherman, has an excellent post about the various aspects of path variables in QGIS beyond just the execution directory. You can check it out at http://spatialgalaxy.net/2013/11/06/getting-paths-with-pyqgis/.

2
Querying Vector Data

In this chapter, we will cover the following recipes:

- Loading a vector layer from a file sample
- Loading a vector layer from a geodatabase
- Examining vector layer features
- Examining vector layer attributes
- Filtering a layer by geometry
- Filtering a layer by attributes
- Buffering a feature
- Measuring the distance between two points
- Measuring distance along a line
- Calculating the area of a polygon
- Creating a spatial index
- Calculating the bearing of a line
- Loading data from a spreadsheet
- Accessing layer metadata

Introduction

This chapter demonstrates how to work with vector data through Python in QGIS. We will first work through loading different sources of vector data. Next, we'll move on to examining the contents of the data. Then, we'll spend the remainder of the chapter performing spatial and database operations on vector data.

Loading a vector layer from a file sample

Vector data stored in a local file is one of the most common geospatial data formats. Vector data typically stores geometry with associated attributes. In this recipe, we'll load a vector data file, in this case a shapefile, as a vector layer in QGIS.

Getting ready

For ease of following the examples in this book, it is recommended that you create a directory called `qgis_data` in your root or user directory,which will provide a short pathname. This setup will help prevent the occurrence of any frustrating errors resulting from path-related issues on a given system. In this recipe, and others, we'll use a point shapefile of the New York City museums, which you can download from `https://github.com/GeospatialPython/Learn/raw/master/NYC_MUSEUMS_GEO.zip`.

Unzip this file and place the shapefile's contents in a directory named `nyc` within your `qgis_data` directory.

How to do it...

Now, we'll walk through the steps of loading a shapefile and adding it to the map, as follows:

1. Start QGIS.
2. From the **Plugins** menu, select **Python Console**.
3. In the Python console, create the layer:

```
layer = QgsVectorLayer("/qgis_data/nyc/NYC_MUSEUMS_GEO.shp",
                        "New York City Museums", "ogr")
```

4. Next, ensure that the layer is created as expected:

```
if not layer.isValid():
    print("Layer {} did not load".format(layer.name()))
```

5. Finally, add the layer to the layer registry:

```
QgsMapLayerRegistry.instance().addMapLayers([layer])
```

6. Verify that your QGIS map looks similar to the following image:

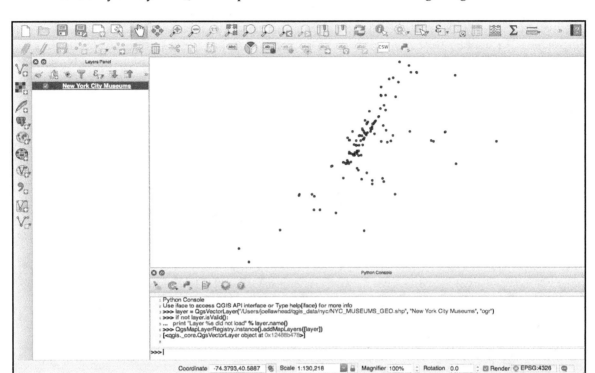

How it works...

The `QgsVectorLayer` object requires the location of the file, a name for the layer in QGIS, and a data provider that provides the right parser and capabilities managed for the file format. Most vector layers are covered by the `ogr` data provider, which attempts to guess the format from the file name extension in order to use the appropriate driver. The possible formats available for this data provider are listed at http://www.gdal.org/ogr_formats.html. You can see which drivers you have installed using the following code:

```
drivers = [ogr.GetDriver(n).GetName() for n in
           range(ogr.GetDriverCount())]
print(drivers)
```

Once we have created the QgsVector object, we do a quick check using the
`layer.isValid()` method to see whether the file was loaded properly. We won't use this
method in every recipe to keep the code short; however, this method is often very
important. It's usually the only indication that something has gone wrong. If you have a
typo in the filename or you try to connect to an online data source but have no network
connection, you won't see any errors. Your first indication will be another method failing
further into your code, which will make tracking down the root cause more difficult.

In the last line, we add the vector layer to `QgsMapLayerRegistry`, which makes it
available on the map. The registry keeps track of all the layers in the project. The reason
why QGIS works this way is so you can load multiple layers, style them, filter them, and do
other operations before exposing them to the user on the map.

Loading a vector layer from a geodatabase

The **PostGIS** geodatabase is based on the open source **Postgres** database. The geodatabase
provides powerful geospatial data management and operations. PyQGIS fully supports
PostGIS as a data source. In this recipe, we'll add a layer from a PostGIS database.

Getting ready

Installing and configuring PostGIS is beyond the scope of this book, so we'll use a sample
geospatial database interface from the excellent service http://www.qgiscloud.com/. It has
its own Python plugin called **QGIS Cloud**. You can sign up for free and create your own
geodatabase online by following the site's instructions, or you can use the example used in
this recipe.

How to do it...

Perform the following steps to load a PostGIS layer into a QGIS map:

1. First, create a new `DataSourceURI` instance:

   ```
   uri = QgsDataSourceURI()
   ```

2. Next, create the database connection string:

```
uri.setConnection("spacialdb.com", "9999", "lzmjzm_hwpqlf",
                  "lzmjzm_hwpqlf", "0e9fcc39")
```

3. Now, describe the data source:

```
uri.setDataSource("public", "islands", "wkb_geometry", "")
```

4. Then, create `layer`:

```
layer = QgsVectorLayer(uri.uri(), "Islands", "postgres")
```

5. Just to be safe, make sure everything works:

```
if not layer.isValid():
    print "Layer %s did not load" % layer.name()
```

6. Finally, add `layer` to the map if everything is okay:

```
QgsMapLayerRegistry.instance().addMapLayers([layer])
```

7. You can see the `Islands` layer in the map, as shown in the following screenshot:

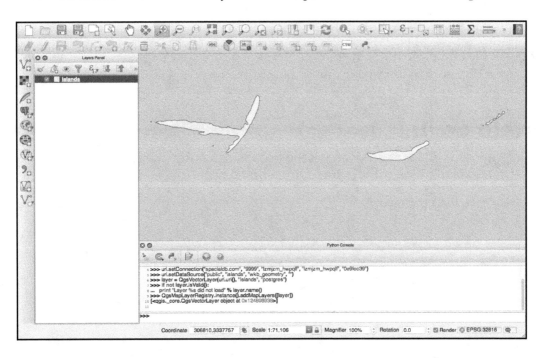

How it works...

PyQGIS provides an object in the API to create a PostGIS data source in `QgsDataSourceURI()`. The `connection` string parameters in the second line of code are database server, port, database name, user, and password. In the example, the database, username, and password are randomly generated unique names. The data source parameters are schema name, table name, geometry column, and an optional SQL `WHERE` to subset the layer as needed.

Examining vector layer features

Once a vector layer is loaded, you may want to investigate the data. In this recipe, we'll load a vector point layer from a shapefile and take a look at the x and y coordinates of the first point.

Getting ready

We'll use the same New York City Museums layer from the *Loading a vector layer from a file* recipe of this chapter. You can download the layer from `https://github.com/GeospatialPython/Learn/raw/master/NYC_MUSEUMS_GEO.zip`.

Unzip that file and place the shapefile's contents in a directory named `nyc` within your `qgis_data` directory, within your root or home directory.

How to do it...

In this recipe, we will load the layer, get the features, grab the first feature, obtain its geometry, and take a look at the values for the first point:

1. First, load the layer:

   ```
   layer = QgsVectorLayer("/qgis_data/nyc/NYC_MUSEUMS_GEO.shp",
                          "New York City Museums", "ogr")
   ```

2. Next, get an iterator of the layer's features:

   ```
   features = layer.getFeatures()
   ```

3. Now, get the first feature from the iterator:

```
f = features.next()
```

4. Then, get the feature's geometry:

```
g = f.geometry()
```

5. Finally, get the point's values:

```
g.asPoint()
```

6. Verify that the Python console output is similar to the following QgsPoint object:

```
(-74.0138,40.7038)
```

How it works...

When you access a layer's features or geometry using the previously demonstrated methods, PyQGIS returns a Python iterator. The iterator data structure allows Python to work efficiently with very large datasets, without keeping the entire dataset in memory. It's important to note the object returned in step six is actually a **QgsPoint**, which is represented as a tuple.

Examining vector layer attributes

A true GIS layer contains both spatial geometry and non-spatial attributes. In this recipe, we'll access a vector point layer's attributes in PyQGIS. We'll use a file-based layer from a shapefile, but once a layer is loaded in QGIS, every vector layer works the same way.

Getting ready

Once again, we'll use the same New York City Museums layer from the *Loading a vector layer from a file* recipe in this chapter. You can download the layer from
`https://github.com/GeospatialPython/Learn/raw/master/NYC_MUSEUMS_GEO.zip`.

Unzip that file and place the shapefile's contents in a directory named `nyc` within your `qgis_data` directory, within your root or home directory.

How to do it...

In the following steps, we'll load the layer, access the `features` iterator, grab the first feature, and then view the attributes as a Python list:

1. First, load the shapefile as a vector layer:

```
layer = QgsVectorLayer("/qgis_data/nyc/NYC_MUSEUMS_GEO.shp",
                       "New York City Museums", "ogr")
```

2. Next, get the `features` iterator:

```
features = layer.getFeatures()
```

3. Now, grab the first feature from the iterator:

```
f = features.next()
```

4. Finally, examine the attributes as a Python list:

```
f.attributes()
```

5. Verify that the Python console's output resembles the following list:

```
[u'Alexander Hamilton U.S. Custom House', u'(212) 514-3700',
 u'http://www.oldnycustomhouse.gov/', u'1 Bowling Grn', NULL,
 u'New York', 10004.0, -74.013756, 40.703817]
```

How it works...

Examining attributes is consistent with accessing the point values of a layer's geometry. Note that all string attribute values are returned as unicode strings, which is the case for all QGIS strings. Unicode allows the internationalization (that is, translation) of QGIS for other languages besides English. It also allows you to read the attributes of layers that use these characters which can only be represented Unicode. It is also important to note that as we move towards QGIS version 3, it will use Python 3 in which all strings default to Unicode.

There's more...

The attribute values don't mean much without the knowledge of what those values represent. You will also need to know the fields. You can get the fields as a list by accessing the `fields` iterator and calling the `name()` method for each field. This operation is easily accomplished with a Python list comprehension:

```
[c.name() for c in f.fields().toList()]
```

This example returns the following result:

```
[u'NAME', u'TEL', u'URL', u'ADRESS1', u'ADDRESS2', u'CITY', u'ZIP',
 u'XCOORD', u'YCOORD']
```

Filtering a layer by geometry

In this recipe, we'll perform a spatial operation to select the subset of a point layer based on the points contained in an overlapping polygon layer. We'll use shapefiles in both the cases, with one being a point layer and the other a polygon. This kind of subset is one of the most common GIS operations.

Getting ready

We will need two new shapefiles that have not been used in the previous recipes. You can download the point layer from
`https://github.com/GeospatialPython/Learn/raw/master/MSCities_Geo_Pts.zip`.

Similarly, you can download the geometry layer from
`https://github.com/GeospatialPython/Learn/raw/master/GIS_CensusTract.zip`.

Unzip these shapefiles and place them in a directory named `ms` within your `qgis_data` directory, within your root or home directory.

How to do it...

In this recipe, we will perform several steps to select features in the point layer that fall within the polygon layer, as follows:

1. First, load the point layer:

```
lyrPts = QgsVectorLayer("/qgis_data/ms/MSCities_Geo_Pts.shp",
                        "MSCities_Geo_Pts", "ogr")
```

2. Next, load the polygon layer:

```
lyrPoly = QgsVectorLayer("/qgis_data/ms/GIS_CensusTract_poly.shp",
                         "GIS_CensusTract_poly", "ogr")
```

3. Add the layers to the map using a list:

```
QgsMapLayerRegistry.instance().addMapLayers([lyrPts,lyrPoly])
```

4. Access the polygon layer's features:

```
ftsPoly = lyrPoly.getFeatures()
```

5. Now, iterate through the polygon's features:

```
for feat in ftsPoly:
```

6. Grab each feature's `geometry`:

```
geomPoly = feat.geometry()
```

7. Access the point features and filter the point features by the polygon's bounding box:

```
bbox = geomPoly.boundingBox()
req = gsFeatureRequest()
filterRect = req.setFilterRect(bbox)
featsPnt = lyrPts.getFeatures(filterRect)
```

8. Iterate through each point and check whether it's within the polygon itself:

```
for featPnt in featsPnt:
    if featPnt.geometry().within(geomPoly):
```

9. If the polygon contains the point, print the point's ID and select the point:

```
print featPnt.id()
lyrPts.select(featPnt.id())
```

10. Now, set the polygon layer as the active map layer:

```
iface.setActiveLayer(lyrPoly)
```

11. Zoom to the polygon layer's extents:

```
iface.zoomToActiveLayer()
```

12. Verify that your map looks similar to the following image:

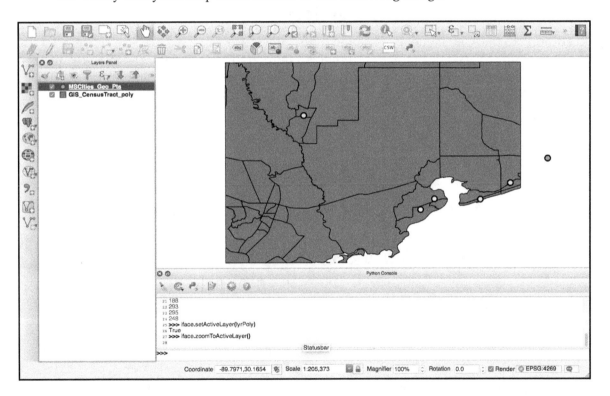

How it works...

While QGIS has several tools for spatial selection, PyQGIS doesn't have a dedicated API for this type of functions. However, there are just enough methods in the API, thanks to the underlying ogr/GEOS library, so that you can easily create your own spatial filters for two layers. Step 7 isn't entirely necessary, but we gain some efficiency by using the bounding box of the polygon to limit the number of point features we're examining. Calculations involving rectangles are far quicker than the detailed point-in-polygon queries. So, we quickly reduce the number of points we need to iterate through for more expensive spatial operations.

Filtering a layer by attributes

In addition to the spatial queries outlined in the previous recipe, we can also subset a layer by its attributes. This type of query resembles a more traditional relational database query and, in fact, uses SQL statements. In this recipe, we will filter a point shapefile-based layer by an attribute.

Getting ready

We'll use the same New York City Museums layer used in the previous recipes in this chapter. You can download the layer from
`https://github.com/GeospatialPython/Learn/raw/master/NYC_MUSEUMS_GEO.zip`.

Unzip that file and place the shapefile's contents in a directory named `nyc` within your `qgis_data` directory, within your root or home directory.

How to do it...

In this recipe, we'll filter the layer by an attribute, select the filtered features, and zoom to them, as follows:

1. First, we load the point layer:

```
lyrPts = QgsVectorLayer("/qgis_data/nyc/NYC_MUSEUMS_GEO.shp",
                        "Museums", "ogr")
```

2. Next, we add the layer to the map in order to visualize the points:

```
QgsMapLayerRegistry.instance().addMapLayers([lyrPts])
```

3. Now, we filter the point layer to points with attributes that match a specific zip code:

```
selection = lyrPts.getFeatures(QgsFeatureRequest()
                    .setFilterExpression(u'"ZIP" = 10002'))
```

4. Then, we use a list comprehension to create a list of feature IDs that are fed to the feature selection method:

```
lyrPts.setSelectedFeatures([s.id() for s in selection])
```

5. Finally, we zoom to the selection:

```
iface.mapCanvas().zoomToSelected()
```

6. Verify that the points layer has three selected features, shown in yellow similar to the following screenshot:

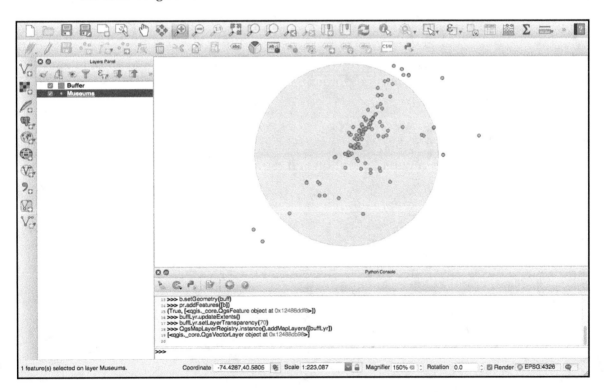

How it works...

This recipe takes advantage of the QGIS filter expressions, highlighted in Step 3. These filter expressions are a subset of SQL. The `QgsFeatureRequest` object handles the query expression as an optional argument to return an iterator with just the features you want. These queries also allow some basic geometrical manipulations. This recipe also introduces the `mapCanvas().zoomToSelected()` method, which is a convenient way to set the map's extent to the features of your interest.

Buffering a feature

Buffering a feature creates a polygon around a feature as a selection geometry or just a simple visualization. In this recipe, we'll buffer a point in a point feature and add the returned polygon geometry to the map.

Getting ready

Once again, we'll use the same New York City Museums layer. You can download the layer from `https://github.com/GeospatialPython/Learn/raw/master/NYC_MUSEUMS_GEO.zip`.

Unzip that file and place the shapefile's contents in a directory named `nyc` within your `qgis_data` directory, within your root or home directory.

How to do it...

This recipe involves both a spatial operation and multiple visualizations. To do this, perform the following steps:

1. First, load the layer:

```
lyr = QgsVectorLayer("/qgis_data/nyc/NYC_MUSEUMS_GEO.shp",
    "Museums", "ogr")
```

2. Next, visualize the layer on the map:

```
QgsMapLayerRegistry.instance().addMapLayers([lyr])
```

3. Access the layer's features:

```
fts = lyr.getFeatures()
```

4. Grab the first feature:

```
ft = fts.next()
```

5. Select this feature:

```
lyr.setSelectedFeatures([ft.id()])
```

6. Create the buffer:

```
buff = ft.geometry().buffer(.2,8)
```

7. Set up a memory layer for the buffer's geometry:

```
buffLyr = QgsVectorLayer('Polygon?crs=EPSG:4326', 'Buffer' ,
          "memory")
```

8. Access the layer's data provider:

```
pr = buffLyr.dataProvider()
```

9. Create a new feature:

```
b = QgsFeature()
```

10. Set the feature's geometry with the buffer geometry:

```
b.setGeometry(buff)
```

11. Add the feature to the data provider:

```
pr.addFeatures([b])
```

12. Update the buffer layer's extents:

```
buffLyr.updateExtents()
```

13. Set the buffer layer's transparency so that you can see other features as well:

```
buffLyr.setLayerTransparency(70)
```

14. Add the buffer layer to the map:

```
QgsMapLayerRegistry.instance().addMapLayers([buffLyr])
```

15. Verify that your map looks similar to the following screenshot:

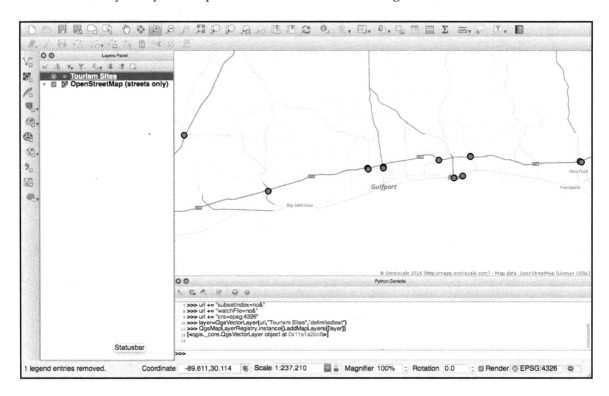

How it works...

The interesting portion of this recipe starts with Step 6, which creates the buffer geometry. The parameters for the `buffer()` method are the distance in map units for the buffer followed by the number of straight line segments used to approximate curves. The more segments you specify, the more the buffer appears like a circle. However, more segments equals greater geometric complexity and, therefore, slower rendering as well as slower geometric calculations. The other interesting feature of this recipe is Step 13, in which we set the transparency of the layer to 70 percent. We also introduce away of creating a new layer, which is done in memory. Later chapters will go more in depth on creating data.

Measuring the distance between two points

In the `QgsDistanceArea` object, PyQGIS has excellent capabilities for measuring the distance. We'll use this object for several recipes, starting with measuring the distance between two points.

Getting ready

If you don't already have the New York City Museums layer used in the previous recipes in this chapter, download the layer from
`https://github.com/GeospatialPython/Learn/raw/master/NYC_MUSEUMS_GEO.zip`.

Unzip that file and place the shapefile's contents in a directory named `nyc` within your `qgis_data` directory, within your root or home directory.

How to do it...

In the following steps, we'll extract the first and last points in the layer's point order and measure the distance between them:

1. First, import the library that contains the QGIS contents:

   ```
   from qgis.core import QGis
   ```

2. Then, load the layer:

   ```
   lyr = QgsVectorLayer("/qgis_data/nyc/NYC_MUSEUMS_GEO.shp",
                        "Museums", "ogr")
   ```

3. Access the features:

   ```
   fts = lyr.getFeatures()
   ```

4. Get the first feature:

   ```
   first = fts.next()
   ```

5. Set a placeholder for the last feature:

   ```
   last = fts.next()
   ```

6. Iterate through the features until you get the last one:

```
for f in fts:
    last = f
```

7. Create a measurement object:

```
d = QgsDistanceArea()
```

8. Measure the distance:

```
m = d.measureLine(first.geometry().asPoint(),
                  last.geometry().asPoint())
```

9. Convert the measurement value from decimal degrees to meters:

```
deg = QGis.DecimalDegrees
met = QGis.Meters
d.convertMeasurement(m, deg, met, False)
```

10. Ensure that your Python console output looks similar to the following tuple:

```
(4401.1622240174165, 0)
```

How it works...

The `QgsDistanceArea` object accepts different types of geometry as input. In this case, we use two points. The map units for this layer are in decimal degrees, which isn't meaningful for a distance measurement. So, we use the `QgsDistanceArea.convertMeasurement()` method to covert the output to meters. The parameters for the method are the measurement output, the input units (in decimal degrees), the output units (meters), and a boolean to denote whether this conversion is an area calculation or a linear measurement.

The returned tuple is the measurement value and the units. The value `0` tells us that the output is in meters.

Measuring distance along a line

In this recipe, we'll measure the distance along a line with multiple vertices.

Getting ready

For this recipe, we'll use a line shapefile with two features. You can download the shapefile as a .zip file from https://github.com/GeospatialPython/Learn/raw/master/paths.zip.

Unzip the shapefile into a directory named qgis_data/shapes within your root or home directory.

How to do it...

The steps for this recipe are fairly straightforward. We'll extract the geometry from the first line feature and pass it to the measurement object, as shown here:

1. First, we must load the QGIS constants library:

   ```
   from qgis.core import QGis
   ```

2. Load the line layer:

   ```
   lyr = QgsVectorLayer("/qgis_data/shapes/paths.shp", "Route", "ogr")
   ```

3. Grab the features:

   ```
   fts = lyr.getFeatures()
   ```

4. Get the first feature:

   ```
   route = fts.next()
   ```

5. Create the measurement object instance:

   ```
   d = QgsDistanceArea()
   ```

6. Then, we must configure the QgsDistanceArea object to use the ellipsoidal mode for accurate measurements in meters:

   ```
   d.setEllipsoidalMode(True)
   ```

7. Pass the line's geometry to the measureLine method:

   ```
   m = d.measureLine(route.geometry().asPolyline())
   ```

8. Convert the measurement output to miles:

```
d.convertMeasurement(m, QGis.Meters, QGis.NauticalMiles, False)
```

9. Ensure that your output looks similar to the following:

```
(2314126.583384674, 7)
```

How it works...

The `QgsDistanceArea` object can perform any type of measurement, based on the method you call. When you convert the measurement from meters (represented by 0) to miles (identified by the number 7), you will get a tuple with the measurement in miles and the unit identifier. The QGIS API documentation shows the values for all the unit constants (`http://qgis.org/api/classQgsDistanceArea.html`).

Calculating the area of a polygon

This recipe measures the area of a polygon. Area calculation can be an end in itself to measure the size of a plot of land or a building. It can also be the input to other calculations such as land use maps.

Getting ready

For this recipe, we'll use a single-feature polygon shapefile, which you can download from the following link:

`https://github.com/GeospatialPython/Learn/raw/master/Mississippi.zip`

Unzip the shapefile and put it in a directory named `qgis_data/ms` within your root or home directory.

How to do it...

Perform the following steps to measure the area of a large polygon:

1. First, import the QGIS constants library, as follows:

```
from qgis.core import QGis
```

2. Load the layer:

```
lyr = QgsVectorLayer("/qgis_data/ms/mississippi.shp",
                     "Mississippi", "ogr")
```

3. Access the layer's features:

```
fts = lyr.getFeatures()
```

4. Get the boundary feature:

```
boundary = fts.next()
```

5. Create the measurement object instance:

```
d = QgsDistanceArea()
```

6. Pass the polygon list to the `measureArea()` method:

```
m = d.measurePolygon(boundary.geometry().asPolygon()[0])
```

7. Convert the measurement from decimal degrees to miles:

```
d.convertMeasurement(m, QGis.Degrees, QGis.NauticalMiles, True)
```

8. Verify that your output looks similar to the following:

```
(42955.47889640281, 7)
```

How it works...

PyQGIS has no `measureArea()` method, but it has a `measurePolygon()` method in the `QgsDistanceArea` object. The method accepts a list of points. In this case, when we convert the measurement output from decimal degrees to miles, we also just specify `True` in the `convertMeasurement()` method so that QGIS knows that it is an area calculation. Note that when we get the boundary geometry as a polygon, we use an index of `0`, suggesting that there is more than one polygon. A polygon geometry can have inner rings, which are specified as additional polygons. The outermost ring, in this case the only ring, is the first polygon.

Creating a spatial index

Until now, the recipes in this book used raw geometry for each layer of operations. In this recipe, we'll take a different approach and create a spatial index for a layer before we run operations on it. A spatial index optimizes a layer for spatial queries by creating additional simpler geometries that can be used to narrow down the field of possibilities within the complex geometry.

Getting ready

If you don't already have the New York City Museums layer used in the previous recipes in this chapter, download the layer from
`https://github.com/GeospatialPython/Learn/raw/master/NYC_MUSEUMS_GEO.zip`.

Unzip that file and place the shapefile's contents in a directory named `nyc` within your `qgis_data` directory, within your root or home directory.

How to do it...

In this recipe, we'll create a spatial index for a point layer and then we'll use it to perform a spatial query, as follows:

1. Load the layer:

```
lyr = QgsVectorLayer("/qgis_data/nyc/NYC_MUSEUMS_GEO.shp",
                     "Museums", "ogr")
```

2. Get the features:

```
fts = lyr.getFeatures()
```

3. Get the first feature in the set:

```
first = fts.next()
```

4. Now, create the spatial index:

```
index = QgsSpatialIndex()
```

5. Begin loading the features:

```
index = QgsSpatialIndex()
```

6. Insert the remaining features:

```
for f in fts:
    index.insertFeature(f)
```

7. Next we add the layer to the canvas:

```
QgsMapLayerRegistry.instance().addMapLayers([lyr])
```

8. Now, select the IDs of three points nearest to the first point. We use the number 4 because the starting point is included in the output:

```
hood = index.nearestNeighbor(first.geometry().asPoint(), 4)
```

9. Finally we can select the ids of those features:

```
lyr.setSelectedFeatures(hood)
```

10. In the following screenshot, the first feature is shown with a star while the nearest three features are selected in lighter yellow:

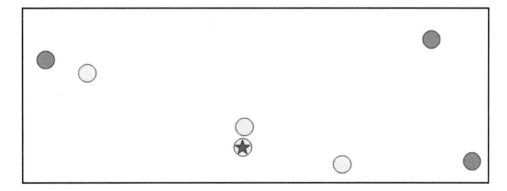

How it works...

The index speeds up spatial operations. However, you must add each feature one by one. Also, note that the nearestNeighbor() method returns the ID of the starting point as part of the output. So, if you want four points, you must specify 5.

Calculating the bearing of a line

Sometimes, you need to know the compass bearing of a line to create specialized symbology or to use as input in a spatial calculation. Even though its name only mentions distance and area, the versatile QgsDistanceArea object includes this function as well. In this recipe, we'll calculate the bearing of the end points of a line. However, this recipe will work with any two points.

Getting ready

We'll use the line shapefile used in *Measuring the distance between two points* recipe. You can download the shapefile as a .zip file from https://github.com/GeospatialPython/Learn/raw/master/paths.zip.

Unzip the shapefile into a directory named qgis_data/shapes within your root or home directory.

How to do it...

The steps to be performed are as simple as getting the two points we need and running them through the bearing function, converting from radians to degrees, and then converting to a positive compass bearing:

1. First, import the Python math module:

   ```
   import math
   ```

2. Next, load the layer:

   ```
   lyr = QgsVectorLayer("/qgis_data/shapes/paths.shp", "Route", "ogr")
   ```

3. Now, grab the features:

   ```
   fts = lyr.getFeatures()
   ```

4. Then, grab the first line feature:

   ```
   route = fts.next()
   ```

5. Create the measurement object:

```
d = QgsDistanceArea()
```

6. We must set the ellipsoidal mode to `True` in order to project the data before calculating the bearing:

```
d.setEllipsoidalMode(True)
```

7. Get all the points as a list:

```
points = route.geometry().asPolyline()
```

8. Get the first point:

```
first = points[0]
```

9. Grab the last point:

```
last = points[-1]
```

10. Calculate the bearing in radians:

```
r = d.bearing(first, last)
```

11. Now convert from radians to degrees:

```
b = math.degrees(r)
```

12. Ensure that the bearing is positive:

```
if b < 0: b += 360
```

13. View the output:

```
print(b)
```

14. Verify that the bearing is close to the following number:

```
320.3356091875395
```

How it works...

The default output of the bearing calculation is in radians. However, the Python `math` module makes converting a snap of the fingers. If the conversion of degrees results in a negative number, most of the time, we will want to add that number to 360 in order to get a compass bearing, as we did here.

Loading data from a spreadsheet

Spreadsheets are one of the most common methods used to collect and store simple geographic data. QGIS can work with text files called **Comma Separated Value (CSV)** files. Any spreadsheet can be converted to a CSV using the spreadsheet program. As long as the CSV data has a column representing x values, one column representing y values, and other columns representing data with the first row containing field names, QGIS can import it. Many organizations distribute geographic information as a CSV, so sooner or later, you will find yourself importing a CSV. Moreover, PyQGIS lets you do it programmatically. Note that a CSV can be delimited by any character as long as it is consistent. Also, the file extension of the CSV file doesn't matter as long as you specify the file type for QGIS.

Getting ready

We'll use a sample CSV file with point features representing points of interest in a region. You can download this sample from
`https://github.com/GeospatialPython/Learn/raw/master/tourism.csv`.

Save this to your `qgis_data/ms` directory in your root or home directory.

How to do it...

We will build a **URI** string to load the CSV as a vector layer. All of the parameters used to describe the structure of the CSV are included in the URI, as follows:

1. First, we build the base URI string with the filename:

```
uri = "file:///qgis_data/ms/tourism.csv?"
```

2. Next, we tell QGIS that the file is a CSV file:

```
uri += "type=csv&"
```

3. Now, the most important part, we specify the x field:

```
uri += "xField=X&"
```

4. Then, we specify the y field:

```
uri += "yField=Y&"
```

5. We decline the spatial index option:

```
uri += "spatialIndex=no&"
```

6. We decline the subset option:

```
uri += "subsetIndex=no&"
```

7. We tell QGIS not to watch the file for changes:

```
uri += "watchFile=no&"
```

8. Finally, we complete `uri` with the CRS of the layer:

```
uri += "crs=epsg:4326"
```

9. We load the layer using the `delimitedtext` data provider:

```
layer=QgsVectorLayer(uri,"Tourism Sites","delimitedtext")
```

10. Finally, we add it to the map:

```
QgsMapLayerRegistry.instance().addMapLayers([layer])
```

11. Verify that your map looks similar to the map shown in the following screenshot, which also has an `OpenStreetMap` service added for reference:

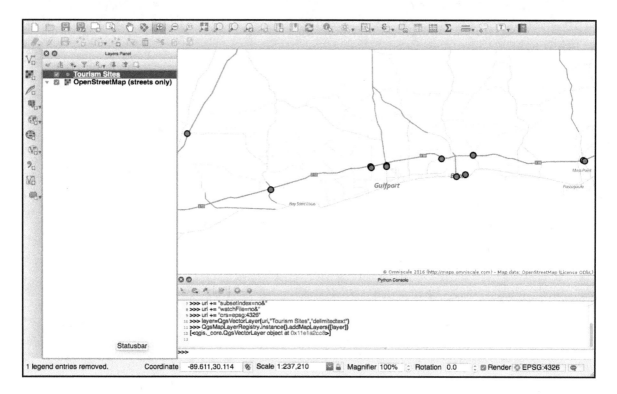

How it works...

The URI is quite extensive but necessary to give QGIS enough information in order to properly load the layer. We used strings in this simple example, but using the `QUrl` object is safer as it handles the encoding for you. The documentation for the `QUrl` class is in the Qt documentation at `http://qt-project.org/doc/qt-4.8/qurl.html`.

Note that in the URI, we tell QGIS that the type is CSV, but when we load the layer, the type is `delimitedtext`. QGIS will ignore empty fields as long as all of the columns are balanced.

There's more...

If you're having trouble loading a layer, you can use the QGIS **Add Delimited Text Layer...** dialog under the **Layer** menu to figure out the correct parameters. Once the layer is loaded, you can take a look at its metadata to see the URI QGIS constructed to load it. You can also get the correct parameters from a loaded delimited text layer using the `layer.source()` method programmatically, and, of course, both of these methods work with any type of layer, not just delimited text. Unlike other layer types, however, you cannot edit delimited text layers in QGIS.

Accessing layer metadata

Layer metadata is, by definition, data about the layer. Metadata includes information such as the extents of the layer, the **coordinate reference system** (**CRS**), the number of features, the data source, and much more. Metadata is an important tool for GIS analysts to understand a dataset. QGIS also uses metadata to properly configure the map, run queries, and perform other management functions. Metadata such as the extents and number of features can be extracted automatically from the data. Other metadata such as the CRS, source, and production methods must be added by the person or software that generates the data. PyQGIS has a method to return layer metadata as an HTML document. To programmatically extract a single metadata attribute, you must parse the HTML. In this recipe, you'll extract the **layer capabilities** from a layer, which tell you if the layer can be edited within PyQGIS. Although there are dozens of ways to parse HTML in Python, you will use some simple string manipulation methods. The metadata in HTML format looks like the following, with the part we are interested in highlighted in bold:

```
u'<html><body><p class="subheaderglossy">General</p>\n<p
class="glossy">Storage type of this layer</p>\n<p>ESRI Shapefile</p>\n<p
class="glossy">Description of this provider</p>\n<p>OGR data provider
(compiled against GDAL/OGR library version 2.1.1, running against GDAL/OGR
library version 2.1.1)</p>\n<p class="glossy">Source for this
layer</p>\n<p> /qgis_data/nyc/NYC_MUSEUMS_GEO.shp</p>\n<p
class="glossy">Geometry type of the features in this layer</p>\n<p>Point
(WKB type: "Point")</p>\n<p class="glossy">The number of features in this
layer</p>\n<p>130</p>\n<p class="glossy">Capabilities of this
layer</p>\n<p>Add Features, Delete Features, Change Attribute Values, Add
Attributes, Delete Attributes, Rename Attributes, Create Spatial Index,
Create Attribute Indexes, Fast Access to Features at ID, Change
Geometries</p>\n<p class="subheaderglossy">Extents</p>\n<p
class="glossy">In layer spatial reference system units</p>\n<p>xMin,yMin
-74.2165,40.5152 : xMax,yMax -73.7257,40.8979</p>\n<p class="glossy">Layer
Spatial Reference System</p>\n<p>+proj=longlat +datum=WGS84
```

```
+no_defs</p>\n</body></html>'
```

Getting ready

In this recipe, once again, we'll use a point shapefile of New York City museums, which you can download from
`https://github.com/GeospatialPython/Learn/raw/master/NYC_MUSEUMS_GEO.zip`.

Unzip this file and place the shapfile's contents in a directory named `nyc` within your `qgis_data` directory.

How to do it...

Add the shapefile to the map as follows, so we can extract the metadata:

1. First, load the layer:

   ```
   lyr = QgsVectorLayer("/qgis_data/nyc/NYC_MUSEUMS_GEO.shp",
                        "Museums", "ogr")
   ```

2. Next, visualize the layer on the map:

   ```
   QgsMapLayerRegistry.instance().addMapLayers([lyr])
   ```

3. Now capture the layer metadata, so we can parse it:

   ```
   m = layer.metadata()
   ```

4. Now, we'll extract the layer capabilities into a list using a chain of string-split commands, grabbing the element we need on each split. We'll split the HTML document on the attribute title, then on HTML tags, and finally split the capabilities list on commas:

   ```
   lyr_cap = m.split("Capabilities of this layer</p>\n<p>")
           [1].split("<")[0].split(",")
   ```

5. Finally, let's strip any leading spaces from the list:

   ```
   lyr_cap = [x.strip() for x in lyr_cap]
   ```

6. Verify that the capabilities list looks like the following:

```
[u'Add Features', u'Delete Features', u'Change Attribute Values',
 u'Add Attributes', u'Delete Attributes', u'Rename Attributes',
 u'Create Spatial Index', u'Create Attribute Indexes',
 u'Fast Access to Features at ID', u'Change Geometries']
```

How it works...

When you're dealing with a predictable document, chopping it up with Python string methods provides a reliable way to easily extract information. We could have broken the series of `split()` methods up into separate lines, but Python's ability to chain a series of commands together without intermediate variables is one of the language's strengths. If you're dealing with unpredictable text, Python's regular expressions are a more powerful and flexible way to search through the text to find the information you want. For HTML or XML, you can also use Python's built-in **ElementTree** library or the robust **BeautifulSoup** third-party parser.

3
Editing Vector Data

In this chapter, we will cover the following recipes:

- Creating a vector layer in memory
- Adding a point feature to a vector layer
- Adding a line feature to a vector layer
- Adding a polygon feature to a vector layer
- Adding a set of attributes to a vector layer
- Adding a field to a vector layer
- Joining a shapefile attribute table to a CSV file
- Changing vector layer geometry
- Changing a vector layer feature's attribute
- Removing data from a vector layer
- Deleting vector layer feature's attributes
- Reprojecting a vector layer
- Converting a shapefile to KML or GeoJSON
- Merging shapefiles
- Splitting a shapefile
- Generalizing a vector layer
- Dissolving vector features
- Performing a union on vector shapes
- Rasterizing a vector layer
- Exporting a layer to the GeoPackage format

Introduction

This chapter details editing the process of QGIS vector data using the Python API. The `QgsVectorLayer` object contains the basics of adding, editing, and deleting features. All other geospatial operations are accessed through the **Processing Toolbox** or even through custom scripts.

Creating a vector layer in memory

Sometimes you need to create a temporary dataset for a quick output, or as an intermediate step in a more complex operation without the overhead of actually writing a file to disk. PyQGIS employs memory layers that allow you to create a complete vector dataset, including the geometry, fields, and attributes, virtually. Once the memory layer is created, you can work with it the same way you would with a vector layer loaded from the disk.

Getting ready

This recipe runs entirely inside the PyQGIS console, so no preparation or outside resources are required.

How to do it...

We will create a point vector layer with a few fields named Layer 1 and then validate it:

1. Start QGIS.
2. From the **Plugins** menu select **Python Console**.
3. In the Python console, create a `QgsVectorLayer`, including fields, and specify it as type memory:

```
vectorLyr = QgsVectorLayer('Point?crs=epsg:4326
                        &field=city:string(25)
                        &field=population:nt',
                        'Layer 1' , "memory")
```

4. Now, validate the layer and ensure the console returns True:

```
vectorLyr.isValid()
```

How it works...

The `QgsVectorLayer` requires three arguments. The last one specifies the type, in this case, `memory`. The second one specifies the layer name. Normally, the first argument is the path to the file on the disk used to create the layer. In the case of a memory layer, the first argument becomes the construction string for the layer. The format uses query parameters following the convention of `key=value`. In this case, we specify the first field, a string for city names, and then an integer field for population.

Adding a point feature to a vector layer

This recipe performs the simplest possible edit to a vector layer instantiated from a shapefile. We will add a point to an existing point layer.

Getting ready

For this recipe, download the following zipped shapefile:

`https://github.com/GeospatialPython/Learn/raw/master/NYC_MUSEUMS_GEO.zip`

Extract the `.shp`, `.shx`, and `.dbf` files to the directory `/qgis_data/nyc`.

How to do it...

We will load the vector layer from the shapefile, create a new geometry object as a point, create a new feature, set the geometry, and add it to the layer's data provider. Finally, we will update the extents of the layer to make sure the bounding box of the layer encapsulates the new point:

1. Start QGIS.
2. From the **Plugins** menu, select **Python Console**.
3. First, load the layer:

```
vectorLyr = QgsVectorLayer('/qgis_data/nyc/NYC_MUSEUMS_GEO.shp',
                           'Museums' , "ogr")
```

4. Now, we will access the layer's data provider:

```
vpr = vectorLyr.dataProvider()
```

5. Next, create a new point using the QgsGeometry API:

```
pnt = QgsGeometry.fromPoint(QgsPoint(-74.80,40.549))
```

6. Now, we will create a new QgsFeature object to house the geometry:

```
f = QgsFeature()
```

7. Next, set the geometry of the feature using our point:

```
f.setGeometry(pnt)
```

8. Then, we place the features into the layer's feature list:

```
vpr.addFeatures([f])
```

9. Finally, we update the layer extents to complete the addition:

```
vectorLyr.updateExtents()
```

10. The following screenshot shows the added point on the far left of the image:

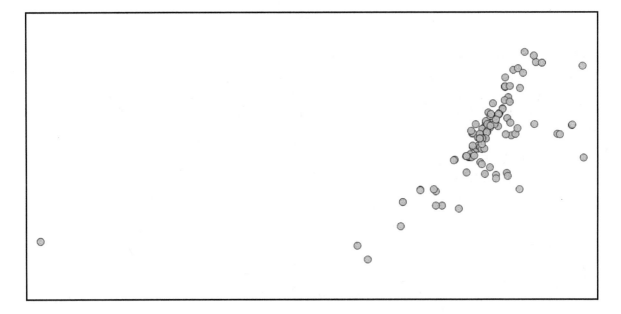

How it works...

PyQGIS abstracts the points within a layer into four levels. At the lowest level is the `QgsPoint` object, which contains nothing more than the coordinates of the point. That object is added to an abstract `QgsGeometry` object. That object becomes the geometry half of a `QgsFeature` object, which also has the ability to store and manage attributes. All the features are managed by the QgsVectorLayer's `QgsDataProvider` object. The data provider manages both the spatial and non-spatial parts of a layer to separate that aspect from styling and other presentation-related portions.

There's more...

When adding any feature to a layer, if the data source is a database such as PostGIS, the `addFeatures()` method will return `true` even if there is an insert error in the database. Insert errors can include common configurations, such as foreign key constraints. If you find you are unable to add a feature, try inserting the feature into the database manually, using SQL to troubleshoot.

Adding a line feature to a vector layer

Adding a line to a vector layer in QGIS is identical to adding a single point, but you just add more points to the `QgsGeometry` object.

Getting ready

For this recipe, you will need to download a zipped line shapefile containing two line features from the following URL:

`https://github.com/GeospatialPython/Learn/raw/master/paths.zip`

Extract the ZIP file to a directory named `paths` in your `/qgis_data` directory.

How to do it...

We will load the line layer from the shapefile, build a list of points, create a new geometry object and add the points as a line, create a new feature, set the geometry, and add it to the layer's data provider. Finally, we will update the extents of the layer to make sure the bounding box of the layer encapsulates the new feature:

1. Start QGIS.
2. From the **Plugins** menu, select **Python Console**.
3. First, we load the line layer and ensure it is valid:

```
vectorLyr=QgsVectorLayer('/qgis_data/paths/paths.shp',
                         'Paths',"ogr")
vectorLyr.isValid()
```

4. Next, we access the layer's data provider:

```
vpr = vectorLyr.dataProvider()
```

5. Now, we build our list of points for a new line:

```
points = []
points.append(QgsPoint(430841.61703,5589485.34838))
points.append(QgsPoint(432438.36523,5575114.61462))
points.append(QgsPoint(447252.64015,5567663.12304))
```

6. Then, we create a geometry object from the line:

```
line = QgsGeometry.fromPolyline(points)
```

7. Create a feature and set its geometry to the line:

```
f = QgsFeature()
f.setGeometry(line)
```

8. Finally, we add the feature to the layer data provider and update the extents:

```
vpr.addFeatures([f])
vectorLyr.updateExtents()
```

How it works...

As with all geometry in QGIS, we use the 4-step building process of points, geometry, feature, and data provider to add the line. Interestingly, the `QgsGeometry` object accepts Python lists for collections of points instead of creating a formal object, as is done with the `QgsPoint` API.

Adding a polygon feature to a vector layer

In this recipe, we'll add a polygon to a layer. A polygon is the most complex kind of geometry; however, in QGIS the API is very similar to a line.

Getting ready

For this recipe, we'll use a simple polygon shapefile which you can download as a ZIP file from the following URL:

`https://github.com/GeospatialPython/Learn/raw/master/polygon.zip`

Extract this shapefile to a folder called `polygon` in your `/qgis_data` directory.

How to do it...

This recipe will follow the standard PyQGIS process of loading a layer, building a feature, and adding it to the layer's data provider:

1. Start QGIS.
2. From the **Plugins** menu, select **Python Console**.
3. First, load the layer and validate it:

```
vectorLyr=  QgsVectorLayer('/qgis_data/polygon/polygon.shp',
                          'Polyon' , "ogr")
vectorLyr.isValid()
```

4. Next, access the layer's data provider:

```
vpr = vectorLyr.dataProvider()
```

5. Now, we build a list of points for the polygon:

```
points = []
points.append(QgsPoint(-123.26072,49.06822))
points.append(QgsPoint(-127.19157,43.07367))
points.append(QgsPoint(-120.70567,35.21197))
points.append(QgsPoint(-115.89037,40.02726))
points.append(QgsPoint(-113.04051,48.47859))
points.append(QgsPoint(-123.26072,49.06822))
```

6. Now, we create a geometry object and ingest the points as a polygon:

```
poly = QgsGeometry.fromPolygon([points])
```

7. Next, we build the feature object and add the points:

```
f = QgsFeature()
f.setGeometry(poly)
```

8. Finally, we add the feature to the layer's data provider and update the extents:

```
vpr.addFeatures([f])
```

How it works...

Adding a polygon is very similar to adding a line, but with one key difference that is a common pitfall. The last point must be identical to the first point in order to close the polygon. If you don't repeat the first point, you won't receive any errors, but the polygon will not display in QGIS, which can be difficult to troubleshoot.

Adding a set of attributes to a vector layer

Each QGIS feature has two parts: the geometry and the attributes. In this recipe, we'll add an attribute for a layer from an existing dataset.

Getting ready...

We will use a point shapefile with museum data for New York City, which you can download as a ZIP file from the following URL:

```
https://github.com/GeospatialPython/Learn/raw/master/NYC_MUSEUMS_GEO.zip
```

Extract this shapefile to the following directory: `/qgis_data/nyc`

How to do it...

While you can add a geometry to a feature without attributes, you must have at least a geometry in order to add attributes. So, we will create a new feature, add some attributes, and then add everything to the layer:

1. Start QGIS.
2. From the **Plugins** menu, select **Python Console**.
3. First, load the layer and validate it:

```
vectorLyr =  QgsVectorLayer('/qgis_data/nyc/NYC_MUSEUMS_GEO.shp',
                            'Museums' , "ogr")
vectorLyr.isValid()
```

4. Next, access the layer's data provider:

```
vpr = vectorLyr.dataProvider()
```

5. Now, we create a point geometry, which, in this case, is a new museum:

```
pnt = QgsGeometry.fromPoint(QgsPoint(-74.13401,40.62148))
```

6. Then, we create a new feature and add the geometry:

```
f = QgsFeature()
```

7. Now, we set the geometry of our new museum feature:

```
f.setGeometry(pnt)
```

8. Now, we are finally able to add a new attribute. We must set at least one attribute, but we don't have to set all of them. We will just add a name, which is at field position 0:

```
f.setAttriibuteMap({0:"Python Museum"})
```

9. Finally, we add the feature to the layer and update the extents:

```
vpr.addFeatures([f])
vectorLyr.updateExtents()
```

How it works...

Just as geometries are created from Python point lists or tuples, PyQGIS attributes are defined as Python dictionaries specifying the field index position as the key and the attribute as the dictionary value. Python lists and dictionaries are very powerful and flexible data structures. This approach makes adding data to QGIS much easier because you can use the full power of Python data types to build your dataset before defining it with the C-based PyQGIS API.

Adding a field to a vector layer

This recipe demonstrates adding a new field to a layer. Each field represents a new column in a data set for which each feature has a new attribute. When you add a new attribute, the attribute value for all existing features are set to NULL for that field index.

Getting ready

We will use the New York City museums shapefile used in other recipes, which you can download as a ZIP file here:

```
https://github.com/GeospatialPython/Learn/raw/master/NYC_MUSEUMS_GEO.zip
```

Extract this shapefile to /qgis_data/nyc.

How to do it...

All data management for a layer is handled through the layer's data provider, and fields are no different. We will load the layer, access the data provider, define the new field, and finalize the change:

1. Start QGIS.
2. From the **Plugins** menu, select **Python Console**.
3. First, we must import the Qt library data types that PyQGIS uses to specify layer field data types:

   ```
   from PyQt4.QtCore import QVariant
   ```

4. Next, load and validate the layer:

```
vectorLyr= QgsVectorLayer('/qgis_data/nyc/NYC_MUSEUMS_GEO.shp',
                          'Museums' , "ogr")
vectorLyr.isValid()
```

5. Then, we access the layer data provider:

```
vpr = vectorLyr.dataProvider()
```

6. Now, we add a Python list of `QgsField` objects, which define the field name and type. In this case, we'll add one field named `Admission` as a double:

```
vpr.addAttributes([QgsField("Admission", QVariant.Double)])
```

7. Finally, we update the fields to complete the change:

```
vectorLyr.updateFields()
```

How it works...

It is important to note that QGIS refers to the column headers as attributes and the feature values as fields. In other GIS packages, you may see this nomenclature reversed.

Joining a shapefile attribute table to a CSV file

Joining attribute tables to other database tables allows you to use a spatial data set to reference a dataset without any geometry, using a common key between the data tables. A very common use case for this is to join a vector dataset of census attributes to a more detailed census attribute dataset. That is the use case we will demonstrate here by linking a US census track file to a detailed **Comma Separated Value** (**CSV**) file containing more in-depth information.

Getting ready

For this recipe you will need a census tract shapefile and a CSV file containing the appropriate census data for the shapefile. You can download the sample dataset from the following URL:

```
https://github.com/GeospatialPython/Learn/raw/master/census.zip
```

Extract the data to a directory named /qgis_data/census.

How to do it...

The join operation is quite involved. We'll perform this operation and save the layer as a new shapefile with the joined attributes. Then, we'll load the new layer and compare the field count to the original layer to ensure the join occurred:

1. Start QGIS.
2. From the **Plugins** menu, select **Python Console**.
3. First, we'll load the county census track layer and validate it:

   ```
   vectorLyr=  QgsVectorLayer("/qgis_data/census/hancock_tracts.shp",
                            "Hancock" , "ogr")
   vectorLyr.isValid()
   ```

4. Now, we'll load the CSV file as a layer and validate it as well:

   ```
   infoLyr = QgsVectorLayer("/qgis_data/census/
                            ACS_12_5YR_S1901_with_ann.csv",
                            "Census" , "ogr")
   infoLyr.isValid()
   ```

5. Now, we must add both layers to the map registry in order for the two layers to interact for the join. However, we will set the visibility to False so that the layers do not appear on the map:

   ```
   QgsMapLayerRegistry.instance().addMapLayers([vectorLyr,infoLyr],
                                              False)
   ```

6. Next, we must create a special join object:

   ```
   info = QgsVectorJoinInfo()
   ```

7. The join object needs the layer ID of the CSV file:

```
info.joinLayerId = infoLyr.id()
```

8. Next, we specify the key field from the CSV file whose values correspond to the values in the shapefile:

```
info.joinFieldName = "GEOid2"
```

9. Then, we specify the corresponding field in the shapefile:

```
info.targetFieldName = "GEOID"
```

10. We then set the `memoryCache` property to `True` to speed up access to the joined data:

```
info.memoryCache = True
```

11. Now, we add the join to the layer:

```
vectorLyr.addJoin(info)
```

12. Next, we will write out the joined shapefile to a new file on disk:

```
QgsVectorFileWriter.writeAsVectorFormat(vectorLyr,
                        "/qgis_data/census/joined.shp",
                        "CP120", None, "ESRI Shapefile")
```

13. Now, we'll load the new shapefile back in as a layer for verification:

```
joinedLyr= QgsVectorLayer("/qgis_data/census/joined.shp","Joined" ,
                        "ogr")
```

14. Next, verify that the field count in the original layer is 12:

```
vectorLyr.dataProvider().fields().count()
```

15. Finally, verify that the new layer has a field count of 142 from the join:

```
joinedLyr.dataProvider().fields().count()
```

How it works...

This recipe reaches out to the very edge of the PyQGIS API, forcing us to use some workarounds. Most recipes for data manipulation can be performed programmatically without writing data to disk or loading layers onto the map. But joins are different. Because the `QgsVectorJoinInfo` object needs the layer ID of the CSV layer we must add both layers to the map layer registry. Fortunately, we can do this without making them visible if we are just trying to write a data manipulation script.

There's more...

You can find an alternate method in a Processing Toolbox script which manually matches up the joined data in Python in the QGIS Join attributes table function. This script creates a whole new shapefile with the joined tables.

Changing vector layer geometry

Sometimes you need to change the location of a feature. You could do this by deleting and re-adding the feature, but PyQGIS provides a simple way to change the geometry.

Getting ready

You will need the New York City museums shapefile, which you can download as a ZIP file from the following URL:

`https://github.com/GeospatialPython/Learn/raw/master/NYC_MUSEUMS_GEO.zip`

Extract this shapefile to `/qgis_data/nyc`.

How to do it...

We will load the shapefile as a vector layer, validate it, define the feature ID we want to change, create the new geometry, and change the feature in the layer.

1. Start QGIS.
2. From the **Plugins** menu, select **Python Console**.

3. First, we load the layer and validate it:

    ```
    vectorLyr = QgsVectorLayer('/qgis_data/nyc/NYC_MUSEUMS_GEO.shp',
                               'Museums' , "ogr")
    vectorLyr.isValid()
    ```

4. Next, we define the feature ID we are interested in changing:

    ```
    feat_id = 22
    ```

5. Now, we create the new point geometry that will become the new location:

    ```
    geom = QgsGeometry.fromPoint(QgsPoint(-74.20378,40.89642))
    ```

6. Finally, we change the geometry and replace it with our new geometry specifying the feature ID:

    ```
    vectorLyr.dataProvider().changeGeometryValues({feat_id : geom})
    ```

How it works...

The `changeGeometryValues` method makes editing a snap. If we had to delete and then re-add the feature, we would have to go through the trouble of reading the attributes, preserving them, and then re-adding them with the new feature. Of course, you must know the feature ID of the feature you want to change. How you determine that ID depends on your application. Typically, you would query the attributes to find a specific value, or you might perform a spatial operation of some sort.

Changing a vector layer feature's attribute

Changing a feature's attribute is very straightforward, and well-supported by the PyQGIS API. In this recipe, we'll change a single attribute, but you can change as many attributes of a feature at once as desired.

Getting ready

You will need the New York City museums shapefile used in other recipes, which you can download as a ZIP file from the following URL:

```
https://github.com/GeospatialPython/Learn/raw/master/NYC_MUSEUMS_GEO.zip
```

Extract this shapefile to `/qgis_data/nyc`.

How to do it...

We will load the shapefile as a vector layer, validate it, define the feature ID whose fields we want to change, define the new attribute value as an attribute index and value, and change the feature in the layer:

1. Start QGIS.
2. From the **Plugins** menu, select **Python Console**.
3. First, load the layer and validate it:

```
vectorLyr = QgsVectorLayer('/qgis_data/nyc/NYC_MUSEUMS_GEO.shp',
                           'Museums' , "ogr")
vectorLyr.isValid()
```

4. Next, define the feature ID we want to change:

```
feat_id = 22
```

5. Now, we'll create the Python dictionary for the attribute index and the new value, which, in this case, is an imaginary phone number:

```
attr = {1:"(555) 555-5555"}
```

6. Now, we use the layer's data provider to update the fields:

```
vectorLyr.dataProvider().changeAttributeValues({feat_id : attr})
```

How it works...

Changing attributes is very similar to changing the geometry within a feature. If you wanted to change more fields at once, you would just expand the Python dictionary with more keys and values.

Removing data from a vector layer

In this recipe, we'll completely remove a feature, including its geometry and attributes, from a layer.

Getting ready

You will need the New York City museums shapefile used in other recipes, which you can download as a ZIP file from the following URL:

```
https://github.com/GeospatialPython/Learn/raw/master/NYC_MUSEUMS_GEO.zip
```

Extract this shapefile to /qgis_data/nyc.

How to do it....

All we need to do is load the layer and then delete the desired features by ID using the layer's data provider:

1. Start QGIS.
2. From the **Plugins** menu, select **Python Console**.
3. First, we load and validate the layer:

```
vectorLyr =  QgsVectorLayer('/qgis_data/nyc/NYC_MUSEUMS_GEO.shp',
                            'Museums' , "ogr")
vectorLyr.isValid()
```

4. Next, we specify a Python list containing feature IDs. In this case, we have two:

```
vectorLyr.dataProvider().deleteFeatures([22, 95])
```

How it works...

This operation couldn't be simpler and better designed. There are a number of ways we could programmatically fill a Python list with feature IDs. Then, we just pass that list to the layer data provider and we are done. Note that the IDs are not stored with the data. They are dynamically assigned when the layer is loaded. If you remove the layer and re-add it, the IDs will be sequential without any missing values.

Deleting a vector layer feature's attribute

In this recipe, we'll remove an entire attribute and all feature fields for a vector layer. Remember, attributes are the column names and fields are the individual values.

Getting ready

You will need the New York City museums shapefile used in other recipes, which you can download as a ZIP file from the following URL:

```
https://github.com/GeospatialPython/Learn/raw/master/NYC_MUSEUMS_GEO.zip
```

Extract this shapefile to `/qgis_data/nyc`.

How to do it...

This operation is straightforward. We'll load and validate the layer, use the layer data provider to delete the attribute by index, and finally update all of the fields to remove the orphaned values:

1. Start QGIS.
2. From the **Plugins** menu, select **Python Console**.
3. First, we load and validate the layer:

```
vectorLyr= QgsVectorLayer('/qgis_data/nyc/NYC_MUSEUMS_GEO.shp',
                          'Museums' , "ogr")
vectorLyr.isValid()
```

4. Then, we delete the first attribute:

```
vectorLyr.dataProvider().deleteAttributes([1])
```

5. Finally, we update the fields:

```
vectorLyr.updateFields()
```

How it works...

Because we are changing the actual structure of the layer data, we must call the `updateFields()` method of the layer to remove the field values, which no longer have an attribute. We have changed the underlying structure of the data and must notify QGIS.

Reprojecting a vector layer

Reprojecting a vector layer is inherent to QGIS; however, to access it from Python, we must use the Processing Toolbox.

Getting ready

For this recipe, we'll need the Mississippi cities shapefile in the Mississippi Transverse Mercator Projection, which can be downloaded as a ZIP file here:

`https://github.com/GeospatialPython/Learn/raw/master/MSCities_MSTM.zip`

Extract the zipped shapefile to a directory named `/qgis_data/ms`.

How to do it...

To reproject the layer, we'll simply call the `qgis:reprojectlayer` processing algorithm specifying the input shapefile, the new projection, and the output file name.

1. Start QGIS.
2. From the **Plugins** menu, select **Python Console**.
3. First, we need to import the processing module:

```
import processing
```

4. Next, we run the reprojection algorithm:

```
processing.runalg("qgis:reprojectlayer",
                  "/qgis_data/ms/MSCities_MSTM.shp","epsg:4326",
                  "/qgis_data/ms/MSCities_MSTM_4326.shp")
```

How it works...

This algorithm is simple as long as the input layer's projection is defined in a `.prj` definition file. You can define the known projection of the layer in PYQGIS using the following code in which we will use EPSG 4326 as the projection:

```
crs = layer.crs()
crs.createFromId(4326)
layer.setCrs(crs)
```

Converting a shapefile to KML or GeoJSON

In this recipe, we'll convert a layer to **KML** and **GeoJSON**. Google KML is an Open GIS Consortium standard and is supported by the underlying OGR library used by QGIS.

Getting ready

For this recipe, download the following zipped shapefile and extract it to a directory named `/qgis_data/hancock`:

`https://github.com/GeospatialPython/Learn/raw/master/hancock.zip`

How to do it...

To convert a shapefile to the KML XML format, we'll load the layer and then use the `QgsVectorFileWriter` object to save it as a KML file:

1. Start QGIS.
2. From the **Plugins** menu, select **Python Console**.
3. First, load the layer and validate it:

```
vectorLyr= QgsVectorLayer('/qgis_data/hancock/hancock.shp',
                          'Hancock' , "ogr")
```

4. Make sure that the layer is loaded correctly:

```
vectorLyr.isValid()
```

5. Next, use the file writer to save it as a KML file by specifying the file type as KML:

```
QgsVectorFileWriter.writeAsVectorFormat(vectorLyr,
                        "/qgis_data/hancock/hancock.kml",
                        "utf-8", None, "KML")
```

How it works...

You will end up with a KML file in the directory next to your shapefile. KML supports styling information. QGIS uses some default styling information that you can change by hand using a text editor or programmatically using an XML library, such as Python's `ElementTree`.

There's more...

Another commonly used format is GeoJSON. Note that GeoJSON should always be projected in WGS84 (EPSG:4326). You can find more information at `https://tools.ietf.org/html/rfc7946#section-4`. Like KML, it is a text format that is both human and computer readable. Instead of using XML like KML, GeoJSON uses **JavaScript Object Notation** syntax, which is much more terse than XML syntax with parsers built in for most programming languages including Python. To save the layer in this example as GeoJSON, it's as simple as just changing the output format:

```
QgsVectorFileWriter.writeAsVectorFormat(vectorLyr,
                        "/qgis_data/hancock/hancock.geojson",
                        "utf-8", dest_crs, "GeoJSON")
```

Merging shapefiles

Merging shapefiles with matching projections and attribute structures is a very common operation. In QGIS, the best way to merge vector datasets is to use another GIS system included with QGIS, called **SAGA**. The **OSGeo4W** QGIS version for Windows includes SAGA. The **KyngChaos** distribution of QGIS for OSX includes SAGA. Most other versions and platforms will need SAGA manually installed. In PyQGIS, you access SAGA functions through the Processing Toolbox.

Getting ready

In this recipe, we'll merge some building footprint shapefiles from the adjoining areas into a single shapefile. You can download the sample dataset from the following URL:

```
https://github.com/GeospatialPython/Learn/raw/master/tiled_footprints.zip
```

Extract the zipped shapefiles to a directory named `/qgis_data/tiled_footprints`.

How to do it...

We will locate all of the `.shp` files in the data directory and hand them to the `saga:mergeshapeslayers` to merge them:

1. Start QGIS.
2. From the **Plugins** menu, select **Python Console**.
3. We will import the Python `glob` module for wildcard file matching:

   ```
   import glob
   ```

4. Next, we import the `processing` module for the merge algorithm:

   ```
   import processing
   ```

5. Now, we'll specify the path of our data directory:

   ```
   pth = "/qgis_data/tiled_footprints/"
   ```

6. Next, we'll locate all the `.shp` files:

   ```
   files = glob.glob(pth + "*.shp")
   ```

7. Then, we specify the output name of the merged shapefile:

   ```
   out = pth + "merged.shp"
   ```

8. Finally, we run the algorithm that will load the merged shapefile onto the map:

   ```
   processing.runandload("saga:mergeshapeslayers",files.pop(0),
                         ";".join(files),out)
   ```

How it works...

The algorithm accepts a base file and then a semi-colon-separated list of additional files to be merged, and finally the output file name. The `glob` module creates the list of files. To get the base file, we use the list `pop()` method to remove and get the first filename. Then, we use the Python string `join()` method to make the required delimited list for the rest.

There's more...

QGIS has its own merge method available through the `processing` module, called `qgis:mergevectorlayers`, but it is limited because it only merges two files. The SAGA method allows for any number of files to be merged.

Splitting a shapefile

Sometimes you need to split a shapefile to break a larger dataset into more manageable sizes, or you want to isolate a specific area of interest. There is a script in the Processing Toolbox that splits a shapefile by attribute. It is very useful, even though it is provided as an example on how to write processing scripts.

Getting ready

We will split a census track shapefile by county. You can download the sample zipped shapefile from the following URL:

```
https://github.com/GeospatialPython/Learn/raw/master/GIS_CensusTract.zip
```

Extract the zipped shapefile to a directory named `/qgis_data/census`.

How to do it...

This recipe is as simple as running the algorithm and specifying the file name and data attribute:

1. Start QGIS.
2. From the **Plugins** menu, select **Python Console**.

3. Import the `processing` module:

   ```
   import processing
   ```

4. Define our data directory as a variable to shorten the processing command:

   ```
   pth = "/qgis_data/census/"
   ```

5. Finally, run the algorithm:

   ```
   processing.runalg("script:splitvectorlayerbyattribute",pth +
                     "GIS_CensusTract_poly.shp","COUNTY_8",
                     pth + "split")
   ```

How it works...

This algorithm splits the data by grouping like attributes. It will will dump the split files in the data directory numbered sequentially. You can select the directory, but not the file names. Because this is a processing Python script, however, you can easily copy and edit it to change the way it works. In QGIS 2.18 there is also a similar OGR function named **Split vector layer**.

Generalizing a vector layer

Generalizing geometry, also known as simplifying, removes points from a vector layer to reduce the space required to store the data. Otherwise, simplification may result in small but acceptable changes within a specified tolerance.

Getting ready

For this recipe, we will use a boundary file for the state of Mississippi, which you can download from the following URL:

```
https://github.com/GeospatialPython/Learn/raw/master/Mississippi.zip
```

Extract the zipped shapefile to a directory named `/qgis_data/ms`.

How to do it...

Generalizing is native to QGIS, but we will access it in PyQGIS through the Processing Toolbox using the `qgis:simplifygeometries` algorithm.

1. Start QGIS.
2. From the **Plugins** menu, select **Python Console**.
3. Import the `processing` module:

```
import processing
```

4. Now, we run the processing algorithm specifying the algorithm name, the input data, a tolerance value spacing between points, and the output dataset name:

```
processing.runandload("qgis:simplifygeometries",
                      "/qgis_data/ms/mississippi.shp",
                      0.3,"/qgis_data/ms/generalize.shp")
```

How it works...

The simplicity of this command makes the operation look simple. However, simplification is quite complex. The same settings rarely produce desirable results across multiple datasets. You should note the simplification operation is not topological and can result in gaps, disconnects, or overlaps between neighboring features.

The shapefile in this recipe starts out quite complex with hundreds of points, as seen in the following visualization:

The simplified version has only ten points as seen in the following image:

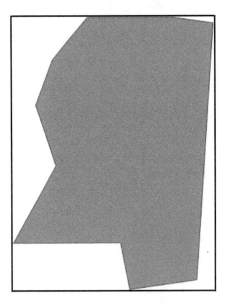

Dissolving vector features

Dissolving a group's geometry allows you to produce a single geometry with common attributes. In this recipe, we'll dissolve some census data into a single dataset.

Getting ready

Download the GIS census tract shapefile, which contains tracts for several counties from the following URL:

```
https://github.com/GeospatialPython/Learn/raw/master/GIS_CensusTract.zip
```

Extract it to your `/qgis_data` directory in a directory called `census`.

How to do it...

We will use the processing toolbox for this recipe and specifically a native QGIS algorithm called `dissolve`:

1. Start QGIS.
2. From the **Plugins** menu, select **Python Console**.
3. We must import the `processing` module:

    ```
    import processing
    ```

4. Next, we run the dissolve algorithm specifying the input data `False` to specify we don't want to dissolve all shapes into one but to use an attribute instead, the attribute we want to use, and the output file name:

    ```
    processing.runandload("qgis:dissolve","/qgis_data/census/
                    GIS_CensusTract_poly.shp",False,"COUNTY_8",
                    "/qgis_data/census/dissovle.shp")
    ```

How it works...

By changing the only boolean in the statement to `True`, we could dissolve all adjoining features into one. It is also very important to note that QGIS will assign the fields of the first features it encounters in each group to the final shape. In most cases, that will make the attributes virtually useless. This operation is primarily a spatial task.

You can see each county boundary has a number of census tracts in the original layer, as shown in the following image:

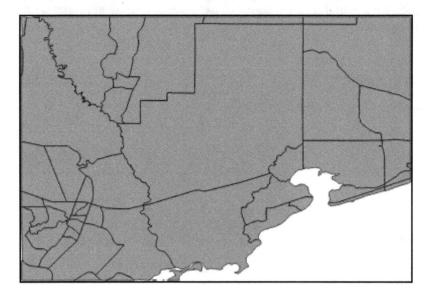

Once the shapes are dissolved, you are left with only the county boundaries, as shown in this image:

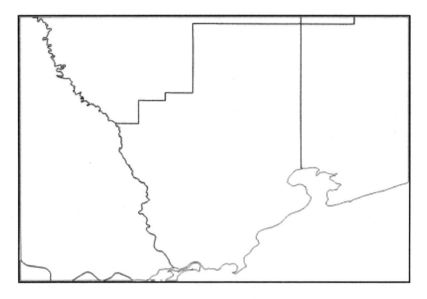

Performing a union on vector shapes

A union turns two overlapping shapes into one. This task can be easily accomplished with the Processing Toolbox. In this recipe, we'll merge the outline of a covered building to the footprint of the main building.

Getting ready

You can download the building files from the following URL and extract them to a directory named /qgis_data/union:

https://github.com/GeospatialPython/Learn/raw/master/union.zip

How to do it...

All we need to do is run the qgis:union algorithm:

1. Start QGIS.
2. From the **Plugins** menu, select **Python Console**.
3. Import the processing module:

```
import processing
```

4. Now, run the algorithm specifying the two input shapes and the single output file:

```
processing.runandload("qgis:union",
                      "/qgis_data/union/building.shp",
                      "/qgis_data/union/walkway.shp",
                      "/qgis_data/union/union.shp")
```

How it works...

As you can tell from the structure of the command, this tool can only combine two shapes at once. It finds where the two geometries meet, and then removes the overlap joining them at the meeting point.

In the original data, the layers starts out as two distinct shapes, as shown in this image:

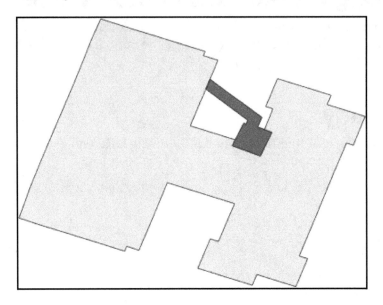

Once the union is complete, the shapes are now one shapefile with the overlap being a separate feature, as shown in this image:

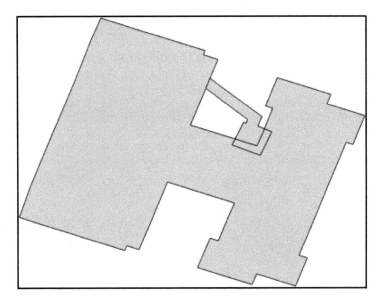

Rasterizing a vector layer

Sometimes, a raster dataset is a more efficient way to display a complex vector that is merely a backdrop in a map. In these cases, you can rasterize a vector layer to turn it into an image.

Getting ready

We will demonstrate rasterizing a vector layer using the following contour shapefile, which you can download:

```
https://github.com/GeospatialPython/Learn/raw/master/contour.zip
```

Extract it to your /qgis_data/rasters directory.

How to do it...

We will run the gdalogr:rasterize algorithm to convert this vector data to a raster:

1. Start QGIS.
2. From the **Plugins** menu, select **Python Console**.
3. Import the processing module:

```
import processing
```

4. Run the algorithm, specifying the input data, the attribute from which to draw raster values, 0 to specify the pixel dimensions for the output instead of map dimensions, then the width and height, and finally the output raster name:

```
processing.runalg("gdalogr:rasterize",
                  "/qgis_data/rasters/contour.shp",
                  "ELEV",0,1000,1000,
                  "/qgis_data/rasters/contour.tif")
```

How it works...

This algorithm is very straightforward. If you want to specify the output dimensions in map units, use 1 instead of 0.

The following image shows the rasterized output of the elevation contour shapefile:

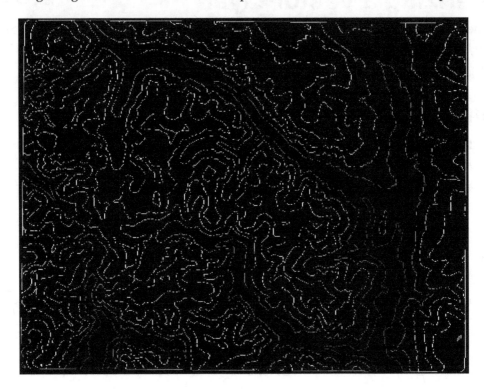

Exporting a layer to the GeoPackage format

The **GeoPackage** format is a developing open standard with recently added support in QGIS. The GeoPackage format has the properties of both the file format and a geodatabase. It overcomes all the limitations of the shapefile format, such as file size limits, attribute name length limits, and many other inconveniences. In a single file, GeoPackages can contain multiple vector and raster datasets. Software can query the file like a database without the overhead of a database server.

Read support for GeoPackages in QGIS is robust; however, write support has some limitations. You can save a single layer to the GeoPackage format using the `QgsVectorLayer` class or the Processing Toolbox. However, if you want to store multiple layers in a GeoPackage, you must use OGR directly. Fortunately, OGR is included in QGIS and available in the Python Console. In this recipe, we'll load two vector layers and save them in a single GeoPackage using OGR.

Getting ready

Download the two vector layers from the following location:

```
https://github.com/GeospatialPython/Learn/raw/master/rivers.zip
```

Unzip the file and place the two shapefiles in a directory named `rivers` in your `/qgis_data` directory.

How to do it...

This recipe will help you in exporting a layer into the GeoPackage format.

1. Start QGIS.
2. From the **Plugins** menu, select **Python Console**.
3. In the Python console, import the following modules:

```
import os
from osgeo import ogr
```

4. Next, set up a path variable for the data:

```
pth = "/qgis_data/rivers/"
```

5. Now, create a path and name for the GeoPackage dataset:

```
gpkg = os.path.join(pth + "rivers.gpkg")
```

6. Create an empty GeoPackage as a data source in OGR:

```
ds = ogr.GetDriverByName("GPKG").CreateDataSource(gpkg)
```

7. Now, open the first shapefile:

```
sf1 = ogr.Open(pth + "rivers.shp")
```

8. Create an OGR layer from the shapefile:

```
sf_lyr1 = sf1.GetLayerByIndex(0)
```

9. Now, copy the shapefile layer into the GeoPackage:

```
ds.CopyLayer(sf_lyr1, "rivers", [])
```

10. In order to add another layer, we first have to close the GeoPackage and reopen it:

```
ds = None
ds = ogr.Open(gpkg, True)
```

11. Now, we just repeat the layer adding process with the second shapefile:

```
sf2 = ogr.Open(pth + "junctions.shp")
sf_lyr2 = sf2.GetLayerByIndex(0)
ds.CopyLayer(sf_lyr2, "junctions", [])
ds = None
```

How it works...

The GeoPackage format is a relatively new format, so we must use a somewhat round about method to save multiple layers to a single GeoPackage. The QGIS team is actively developing additional GeoPackage format support. As the standard and supporting software continues to develop, GeoPackages will be used more and more.

4
Using Raster Data

In this chapter, we will cover the following recipes:

- Loading a raster layer
- Loading a NetCDF file
- Getting the cell size of a raster layer
- Obtaining the width and height of a raster
- Counting raster bands
- Swapping raster bands
- Querying the value of a raster at a specified point
- Reprojecting a raster
- Creating an elevation hillshade
- Creating vector contours from elevation data
- Sampling a raster dataset using a regular grid
- Adding elevation data to a line using a digital elevation model
- Creating a common extent for rasters
- Resampling raster resolution
- Counting the unique values in a raster
- Mosaicing rasters
- Converting a TIFF image to a JPEG image
- Creating pyramids for a raster
- Converting a pixel location to a map coordinate
- Converting a map coordinate to a pixel location
- Creating a KML image overlay for a raster
- Classifying a raster

- Converting a raster to a vector
- Georeferencing a raster from ground control points
- Clipping a raster using a shapefile

Introduction

This chapter shows you how to bring raster data into a GIS and create derivative raster products using QGIS and Python. QGIS is equally adept at working with raster data as with vector data by incorporating leading-edge open source libraries and algorithms, including **GDAL**, **SAGA**, and the **Orfeo Toolbox**. QGIS provides a consistent interface for a large array of remote sensing tools. We will switch back and forth between visually working with raster data and using QGIS as a processing engine via the Processing Toolbox to completely automate remote sensing workflows.

Raster data consists of rows and columns of cells or pixels, with each cell representing a single value. The easiest way to think of raster data is as images, which is how they are typically represented by software. However, raster datasets are not necessarily stored as images. They can also be ASCII text files or **binary large objects** (**BLOBs**) in databases.

Another difference between geospatial raster data and regular digital images is their resolution. Digital images express resolution as dots-per-inch if they are printed in full size. Resolution can also be expressed as the total number of pixels in the image, defined in megapixels. However, geospatial raster data uses the ground distance that each cell represents. For example, a raster dataset with a two-foot resolution means that a single cell represents two feet on the ground. It also means that only objects larger than two feet can be identified visually in the dataset.

Raster datasets may contain multiple bands, meaning that different wavelengths of light or other energy returns can be collected at the same time over the same area. Often, this range is from 3 to 7 bands wide, but it can be several hundred bands wide in hyperspectral systems. These bands are viewed individually or swapped in and out as the RGB bands of an image. They can also be recombined using mathematics into a derived single band image and then recolored using a set number of classes, representing similar values within the dataset.

Loading a raster layer

The QGSRasterLayer API provides a convenient, high-level interface to raster data. To use this interface, we must load a layer into QGIS. The API allows you to work with a layer without adding it to the map. In this way, we'll load a layer and then add it to the map.

Getting ready

As with the other recipes in this book, you need to create a directory called qgis_data in our root or user directory, which provides a short path name without spaces. This setup will help prevent any frustrating errors that result from path-related issues on a given system. In this recipe, and the others, we'll use a Landsat satellite image of the Mississippi Gulf Coast, which you can download from
https://github.com/GeospatialPython/Learn/raw/master/SatImage.zip.

Unzip the SatImage.tif and SatImage.tfw files and place them in a directory named rasters within your qgis_data directory.

How to do it...

Now we'll go through how to load a raster layer and then add it step by step to the map:

1. Start QGIS.
2. From the **Plugins** menu, select **Python Console**.
3. Then, in the Python console, create the layer by specifying the source file and layer name:

```
rasterLyr = QgsRasterLayer("/qgis_data/rasters/SatImage.tif",
                           "Gulf Coast")
```

4. Next, ensure that the layer is created as expected. The following command should return True:

```
rasterLyr.isValid()
```

5. Finally, add the layer to the layer registry:

```
QgsMapLayerRegistry.instance().addMapLayers([rasterLyr])
```

6. Verify that your QGIS map looks similar to the following image:

How it works...

The `QgsRasterLayer` object requires the location of the file and a name for the layer in QGIS. The underlying GDAL library determines the appropriate method of loading the layer. This approach contrasts with the `QgsVectorLayer()` method, which requires you to specify a data provider. Raster layers also have a data provider, but unlike vector layers, all raster layers are managed through GDAL. One of the best features of QGIS is that it combines the best-of-breed open source geospatial tools into one package. GDAL can be used as a library; as we are using it here from Python or as a command-line tool.

Once we have created the `QgsRasterLayer` object, we do a quick check using the `rasterLayer.isValid()` method to see whether the file was loaded properly. This method will return `True` if the layer is valid. We won't use this method in every recipe; however, it is a best practice, especially when building dynamic applications that accept user input. Because most of the PyQGIS API is built around C libraries, many methods do not throw exceptions if an operation fails. You must use specialized methods to verify the output.

Finally, we add the layer to the map layer registry, which makes it available on the map and in the legend. The registry keeps track of all the loaded layers by separating, loading, and visualizing the layers. QGIS allows you to work behind the scenes in order to perform unlimited intermediate processes on a layer before adding the final product to the map.

Loading a NetCDF file

NetCDF stands for **Network Common Data Form** and is an open geospatial and scientific data format. Features of the format include machine independent data storage, the ability to store vector, raster, and statistical data, as well as multi-dimensional data, and widespread software read and write support. NetCDF is commonly used for meteorological data, which is what we'll use in this example. Loading NetCDF data in QGIS is a little different from the other types of raster data because of its multi-dimensional capability.

Getting ready

Download the sea surface temperature sample NetCDF file from the following URL:

```
https://github.com/GeospatialPython/Learn/raw/master/tos_O1_2001-2002.nc
```

Place that file in your `/qgis_data/rasters` directory.

How to do it...

1. In the QGIS Python Console, create a variable for the path or URI for the NetCDF file. Note that we must specify at the beginning that this file is a NetCDF file, and at the end of the URI, we must specify which of the variables stored in the NetCDF file we want to view. In this case, the temperature data is stored in the `tos` variable:

   ```
   uri='NETCDF:"/qgis_data/rasters/tos_O1_2001-2002.nc":tos'
   ```

2. Now, we can use the URI to load the layer and make sure it is valid:

   ```
   rlayer = QgsRasterLayer(uri,'Sea Surface Temperature')
   rlayer.isValid()
   ```

3. Finally, we can add the layer to QGIS:

```
QgsMapLayerRegistry.instance().addMapLayer(rlayer)
```

4. Verify that the layer looks similar to the following screenshot:

How it works...

You specify the variable of interest because this same dataset could also contain information for precipitation or any number of other factors in a single file. Note that the data is rendered as a grayscale raster. Typically you would apply a pseudocolor style using a color ramp to render cooler temperatures in blue and warmer temperatures in red. Later in the book, we'll do exactly that in *Rendering a single band raster using a color ramp algorithm* recipe from Chapter 5, *Creating Dynamic Maps*.

Getting the cell size of a raster layer

The first key element of a geospatial raster is the width and height in pixels. The second key element is the ground distance of each pixel, also called the **pixel size**. Once you know the cell size and a coordinate somewhere on the image (usually the upper-left corner), you can begin using remote sensing tools on the image. In this recipe, we'll query the cell size of a raster.

Getting ready

Once again, we will use the SatImage raster available at
`https://github.com/GeospatialPython/Learn/raw/master/SatImage.zip`.

Place this raster in your `/qgis_data/rasters` directory.

How to do it...

We will load the raster as a layer and then use the `QgsRasterLayer` API to get the cell size for the *x* and *y* axis. To do this, we need to perform the following steps:

1. Start QGIS.
2. From the **Plugins** menu, select **Python Console**.
3. Load the layer and validate it:

```
rasterLyr = QgsRasterLayer("/qgis_data/rasters/satimage.tif",
                            "Satellite Image")
rasterLyr.isValid()
```

4. Now, call the *x* distance method, which should return `0.00029932313140079714`:

```
rasterLyr.rasterUnitsPerPixelX()
```

5. Then, call the *y* distance, which should be `0.00029932313140079714`:

```
rasterLyr.rasterUnitsPerPixelY()
```

How it works...

GDAL provides this information, which is passed through to the layer API. The pixel sizes are in the unit of the coordinate system. Note that while the x and y values are essentially the same in this case, it is entirely possible for the x and y distances to be different–especially if an image is projected or warped in some way.

Obtaining the width and height of a raster

All raster layers have a width and height in pixels. Because remote sensing data can be considered an image as well as an array or matrix, you will often see different terms used, including columns and rows or pixels and lines. These different terms surface many times within the QGIS API.

Getting ready

We will use the SatImage raster again, which is available at `https://github.com/GeospatialPython/Learn/raw/master/SatImage.zip`.

Place this raster in your `/qgis_data/rasters` directory.

How to do it...

1. Start QGIS.
2. From the **Plugins** menu, select **Python Console**.
3. In the Python console, load the layer and ensure that it is valid:

```
rasterLyr = QgsRasterLayer("/qgis_data/rasters/satimage.tif",
                           "Satellite Image")
rasterLyr.isValid()
```

4. Check the name of the SatImage after unzipping.
5. Obtain the layer's width, which should be `2592`:

```
rasterLyr.width()
```

6. Now, get the raster's height, which will return `2693`:

```
rasterLyr.height()
```

How it works...

The width and height of a raster are critical pieces of information for many algorithms, including those used to calculate the map units that the raster occupies. You will see this technique used again in other recipes.

Counting raster bands

A raster might have one or more bands. Bands represent layers of information within a raster. Each band has the same number of columns and rows.

Getting ready

We will again use the SatImage raster available at
`https://github.com/GeospatialPython/Learn/raw/master/SatImage.zip`.

Place this raster in your `/qgis_data/rasters` directory.

How to do it...

We will load the layer and then print the band count to the console. To do this, we need to perform the following steps:

1. Start QGIS.
2. From the **Plugins** menu, select **Python Console**.
3. In the Python console, load the layer and ensure that it is valid:

```
rasterLyr = QgsRasterLayer("/qgis_data/rasters/satimage.tif",
                           "Sat Image")
rasterLyr.isValid()
```

4. Now, get the band count, which should be 3 in this case:

```
rasterLyr.bandCount()
```

How it works...

It is important to note that raster bands are not zero-based indexes. When you want to access the first band, you reference it as 1 instead of 0. Most sequences in Python and C within a programming context start with 0.

Swapping raster bands

Computer displays render images in the visible spectrum of red, green, and blue light (RGB). However, raster images may contain bands outside the visible spectrum. Such rasters make poor visualizations, so you will often want to recombine the bands to change the RGB values.

Getting ready

For this recipe, we will use a false-color image, which you can download from `https://github.com/GeospatialPython/Learn/raw/master/FalseColor.zip`.

Unzip this `.tif` file and place it in your `/qgis_data/rasters` directory.

How to do it...

We will load this raster and swap the order of the first and second bands. Then, we will add it to the map. To do this, we need to perform the following steps:

1. Start QGIS.
2. From the **Plugins** menu, select **Python Console**.
3. In the Python console, load the layer and ensure that it is valid:

```
rasterLyr = QgsRasterLayer("/qgis_data/rasters/FalseColor.tif",
                            "Band Swap")
rasterLyr.isValid()
```

4. Now, we must access the layer renderer in order to manipulate the order of the bands displayed. Note that this change does not affect the underlying data:

```
ren = rasterLyr.renderer()
```

5. Next, we will set the red band to band 2:

    ```
    ren.setRedBand(2)
    ```

6. Now, we will set the green band to band 1:

    ```
    ren.setGreenBand(1)
    ```

7. Finally, add the altered raster layer to the map:

    ```
    QgsMapLayerRegistry.instance().addMapLayers([rasterLyr])
    ```

How it works...

Load the source image into QGIS as well to compare the results. In the false-color image, vegetation appears red, while in the band-swapped image, trees appear a more natural green and the water is blue. QGIS uses the RGB order to allow you to continue to reference the bands by number. Even though band 2 is displayed first, it is still referenced as band 2. Also, note that the band order is controlled by a `QgsMultiBandColorRenderer` object instantiated by the layer rather than the layer itself. The type of renderer that is needed is determined at load time by the data type and number of bands.

There's more...

The `QgsMultiBandColorRenderer()` method has other methods to control contrast enhancement for each band, such as `setRedContrastEnhancement()`. You can learn more about raster renderers for different types of data in the QGIS API documentation at `http://qgis.org/api/classQgsRasterRenderer.html`.

Querying the value of a raster at a specified point

A common remote sensing operation is to get the raster data value at a specified coordinate. In this recipe, we'll query the data value in the center of the image. It so happens that the raster layer will calculate the center coordinate of its extent for you.

Getting ready

As with many recipes in this chapter, we will again use the SatImage raster, which is available at `https://github.com/GeospatialPython/Learn/raw/master/SatImage.zip`.

Place this raster in your `/qgis_data/rasters` directory.

How to do it...

We will load the layer, get the center coordinate, and then query the value. To do this, we need to perform the following steps:

1. First, load and validate the layer:

   ```
   rasterLyr = QgsRasterLayer("/qgis_data/rasters/satimage.tif",
                              "Sat Image")
   rasterLyr.isValid()
   ```

2. Next, get the layer's center point from its `QgsRectangleextent` object, which will return a QGSPoint which looks and behaves like a tuple and contains the *x* and *y* values:

   ```
   c = rasterLyr.extent().center()
   ```

3. Now, using the layer's data provider, we can query the data value at that point using the `identify()` method:

   ```
   qry = rasterLyr.dataProvider()
         .identify(c,QgsRaster.IdentifyFormatValue)
   ```

4. Because a query error won't throw an exception, we must validate the query:

   ```
   qry.isValid()
   ```

5. Finally, we can view the query results, which will return a Python dictionary with each band number as the key pointing to the data values in that band:

   ```
   qry.results()
   ```

6. Verify that you get the following output:

   ```
   {1: 17.0, 2: 66.0, 3: 56.0}
   ```

How it works...

This recipe is short compared to some of the others; however, we have touched upon several features of the PyQGIS raster API. First, start with a raster layer and get the extents. Then, calculate the center and create a point at the center coordinates. Lastly, query the raster at that point. If we were to perform this same, seemingly simple operation using the Python API of the underlying GDAL library, which does the work, this example would have been approximately seven times longer.

Reprojecting a raster

A core requirement for all geospatial analysis is the ability to change the map projection of data in order to allow different layers to be displayed on the same map. Reprojection can be challenging, but QGIS makes it a piece of cake. Starting with this recipe, we will begin using the powerful QGIS Processing Toolbox. The Processing Toolbox wraps over 600 algorithms into a highly consistent API available to Python and also as interactive tools. This toolbox was originally a third-party plugin named **SEXTANTE** but is now a standard plugin distributed with QGIS.

Getting ready

As with many recipes in this chapter, we will use the SatImage raster available at https://github.com/GeospatialPython/Learn/raw/master/SatImage.zip.

Place this raster in your /qgis_data/rasters directory.

How to do it...

In this recipe, we will use the gdalwarp algorithm of the processing module to reproject our image from EPSG 4326 to 3722. To do this, we need to perform the following steps:

1. Start QGIS.
2. From the **Plugins** menu, select **Python Console**.
3. The first line of code is used to import the processing module:

```
import processing
```

4. Next, we load our raster layer and validate it:

```
rasterLyr = QgsRasterLayer("/qgis_data/rasters/SatImage.tif",
                           "Reproject")
rasterLyr.isValid()
```

5. Finally, we run the `gdalwarp` algorithm by inserting the correct parameters, including the algorithm name, inputting the data reference, source projection, destination projection, no data value, output resolution, 0 to select nearest neighbor resampling, the raster extent, the optional CRS of the raster extent, the output raster type (0 represents **Float32**), GeoTIFF compression type, optional JPEG compression level, optional LZW/DEFLATE compression level, lzw/deflate compression predictor, tiled output flag, TIFF type, TFW file creation flag, additional optional parameters, and an output name for the reprojected image:

```
processing.runalg("gdalogr:warpreproject",
                  "C:/qgis_data/rasters/SatImage.tif",
                  "EPSG:4326","EPSG:3722","0",0,1,None,None,
                  0,4,75,6,1,False,0,False,"",
                  "/qgis_data/rasters/warped.tif")
```

6. Verify that the output image, `warped.tif`, was properly created in the filesystem.

How it works...

In most cases, the Processing Toolbox is essentially a wrapper for command-line tools. However, unlike the tools it accesses, the toolbox provides a consistent and mostly predictable API. Users familiar with **Esri's ArcGIS ArcToolbox** will find this approach familiar. Besides consistency, the toolbox adds additional validation of parameters and logging, making these tools more user-friendly. It is important to remember that you must explicitly import the `processing` module. PyQGIS automatically loads the QGIS API, but this module is not yet included. Remember that it was a third-party plugin named SEXTANTE until version 2.0.

There's more...

The `runalg()` method, short for **run algorithm**, is the most common way to run processing commands. There are other processing methods that you can use, though. If you want to load the output of your command straight into QGIS, you can swap `runalg()` for the `runandload()` method. All arguments to the method remain the same. You can also get a list of processing algorithms with descriptions by running `processing.alglist()`. For any given algorithm, you can run the `alghelp()` command to see the types of input it requires, such as `processing.alghelp("gdalogr:warpproject")`. You can also write your own processing scripts based on combinations of algorithms and add them to the Processing Toolbox. There is also a visual modeler for chaining processing commands together similar to the **Model Builder** in **Esri ArcGIS**.

Creating an elevation hillshade

A hillshade, or shaded relief, is a technique to visualize elevation data in order to make it photorealistic for presentation as a map. This capability is part of GDAL and is available in QGIS in two different ways. It is a tool in the **Terrain Analysis** menu under the **Raster** menu, and it is also an algorithm in the Processing Toolbox.

Getting ready

You will need to download a **Digital Elevation Model (DEM)** from `https://github.com/GeospatialPython/Learn/raw/master/dem.zip`.

Unzip the file named `dem.asc` and place it in your `/qgis_data/rasters` directory. A DEM is a 3D representation of a terrain's surface.

How to do it...

In this recipe, we will load the DEM layer and run the `Hillshade` processing algorithm against it. To do this, we need to perform the following steps:

1. Start QGIS.
2. From the **Plugins** menu, select **Python Console**.
3. Import the `processing` module:

```
import processing
```

4. Load and validate the layer:

```
rasterLyr = QgsRasterLayer("/qgis_data/rasters/dem.asc",
                           "Hillshade")
rasterLyr.isValid()
```

5. Run the `Hillshade` algorithm, providing the algorithm name, layer reference, band number, compute edges option, zevenbergen option for smoother terrain, z-factor elevation exaggeration number, scaling ratio of vertical to horizontal units, azimuth (angle of the light source), altitude (height of the light source), and the output image's name:

```
processing.runandload("gdalogr:hillshade", rasterLyr, 1, False,
                      False,1.0, 1.0, 315.0, 45.0,
                      "/qgis_data/rasters/hillshade.tif")
```

6. Verify that the output image, `hillshade.tif`, looks like the following image in QGIS. It should be automatically loaded into QGIS via the `processing.runandload()` method:

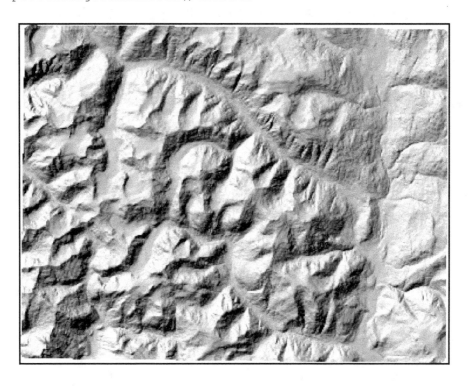

How it works...

The `Hillshade` algorithm simulates a light source over an elevation dataset to make it more visually appealing. Most of the time, the only variables in the algorithm you need to alter are the z-factor, azimuth, and altitude to get different effects. However, if the resulting image doesn't look right, you may need to alter the scale. According to the GDAL documentation, if your DEM is in degrees, you should set a scale of `111120`, and if it is in meters, you should set a scale of `370400`. This dataset covers a small area such that a scale of `1` is sufficient. For more information on these values, see the gdaldem documentation at `http://www.gdal.org/gdaldem.html`.

There's more...

DEM data are rasters, but typical pseudocolor algorithms aren't as effective as this `hillshade` method for an intuitive visualization. There are other recipes in this book using elevation data and nearly all of them benefit from adding this type of visualization as a backdrop. Note that while this recipe creates a new raster, version 2.16 of QGIS also added a live hillshade renderer for quick visualization. You could modify the previous example to get a similar result:

```
lyr = QgsRasterLayer("/qgis_data/rasters/dem.asc", "Hillshade")
r = QgsHillshadeRenderer(lyr.dataProvider(), 1, 315, 45)
lyr.setRenderer(r)
QgsMapLayerRegistry.instance().addMapLayer(lyr)
```

Creating vector contours from elevation data

Contours provide an effective visualization of terrain data by tracing isolines along the same elevation to form a loop at set intervals in the dataset. Similar to the hillshade capability in QGIS, the **Contour** tool is provided by GDAL, both as a menu option under the **Raster** menu in the **Extraction category** and as a Processing Toolbox algorithm.

Getting ready

This recipe uses the DEM from
`https://github.com/GeospatialPython/Learn/raw/master/dem.zip`, which is used in the other recipes as well.

Unzip the file named `dem.asc` and place it in your `/qgis_data/rasters` directory.

How to do it…

In this recipe, we will load and validate the DEM layer, add it to the map, and then produce and load the contour vector as a layer. To do this, we need to perform the following steps:

1. Start QGIS.
2. From the **Plugins** menu, select **Python Console**.
3. Import the `processing` module.

   ```
   import processing
   ```

4. Load and validate the DEM:

   ```
   rasterLyr = QgsRasterLayer("/qgis_data/rasters/dem.asc", "DEM")
   rasterLyr.isValid()
   ```

5. Add the DEM to the map using the `mapLayerRegistry` method:

   ```
   QgsMapLayerRegistry.instance().addMapLayers([rasterLyr])
   ```

6. Run the contour algorithm and draw the results on top of the DEM layer, specifying the algorithm name, layer reference, interval between contour lines in map units, name of the vector data attribute field that will contain the elevation value, any extra parameters, and output filename:

   ```
   processing.runandload("gdalogr:contour", rasterLyr, 50.0, "Elv",
                         None, "/qgis_data/rasters/contours.shp")
   ```

7. Verify that the output in QGIS looks similar to the following screenshot:

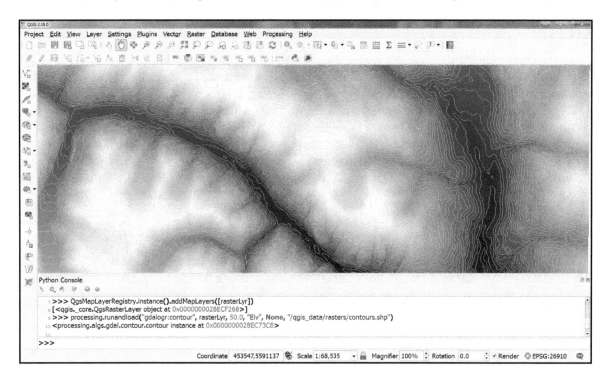

How it works...

The contour algorithm creates a vector dataset, which is a shapefile. The layer attribute table contains the elevation values for each line. Depending on the resolution of the elevation dataset, you may need to change the contour interval to stop the contours from becoming too crowded or too sparse at your desired map resolution. Usually, auto-generated contours like this are a starting point, and you must manually edit the result to make it visually appealing. You may want to smoothen the lines or remove unnecessary small loops.

Sampling a raster dataset using a regular grid

Sometimes, you need to sample a raster dataset at regular intervals in order to provide summary statistics or for quality assurance purposes on the raster data. A common way to accomplish this regular sampling is to create a point grid over the dataset, query the grid at each point, and assign the results as attributes to those points. In this recipe, we will perform this type of sampling over a satellite image. QGIS has a tool to perform this operation called regular points, which is in the **Vector** menu under **Research Tools**. However, there is no tool in the QGIS API to perform this operation programmatically. Instead, we can implement this algorithm directly using Python's `numpy` module.

Getting ready

In this recipe, we will use the previously used SatImage raster, available at `https://github.com/GeospatialPython/Learn/raw/master/SatImage.zip`.

Place this raster in your `/qgis_data/rasters` directory. You may need to install Numpy for Python. You can find instructions for installing Numpy at `https://docs.scipy.org/doc/numpy/user/index.html`.

How to do it...

The order of operation for this recipe is to load the raster layer, create a vector layer in memory, add points at regular intervals, sample the raster layer at these points, and then add the sampling data as attributes for each point. To do this, we need to perform the following steps:

1. Start QGIS.
2. From the **Plugins** menu, select **Python Console**.
3. We will need to import the `numpy` module, which is included with QGIS, as well as the `QtCore` module:

```
import numpy
from PyQt4.QtCore import *
```

4. Now, we will create a `spacing` variable to control how far apart the points are in map units:

```
spacing = .1
```

5. Next, we will create an `inset` variable to determine how close to the edge of the image the points start, in map units:

```
inset = .04
```

6. Now, we load and validate the raster layer:

```
rasterLyr = QgsRasterLayer("/qgis_data/rasters/satimage.tif",
                           "Sat Image")
rasterLyr.isValid()
```

7. Next, we collect the coordinate reference system and extent from the raster layer in order to transfer it to the point layer:

```
rpr = rasterLyr.dataProvider()
epsg = rasterLyr.crs().postgisSrid()
ext = rasterLyr.extent()
```

8. Now, we create an in-memory vector point layer, which won't be written to disk:

```
vectorLyr = QgsVectorLayer('Point?crs=epsg:%s' % epsg, 'Grid',
                           "memory")
```

9. In order to add points to the vector layer, we must access its data provider:

```
vpr = vectorLyr.dataProvider()
qd = QVariant.Double
```

10. Next, we create the attributes' fields to store the raster data samples:

```
vpr.addAttributes([QgsField("Red", qd), QgsField("Green", qd),
                   QgsField("Blue", qd)])
vectorLyr.updateFields()
```

11. We use the `inset` variable to set up the layer's extents inside the raster layer:

```
xmin = ext.xMinimum() + inset
xmax = ext.xMaximum()
ymin = ext.yMinimum() + inset
ymax = ext.yMaximum() - inset
```

12. Now, we use the `numpy` module to efficiently create the coordinates of the points in our regular grid:

```
pts = [(x,y) for x in (i for i in numpy
                          .arange(xmin, xmax, spacing))
          for y in (j for j in numpy.arange(ymin, ymax, spacing))]
```

13. Then, we create a list to store the point features we will create:

```
feats = []
```

14. In one loop, we create the point features, query the raster, and then update the attribute table. We store the points in a list for now:

```
for x,y in pts:
    f = QgsFeature()
    f.initAttributes(3)
    p = QgsPoint(x,y)
    qry = rasterLyr.dataProvider().identify(p,
        QgsRaster.IdentifyFormatValue)
    r = qry.results()
    f.setAttribute(0, r[1])
    f.setAttribute(1, r[2])
    f.setAttribute(2, r[3])
    f.setGeometry(QgsGeometry.fromPoint(p))
    feats.append(f)
```

15. Next, we pass the list of points to the data provider of the points layer:

```
vpr.addFeatures(feats)
```

16. Now, we update the layer's extents:

```
vectorLyr.updateExtents()
```

17. Then, we add both the raster and vector layers to the map in the list. The last item in the list is on top:

```
QgsMapLayerRegistry.instance().addMapLayers([vectorLyr, rasterLyr])
```

18. Finally, we refresh the map to see the result:

```
canvas = iface.mapCanvas()
canvas.setExtent(rasterLyr.extent())
canvas.refresh()
```

How it works...

The following screenshot shows the end result, with one of the points in the grid identified using the **Identify Features** map tool. The results dialog shows the raster values of the selected point:

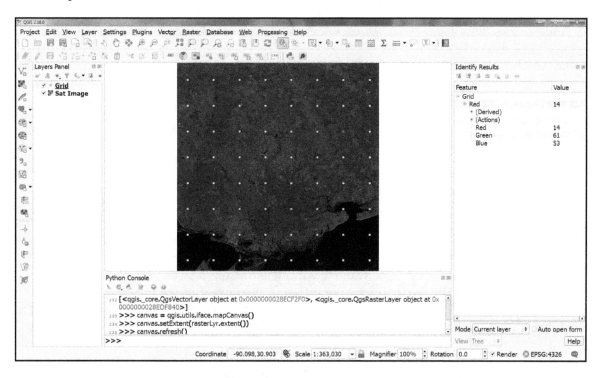

Using memory layers in QGIS is an easy way to perform quick, one-off operations, without the overhead of creating files on disk. Memory layers also tend to be fast if your machine has the resources to spare.

There's more...

In this example, we used a regular grid, but we could have just as easily modified the numpy-based algorithm to create a random points grid, which in some cases is more useful. However, the Processing Toolbox also has a simple algorithm for random points called `grass:v.random`.

Adding elevation data to a line vertices using a digital elevation model

If you have a transportation route through some terrain, it is useful to know the elevation profile of that route. This operation can be accomplished using the points that make up the line along the route to query a DEM and to assign elevation values to that point. In this recipe, we'll do exactly that.

Getting ready

You will need an elevation grid and a route. You can download this dataset from `https://github.com/GeospatialPython/Learn/raw/master/path.zip`.

Unzip the `path` directory containing a shapefile and the elevation grid. Place the whole path directory in your `qgis_data/rasters` directory.

How to do it...

We will need two processing algorithms to complete this recipe. We will load the raster and vector layers, convert the line feature to points, and then use these points to query the raster. The resulting point dataset will serve as the elevation profile for the route. To do this, we need to perform the following steps:

1. Start QGIS.
2. From the **Plugins** menu, select **Python Console**.
3. Import the `processing` module:

   ```
   import processing
   ```

4. Set up the filenames as variables, so they can be used throughout the script:

   ```
   pth = "/qgis_data/rasters/path/"
   rasterPth = pth + "elevation.asc"
   vectorPth = pth + "path.shp"
   pointsPth = pth + "points.shp"
   elvPointsPth = pth + "elvPoints.shp"
   ```

5. Load and validate the source layers, disabling and then re-enabling the QGIS pop-up asking for the layer's projection:

```
settings = QSettings()
originalSetting = settings.value("/Projections/defaultBehaviour",
                                 "prompt", type=str)
settings.setValue("/Projections/defaultBehaviour", "useProject")

rasterLyr = QgsRasterLayer(rasterPth, "Elevation")
crs = QgsCoordinateReferenceSystem()
crs.createFromSrid(4326)
rasterLyr.setCrs(crs)
settings.setValue( "/Projections/defaultBehaviour",
                   originalSetting)

rasterLyr.isValid()
```

6. Add the layers to the map:

```
QgsMapLayerRegistry.instance().addMapLayers([vectorLyr, rasterLyr])
```

7. Create an intermediate point dataset from the line using a SAGA algorithm in the Processing Toolbox:

```
processing.runalg("saga:convertlinestopoints", vectorLyr, False, 1,
                  pointsPth)
```

8. Finally, use another processing algorithm from SAGA to create the final dataset with the grid values assigned to the points:

```
processing.runandload("saga:addgridvaluestopoints", pointsPth,
                      rasterPth, 0, elvPointsPth)
```

How it works...

The following image saved from QGIS shows the DEM, route line, and elevation points with elevation labels, all displayed on the map, with some styling:

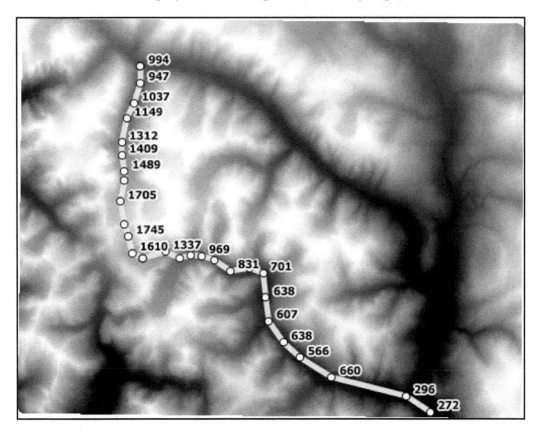

It is necessary to convert the lines to points because a line feature can only have one set of attributes. You can perform the same operation with a polygon as well. This DEM is an ASCII file, so it has no projection information. So, when we loaded the raster layer, we also changed the QGIS setting, which prompts the user to provide that information. QGIS then defaults the layer to the map project's default projection. But to be safe, we change the layer CRS to the correct projection in case it's different from the map project. Once the layer is loaded, we change QGIS back to its default setting.

There's more...

Instead of running two algorithms, we can build a processing script that combines these two algorithms into one interface and then add it to the toolbox. In the Processing Toolbox, there is a category called **Scripts**, which has a tool called **Create new script**. Double-clicking on this tool will bring up an editor that lets you build your own processing scripts. Depending on your platform, you may need to install or configure SAGA to use this algorithm. You can find binary packages for Linux at
`http://sourceforge.net/p/saga-gis/wiki/Binary%20Packages/`.

Also, on Linux, you may need to change the following option:

1. In the **Processing** menu, select **Options...**.
2. In the **Options** dialog, open the **Providers** tree menu and then open the **Saga** tree menu.
3. Uncheck **the Use 2.0.8 syntax** option.

Creating a common extent for rasters

If you are trying to compare two raster images, it is important that they have the same extent and resolution. Most software packages won't even allow you to attempt to compare images if they don't have the same extent. Sometimes, you have images that overlap but do not share a common extent and/or are of different resolutions. The following illustration is an example of this scenario:

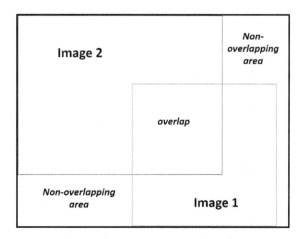

In this recipe, we'll take two overlapping images and clip them to the common extents.

Getting ready

You can download two overlapping images from
`https://github.com/GeospatialPython/Learn/raw/master/overlap.zip`.

Unzip the images and place them in your `/qgis_data/rasters` directory.

You will also need to download the processing script from the following link:

`https://github.com/GeospatialPython/Learn/raw/master/unify_extents.zip`

Unzip the contents and place the scripts in your `\.qgis2\processing\scripts` directory, found within your user directory. For example, on a Windows 64-bit machine, the directory will be `C:\Users\<username>\.qgis2\processing\scripts`, replacing `<username>` with your username.

Make sure you restart QGIS. This script is a modified version of the one created by **Yury Ryabov** on his blog at
`http://ssrebelious.blogspot.com/2014/01/unifying-extent-and-resolution-of.html`.

The original script used a confirmation dialog that required user interaction. The modified script adheres to the Processing Toolbox programming conventions and allows you to use it programmatically as well.

How to do it...

The only step in QGIS is to run the newly created processing command. To do this, we need to perform the following steps:

1. Start QGIS.
2. From the **Plugins** menu, select **Python Console**.
3. Import the `processing` module:

   ```
   import processing
   ```

4. Run the newly added processing algorithm, specifying the algorithm name, the path to the two images, an optional no data value, an output directory for the unified images, and a boolean flag to load the images into QGIS:

   ```
   processing.runalg("script:unifyextentandresolution",
                     "/qgis_data/rasters/Image2.tif;
                     /qgis_data/rasters/Image1.tif",
                     -9999,"/qgis_data/rasters",True)
   ```

5. In the QGIS table of contents, verify that you have two images named as follows:

```
Image1_unified.tif
Image2_unified.tif
```

How it works...

The following screenshot shows the common extent for the rasters by setting the transparency of `Image1_unified.tif` to the pixel `0,0,0`:

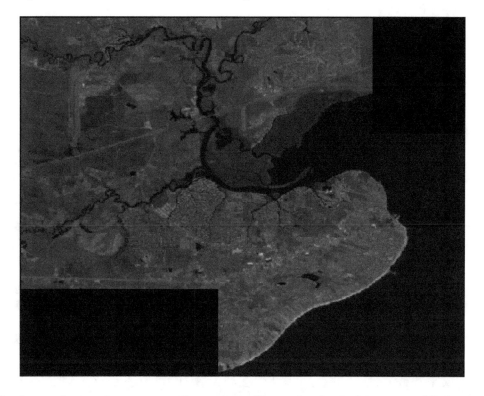

If you don't use the transparency setting, you will see that both the images fill the non-overlapping areas with no data within the minimum bounding box of both extents. The no data values, specified as `-9999`, will be ignored by other processing algorithms.

Resampling raster resolution

Resampling an image allows you to change the current resolution of an image to a different resolution. Resampling to a lower resolution, also known as downsampling, requires you to remove pixels from the image while maintaining the geospatial referencing integrity of the dataset. In the QGIS Processing Toolbox, the `gdalogr:warpproject` algorithm is used, which is the same as the algorithm used for reprojection.

Getting ready

We will again use the SatImage raster available at `https://github.com/GeospatialPython/Learn/raw/master/SatImage.zip`.

Place this raster in your `/qgis_data/rasters` directory.

How to do it...

There's an extra step in this process where we will get the current pixel resolution of the raster as a reference to calculate the new resolution and pass it to the algorithm. To do this, we need to perform the following steps:

1. Start QGIS.
2. From the **Plugins** menu, select **Python Console**.
3. Import the `processing` module:

    ```
    import processing
    ```

4. Load and validate the raster layer:

    ```
    rasterLyr = QgsRasterLayer("/qgis_data/rasters/SatImage.tif",
                               "Resample")
    rasterLyr.isValid()
    ```

5. The algorithm requires projection information. We are not changing it, so just assign the current projection to a variable:

    ```
    epsg = rasterLyr.crs().postgisSrid()
    srs = "EPSG:%s" % epsg
    ```

6. Get the current pixel's ground distance and multiply it by 2 to calculate half the ground resolution. We only use the X distance because in this case, it is identical to the Y distance:

```
res = rasterLyr.rasterUnitsPerPixelX() * 2
```

7. Run the resampling algorithm, specifying the algorithm name, layer reference, input and output spatial reference system, desired resolution, resampling algorithm (0 is the nearest neighbor), any additional parameters, 0 for output raster data type, and the output filename:

```
processing.runalg("gdalogr:warpreproject",
                   rasterLyr,srs,srs,res,0,0,None,
                   "EPSG:4326",5,4,75,6,1,False,0,False,"",
                   "/qgis_data/rasters/resampled.tif")
```

8. Verify that the `resampled.tif` image was created in your `/qgis_data/rasters` directory.

How it works...

It is counter intuitive at first to reduce the resolution by multiplying it. However, by increasing the spatial coverage of each pixel, it takes fewer pixels to cover the extent of the raster. You can easily compare the difference between the two in QGIS visually by loading both the images and zooming to an area with buildings or other detailed structures and then turning one layer off or on.

Counting the unique values in a raster

Remotely-sensed images are not just pictures; they are data. The value of the pixels has a meaning that can be automatically analyzed by a computer. The ability to run statistical algorithms on a dataset is the key to remote sensing. This recipe counts the number of unique combinations of pixels across multiple bands. A use case for this recipe will be to assess the results of image classification, which is a recipe that we'll cover later in this chapter. This recipe is in contrast to the typical histogram function, which totals the unique values and the frequency of each value per band.

Getting ready

We will use the SatImage raster available at
`https://github.com/GeospatialPython/Learn/raw/master/SatImage.zip`.

Place this raster in your `/qgis_data/rasters` directory.

How to do it...

This algorithm relies completely on the `numpy` module. Numpy can be accessed through the GDAL package's `gdalnumeric` module. To do this, we need to perform the following steps:

1. Start QGIS.
2. From the **Plugins** menu, select **Python Console**.
3. First, we must import the bridge module called `gdalnumeric`, which connects GDAL to Numpy in order to perform an array math on geospatial images:

   ```
   import gdalnumeric
   ```

4. Now, we will load our raster image directly into a multidimensional array:

   ```
   a = gdalnumeric.LoadFile("/qgis_data/rasters/satimage.tif")
   ```

5. The following code counts the number of pixel combinations in the image:

   ```
   b = a.T.ravel()
   c=b.reshape((b.size/3,3))
   order = gdalnumeric.numpy.lexsort(c.T)
   c = c[order]
   diff = gdalnumeric.numpy.diff(c, axis=0)
   ui = gdalnumeric.numpy.ones(len(c), 'bool')
   ui[1:] = (diff != 0).any(axis=1)
   u = c[ui]
   ```

6. Now, we can take a look at the size of the resulting one-dimensional array to get the unique values count:

   ```
   u.size
   ```

7. Lastly, verify that the result is `16085631`.

How it works...

The `numpy` module is an open source equivalent of the commercial package `Matlab`. You can learn more about Numpy at `http://www.numpy.org/`.

When you load an image using Numpy, it is loaded as a multidimensional array of numbers. Numpy allows you to do an array math on the entire array using operators and specialized functions in the same way you would on variables containing a single numeric value.

Mosaicing rasters

Mosaicing rasters is the process of fusing multiple geospatial images with the same resolution and map projection into one raster. In this recipe, we'll combine two overlapping satellite images into a single dataset.

Getting ready

You will need to download the overlapping dataset from `https://github.com/GeospatialPython/Learn/raw/master/overlap.zip` if you haven't downloaded it from a previous recipe.

Place the two images in your `/qgis_data/rasters/` directory.

How to do it...

This process is relatively straightforward and has a dedicated algorithm within the Processing Toolbox. Perform the following steps:

1. Start QGIS.
2. From the **Plugins** menu, select **Python Console**.
3. Run the `gdalogr:merge` algorithm, specifying the process name, two images, a boolean to use the pseudocolor palette from the first image, a boolean to stack each image into a separate band, and the output filename:

```
processing.runalg("gdalogr:merge",
                  "/qgis_data/rasters/Image2.tif;
                  /qgis_data/rasters/Image1.tif", False,False,0,
                  "/qgis_data/rasters/merged.tif")
```

4. Verify that the `merged.tif` image has been created and displays the two images as a single raster within QGIS.

How it works...

The merge processing algorithm is a simplified version of the actual `gdal_merge` command-line utility. This algorithm is limited to the GDAL output and aggregates the extent of input rasters. It can only merge two rasters at a time. The `gdal_merge` tool has far more options, including additional output formats, the ability to merge more than two rasters at once, the ability to control the extent, and more. You can also use the GDAL API directly to take advantage of these features, but it will take far more code than what is used in this simple example.

Converting a TIFF image to a JPEG image

Image format conversion is a part of nearly every geospatial project. Rasters come in dozens of different specialized formats, making conversion to a more common format a necessity. The GDAL utilities include a tool called `gdal_translate` specifically for format conversion. Unfortunately, the algorithm in the Processing Toolbox is limited in functionality. For format conversion, it is easier to use the core GDAL API.

Getting ready

We will use the SatImage raster available at
`https://github.com/GeospatialPython/Learn/raw/master/SatImage.zip`.

Place this raster in your `/qgis_data/rasters` directory.

How to do it...

In this recipe, we'll open a TIFF image using GDAL and copy it to a new dataset as a JPEG2000 image, which allows you to use the JPEG format while maintaining geospatial information. To do this, we need to perform the following steps:

1. Start QGIS.
2. From the **Plugins** menu, select **Python Console**.

3. Import the `gdal` module:

```
from osgeo import gdal
```

4. Get a GDAL driver for our desired format:

```
drv = gdal.GetDriverByName("JP2OpenJPEG")
```

5. Open the source image:

```
src = gdal.Open("/qgis_data/rasters/satimage.tif")
```

6. Copy the source dataset to the new format:

```
tgt = drv.CreateCopy("/qgis_data/rasters/satimage.jp2", src)
```

How it works...

For the straight format conversion of an image format, the core GDAL library is extremely fast and simple. GDAL supports the creation of over 60 raster formats and the reading of over 130 raster formats.

Creating pyramids for a raster

Pyramids, or overview images, sacrifice the disk space for map rendering speed by storing resampled, lower-resolution versions of images in the file alongside the full resolution image. Once you have finalized a raster, building pyramid overviews is a good idea.

Getting ready

For this recipe, we will use a false-color image, which you can download from https://github.com/GeospatialPython/Learn/raw/master/FalseColor.zip.

Unzip this `.tif` file and place it in your `/qgis_data/rasters` directory.

How to do it...

The Processing Toolbox has a dedicated algorithm for building pyramid images. Perform the following steps to create pyramids for a raster:

1. Start QGIS.
2. From the **Plugins** menu, select **Python Console**.
3. Import the `processing` module:

   ```
   import processing
   ```

4. Run the `gdalogr:overviews` algorithm, specifying the process name, input image, overview levels, the option to remove existing overviews, resampling method (`0` is the nearest neighbor), and overview format (`1` is internal):

   ```
   processing.runalg("gdalogr:overviews",
                     "/qgis_data/rasters/FalseColor.tif",
                     "2 4 8 16",True,0,1)
   ```

5. Now, load the raster into QGIS by dragging and dropping it from the file system onto the map canvas.
6. Double-click on the layer name in the map's legend to open the **Layer Properties** dialog.
7. In the **Layer Properties** dialog, click on the **Pyramids** tab and verify that the layer has multiple resolutions listed.

How it works...

The concept of overview images is quite simple. You resample the images several times, and then a viewer chooses the smallest, most appropriate file to load on the map, depending on scale. The overviews can be stored in the header of the file for certain formats or as an external file format. The level of overviews needed depends largely on the file size and resolution of your current image, but is really arbitrary. In this example, we double the scale by a factor of 2, which is a common practice. Most of the zoom tools in the applications will double the scale when you click to zoom in. The factor of 2 gives you enough zooming levels so that you usually won't zoom to a level where there is no pyramid image. There is a point of diminishing returns if you create too many levels because pyramids take up additional disk space. Usually 4 to 5 levels are effective.

Converting a pixel location to a map coordinate

The ability to view rasters in a geospatial context relies on the conversion of pixel locations to coordinates on the ground. Sooner or later, when you use Python to write geospatial programs, you'll have to perform this conversion yourself.

Getting ready

We will use the SatImage raster available
at https://github.com/GeospatialPython/Learn/raw/master/SatImage.zip

Place this raster in your /qgis_data/rasters directory.

How to do it...

We will use GDAL to extract the information needed to convert pixels to coordinates and then use pure Python to perform the calculation. We'll use the center pixel of the image as the location to convert.

1. Start QGIS.
2. From the **Plugins** menu, select **Python Console**.
3. We need to import the gdal module:

```
from osgeo import gdal
```

4. Then, we need to define the reusable function that does the conversion as accepting a GDAL GeoTransform object, containing the raster georeferencing information and the pixel's *x, y* values:

```
def Pixel2world(geoMatrix, x, y):
    ulX = geoMatrix[0]
    ulY = geoMatrix[3]
    xDist = geoMatrix[1]
    yDist = geoMatrix[5]
    coorX = (ulX + (x * xDist))
    coorY = (ulY + (y * yDist))
    return (coorX, coorY)
```

5. Now, we'll open the image in GDAL:

```
src = gdal.Open("/qgis_data/rasters/Satimage.tif")
```

6. Next, get the `GeoTransform` object from the image:

```
geoTrans = src.GetGeoTransform()
```

7. Now, calculate the center pixel of the image:

```
centerX = src.RasterXSize/2
centerY = src.RasterYSize/2
```

8. Finally, perform the conversion by calling our function:

```
Pixel2world(geoTrans, centerX, centerY)
```

9. Verify that the coordinates returned are close to the following output:

```
(-89.59486002580364, 30.510227817850406)
```

How it works...

Pixel conversion is just a scaling ratio between two planes: the image coordinate system and the Earth coordinate system. When dealing with large areas, this conversion can become a more complex projection because the curvature of the Earth comes into play. The GDAL website has a nice tutorial about the `Geotransform` object at `http://www.gdal.org/gdal_tutorial.html`

Converting a map coordinate to a pixel location

When you receive a map coordinate as user input or from some other source, you must be able to convert it back to the appropriate pixel location on a raster.

Getting ready

We will use the SatImage raster available at `https://github.com/GeospatialPython/Learn/raw/master/SatImage.zip`

Place this raster in your /qgis_data/rasters directory.

How to do it...

Similar to the previous recipe, we will define a function, extract the GDAL GeoTransform object from our raster, and use it for the conversion.

1. Start QGIS.
2. From the **Plugins** menu, select **Python Console**.
3. We need to import the gdal module:

```
from osgeo import gdal
```

4. Then, we need to define the reusable function that does the coordinate to pixel conversion. We get the GDAL GeoTransform object containing the raster georeferencing information and the map *x, y* coordinates:

```
def world2Pixel(geoMatrix, x, y):
    ulX = geoMatrix[0]
    ulY = geoMatrix[3]
    xDist = geoMatrix[1]
    yDist = geoMatrix[5]
    rtnX = geoMatrix[2]
    rtnY = geoMatrix[4]
    pixel = int((x - ulX) / xDist)
    line = int((y - ulY) / yDist)
    return (pixel, line)
```

5. Next, we open the source image:

```
src = gdal.Open("/qgis_data/rasters/satimage.tif")
```

6. Now, get the GeoTransform object:

```
geoTrans = src.GetGeoTransform()
```

7. Finally, perform the conversion:

```
world2Pixel(geoTrans, -89.59486002580364, 30.510227817850406)
```

8. Verify that your output is the following:

```
(1296, 1346)
```

How it works...

This conversion is very reliable over small areas, but as the area of interest expands, you must account for elevation as well, which requires a far more complex transformation depending on how an image was generated.

 The following presentation from the University of Massachusetts does an excellent job of explaining the challenges of georeferencing data:
`http://courses.umass.edu/nrc592g-cschweik/pdfs/Class_3_Georefere ncing_concepts.pdf`

Creating a KML image overlay for a raster

Google Earth is one of the most widely available geospatial viewers in existence. The XML data format used by Google Earth for geospatial data is called **KML**. The Open Geospatial Consortium adopted KML as a data standard. Converting rasters into a KML overlay compressed in a **KMZ** archive file is a very popular way to make data available to end users who know how to use Google Earth.

Getting ready

We will use the SatImage raster again available at the following URL if you haven't downloaded it from previous recipes:

`https://github.com/GeospatialPython/Learn/raw/master/SatImage.zip`

Place this raster in your `/qgis_data/rasters` directory.

How to do it...

In this recipe, we'll create a KML document describing our image. Then we'll convert the image to a JPEG in memory using GDAL's specialized virtual file system and write all of the contents directly to a KMZ file using Python's `zipfile` module.

1. Start QGIS.
2. From the **Plugins** menu, select **Python Console**.

3. We need to import the `gdal` module as well as the Python `zipfile` module:

```
from osgeo import gdal
import zipfile
```

4. Next, we'll open our satellite image in `gdal`:

```
srcf = "/qgis_data/rasters/Satimage.tif"
```

5. Now, we'll create a variable with our virtualized file name using the GDAL virtual file naming convention, beginning with `vismem`:

```
vfn = "/vsimem/satimage.jpg"
```

6. We create the JPEG `gdal` driver object for the output format:

```
drv = gdal.GetDriverByName('JPEG')
```

7. Now, we can open the source file:

```
src = gdal.Open(srcf)
```

8. Then, we can copy that source file to our virtual JPEG:

```
tgt = drv.CreateCopy(vfn, src)
```

9. Now, we are going to create a raster layer in QGIS for our raster, just for the benefit of it calculating the image's extent:

```
rasterLyr = QgsRasterLayer(srcf, "SatImage")
```

10. Next, we get the layer's extent:

```
e = rasterLyr.extent()
```

11. Next, we format our KML document template and insert the image extents:

```
kml = """<?xml version="1.0" encoding="UTF-8"?>
  <kmlxmlns="http://www.opengis.net/kml/2.2">
    <Document>
      <name>QGISKML Example</name>
      <GroundOverlay>
        <name>SatImage</name>
        <drawOrder>30</drawOrder>
        <Icon>
          <href>SatImage.jpg</href>
        </Icon>
        <LatLonBox>
          <north>%s</north>
          <south>%s</south>
          <east>%s</east>
          <west>%s</west>
        </LatLonBox>
      </GroundOverlay>
    </Document>
</kml>""" %(e.yMaximum(), e.yMinimum(), e.xMaximum(), e.xMinimum())
```

12. Now, we open our virtual JPEG in GDAL and prepare it for reading:

```
vsifile = gdal.VSIFOpenL(vfn,'r')
gdal.VSIFSeekL(vsifile, 0, 2)
vsileng = gdal.VSIFTellL(vsifile)
gdal.VSIFSeekL(vsifile, 0, 0)
```

13. Finally, we write our KML document and virtual JPEG into a zipped KMZ file:

```
z = zipfile.ZipFile("/qgis_data/rasters/satimage.kmz", "w",
                    zipfile.ZIP_DEFLATED)
z.writestr("doc.kml", kml)
z.writestr("SatImage.jpg", gdal.VSIFReadL(1, vsileng, vsifile))
z.close()
```

14. Now, open the KMZ file in Google Earth and verify that it looks like the following screenshot:

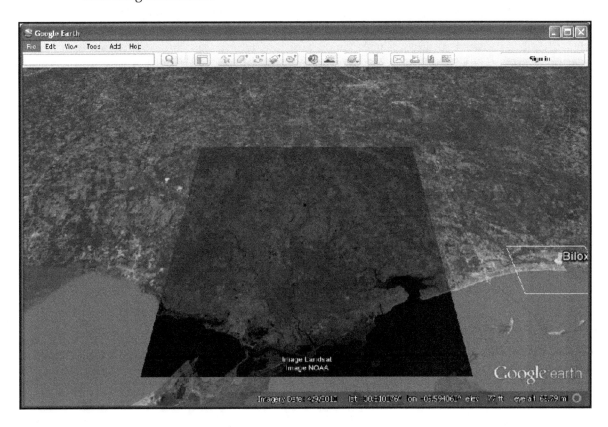

How it works...

KML is a straightforward XML format. There are entire libraries in Python dedicated to reading and writing it, but for a simple export to share an image or two, the PyQGIS console is more than adequate. While we run this script in the QGIS Python interpreter, it could be run outside of QGIS using just GDAL.

There's more...

The Orfeo Toolbox has a processing algorithm called otb:imagetokmzexport, which has a much more sophisticated KMZ export tool for images.

Classifying a raster

Image classification is one of the most complex aspects of remote sensing. While QGIS is able to color pixels based on values for visualization, it stops short of doing much classification. It does provide a Raster Calculator tool where you can perform arbitrary math formulas on an image; however, it does not attempt to implement any common algorithms. The Orfeo Toolbox is dedicated purely to remote sensing and includes an automated classification algorithm called **K-Means Clustering**, which groups pixels into an arbitrary number of similar classes to create a new image. We can do a nice demonstration of image classification using this algorithm.

Getting ready

For this recipe, we will use a false color image, which you can download here:

```
https://github.com/GeospatialPython/Learn/raw/master/FalseColor.zip
```

Unzip this TIF file and place it in your /qgis_data/rasters directory.

How to do it...

All we need to do is run the algorithm on our input image. The important parameters are the second, third, sixth, and tenth parameters. They define the input image name, the amount of RAM to dedicate to the task, the number of classes, and the output name respectively:

1. First, import the processing module in the QGIS **Python Console**:

   ```
   import processing
   ```

2. Next, run the otb algorithm using the processing.runandload() method to display the output in QGIS:

   ```
   processing.runandload("otb:unsupervisedkmeansimageclassification",
                   "/qgis_data/rasters/FalseColor.tif",
                   128,None,100,3,1000,0.95,
                   "/qgis_data/rasters/class.tif",None)
   ```

3. When the image loads in QGIS, double-click the layer name in the **Table of Contents**.

4. In the **Layer Properties** dialog, choose **Style**.
5. Change the **Render** type menu to **Single band pseudocolor**.
6. Change the **color map** menu on the right to **Spectral**.
7. Click the **Classify** button.
8. Choose the **Ok** button at the bottom of the window.
9. Verify your image looks similar to the following image, except without the class labels:

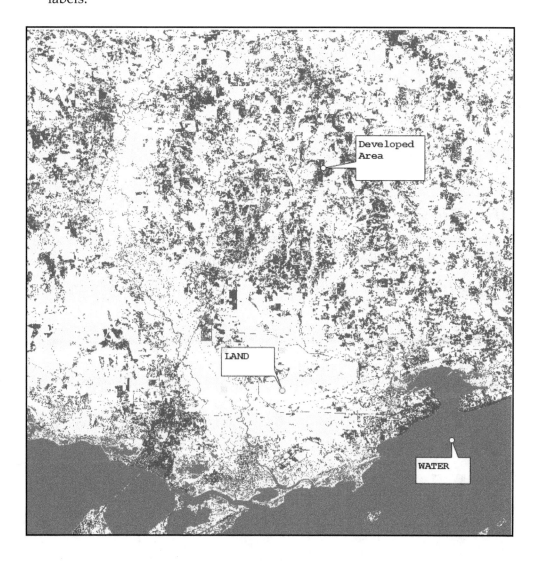

How it works...

Keeping the class number low allows the automated classification algorithm to focus on the major features in the image and helps us to achieve a very high level of accuracy, determining overall land use. Additional automated classification would require supervised analysis with training data sets and more in-depth preparation. But the overall concept would remain the same. QGIS has a nice plugin for semi-automatic classification. You can learn more about it

at `https://plugins.qgis.org/plugins/SemiAutomaticClassificationPlugin/`

Converting a raster to a vector

Raster datasets represent real-world features efficiently, but can have limited usage for geospatial analysis. Once you have classified an image into a manageable data set, you can convert those raster classes into a vector data set for more sophisticated GIS analysis. GDAL has a function for this operation called **polygonize**.

Getting ready

You will need to download the following classified raster and place it in your `/qgis_data/rasters` directory:

`https://github.com/GeospatialPython/Learn/raw/master/landuse_bay.zip`

How to do it...

Normally, you would save the output of this recipe as a shapefile. We won't specify an output file name. The Processing Toolbox will assign it a temporary filename and return that filename. We'll simply load the temporary file into QGIS. The algorithm allows you to write to a shapefile by specifying it as the last parameter. Perform the following steps:

1. In the QGIS **Python Console**, import the `processing` module:

```
import processing
```

2. Next, run the algorithm specifying the process name, input image, the field name for the class number, and optionally, the output shapefile:

```
processing.runandload("gdalogr:polygonize",
                      "/qgis_data/rasters/landuse_bay.tif",
                      "DN",None)
```

3. You should get a vector layer with three classes, defined as polygons, denoting developed areas. In the following sample image, we have assigned unique shades to each class: developed area (darkest), water (mid tones), and land (lightest color):

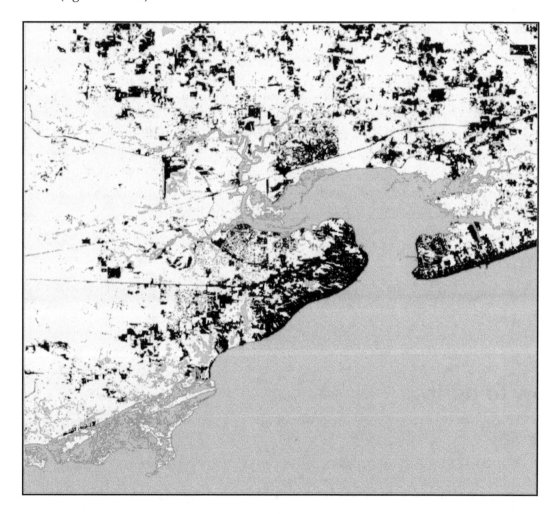

How it works...

GDAL looks for clusters of pixels and creates polygons around them. It is important to have as few classes as possible. If there is too much variation in the pixels, then GDAL will create a polygon around each pixel in the image. You can turn this recipe into a true analysis product by using the *Calculating the area of a polygon* recipe in `Chapter 1`, *Automating QGIS* to quantify each class of land use.

Georeferencing a raster from control points

Sometimes, a raster that represents features on the earth is just an image with no georeferencing information. That is certainly the case with historical scanned maps. However, you can use a referenced data set of the same area to create tie points, or ground control points, and then use an algorithm to warp the image to fit the model of the earth. It is common for data collection systems to just store the **ground control points** (**GCP**) along with the raster to keep the image in as raw a format as possible. Each change to an image holds the possibility of losing data, so georeferencing an image on demand is often the best approach.

In this recipe, we'll georeference a historical survey map of the Louisiana and Mississippi Gulf Coast from 1853. The control points were manually created with the QGIS Georeferencer plugin and saved to a standardized control point file.

Getting ready

Download the following ZIP file, unzip the contents, and put the `georef` directory in `/qgis_data/rasters`:

https://github.com/GeospatialPython/Learn/raw/master/georef.zip

How to do it...

We will use a low-level module of the processing API to access some specialized GDAL utility functions:

1. In the QGIS **Python Console**, import the `GdalUtils` module:

```
from processing.algs.gdal.GdalUtils import GdalUtils
```

2. Now, we will set up some path names for source and target data, which will be used multiple times:

```
src = "/qgis_data/rasters/georef/1853survey.jpg"
points = "/qgis_data/rasters/georef/1853Survey.points"
trans = "/qgis_data/rasters/georef/1835survey_trans.tif"
final = "/qgis_data/rasters/georef/1835survey_georef.tif"
```

3. Next, we will open up our GCP file and read past the header line:

```
gcp = open(points, "rb")
hdr = gcp.readline()
```

4. Then, we can begin building our first `gdal` utility command:

```
command = ["gdal_translate"]
```

5. Loop through the GCP file and append the points to the command arguments:

```
for line in gcp:
    x,y,col,row,e = line.split(",")
    command.append("-gcp")
    command.append("%s" % col)
    command.append("%s" % abs(float(row)))
    command.append("%s" % x)
    command.append("%s" % y)
```

6. Now, add the input and output file to the command:

```
command.append(src)
command.append(trans)
```

7. Next, we execute the first command:

```
GdalUtils.runGdal(command, None)
```

8. Next, we change the command to warp the image:

```
command = ["gdalwarp"]
command.extend(["-r", "near", "-order", "3", "-co",
                "COMPRESS=NONE", "-dstalpha"])
```

9. Add the output of the last command as the input and use the final image path as the output:

```
command.append(trans)
command.append(final)
```

10. Now, run the warp command to complete the task:

```
GdalUtils.runGdal(command, None)
```

How it works...

The `GdalUtils` API exposes the underlying tools used by the Processing Toolbox algorithm, yet it provides a robust cross-platform approach that is better than other traditional methods of accessing external programs from Python. If you pull the output image into QGIS and compare it to the USGS coastline shapefile, you can see the results are fairly accurate and could be improved with additional control points and referenced data. The number of GCPs required for a given image is a matter of trial and error. Adding more GCPs won't necessarily lead to better results. You can find out more about creating GCPs from the QGIS documentation at `http://docs.qgis.org/testing/en/docs/user_manual/plugins/plugins_georeference r.html`

Clipping a raster using a shapefile

Sometimes, you need to use a subset of an image which covers an area of interest for a project. In fact, areas of an image outside your area of interest can distract your audience from the idea you are trying to convey. Clipping a raster to a vector boundary allows you to only use the portions of the raster you need. It can also save processing time by eliminating areas outside your area of interest.

Getting ready

We will use the SatImage raster again, available at the following URL if you haven't downloaded it from the previous recipes:

`https://github.com/GeospatialPython/Learn/raw/master/SatImage.zip`

Place this raster in your `/qgis_data/rasters` directory.

How to do it...

Clipping is a common operation and GDAL is well suited for it. Perform the following steps:

1. First, in the QGIS **Python Console**, import the processing module:

```
import processing
```

2. Next, run the processing command specifying the input image name as the second argument and the output image as the seventh argument:

```
processing.runandload("gdalogr:cliprasterbymasklayer",
                      "/qgis_data/rasters/SatImage.tif",
                      "/qgis_data/hancock/hancock.shp",
                      None,False,False,False,0,4,75,6,
                      1,False,0,False,"",None)
```

3. Verify that your output raster looks like the following screenshot:

How it works...

GDAL creates a no-data mask outside the shapefile boundary. The extent of the original image remains the same. However, you no longer visualize it, and processing algorithms will ignore the no data values.

5
Creating Dynamic Maps

In this chapter, we will cover the following recipes:

- Accessing the map canvas
- Changing the map units
- Iterating over layers
- Symbolizing a vector layer
- Setting a transparent layer fill
- Using a filled marker symbol
- Rendering a single band raster using a color ramp algorithm
- Setting a feature's color using a column in a CSV file
- Creating a complex vector layer symbol
- Using icons as vector layer symbols
- Using an outline for font markers
- Using the arrow symbol
- Creating a graduated vector layer symbol
- Creating a categorized vector layer symbol
- Using live layer effects
- Creating inverted polygon shapeburst fills
- Creating a map bookmark
- Navigating to a map bookmark
- Setting scale-based visibility for a layer
- Using SVG for layer symbols
- Using pie charts for symbols
- Using the 2.5D renderer
- Using XYZ tiled map services

- Using Esri ArcGIS map services
- Labeling a feature
- Using null symbols
- Changing map layer transparency
- Adding standard map tools to the canvas
- Using a map tool to draw points on the canvas
- Using a map tool to draw polygons or lines on the canvas
- Building a custom selection tool
- Creating a mouse coordinate tracking tool

Introduction

In this chapter, we'll programmatically create dynamic maps using Python to control every aspect of the QGIS map canvas. We'll learn to dynamically apply symbology from data in a CSV file. We'll also learn how to use some newer QGIS custom symbology, including font markers, arrow symbols, null symbols, and the powerful new 2.5D renderer for buildings. We'll use labels and map bookmarks. We'll learn the new way in which QGIS handles map services, which formerly required a plugin. We'll also go beyond the canvas to create custom map tools. You will see that every aspect of QGIS is up for grabs with Python, to write your own application. Sometimes, the PyQGIS API may not directly support your application goal, but there is nearly always a way to accomplish what you set out to do with QGIS.

Accessing the map canvas

Maps in QGIS are controlled through the map canvas. In this recipe, we'll access the canvas and then check one of its properties to ensure that we have control over the object.

Getting ready

The only thing you need to do for this recipe is to open QGIS and select **Python Console** from the **Plugins** menu.

How to do it...

We will assign the map canvas to a variable named `canvas`. Then, we'll check the `size` property of the canvas to get its size in pixels. To do this, perform the following steps:

1. Enter the following line in the QGIS **Python Console**:

   ```
   canvas = qgis.utils.iface.mapCanvas()
   ```

2. Now, to ensure that we have properly accessed the canvas, check its size in pixels using the following line of code:

   ```
   canvas.size()
   ```

3. Verify that QGIS returns a `QSize` object that contains the canvas's pixel size as width and height respectively, similar to the following format. The actual width and height will vary based on the size of your QGIS window and screen size:

   ```
   PyQt4.QtCore.QSize(698, 138)
   ```

How it works...

Everything in QGIS centers around the canvas. The canvas is part of the QGIS interface or **iface** API. Anything you see on the screen when using QGIS is generated through the iface API. Note that the `iface` object is only available to scripts and plugins. When you are building a standalone application, you must initialize your own `QgsMapCanvas` object.

Changing the map units

Changing the units of measure on a map, or map units, is a very common operation, depending on the purpose of your map or the standards of your organization or country. In this recipe, we'll read the map units used by QGIS and then change them for your project.

Getting ready

The only preparation you need for this recipe is to open QGIS and select **Python Console** from the **Plugins** menu.

How to do it...

In the following steps, we'll access the map canvas, check the map unit type, and then alter it to a different setting:

1. First, access the map canvas, as follows:

```
canvas = iface.mapCanvas()
```

2. Now, get the map units type. By default, it should be the number 2:

```
canvas.mapUnits()
```

3. Now, let's set the map units to meters, which is represented by the number 0:

```
canvas.setMapUnits(0)
```

How it works...

QGIS has seven different map units, which are enumerated in the following order:

- 0 = Meters
- 1 = Feet
- 2 = Degrees
- 3 = UnknownUnit
- 4 = DecimalDegrees
- 5 = DegreesMinutesSeconds
- 6 = DegreesDecimalMinutes
- 7 = NauticalMiles

It is important to note that changing the map units just changes the unit of measurement for the measurement tool and the display in the status bar; it does not change the underlying map projection. You'll notice this difference if you try to run an operation in the Processing Toolbox, which depends on the projected data in meters if the data is unprojected. The most common use case for changing the map units is to switch between imperial and metric units, depending on the user's preference.

Iterating over layers

For many GIS operations, you need to loop through the map layers to look for specific information or to apply a change to all the layers. In this recipe, we'll loop through the layers and get information about them.

Getting ready

We'll need two layers in the same map projection to perform this recipe. You can download the first layer as a ZIP file from
`https://github.com/GeospatialPython/Learn/raw/master/MSCities_Geo_Pts.zip`.

You can download the second zipped layer from
`https://github.com/GeospatialPython/Learn/raw/master/Mississippi.zip`.

Unzip both of these layers into a directory named `ms` within your `qgis_data` directory.

How to do it...

We will add the layers to the map through the map registry. Then, we will iterate through the map layers and print each layer's title. To do this, perform the following steps:

1. First, let's open the polygon and the point layer using **Python Console**:

   ```
   lyr_1 = QgsVectorLayer("/qgis_data/ms/mississippi.shp",
                          "Mississippi", "ogr")
   lyr_2 = QgsVectorLayer("/qgis_data/ms/MSCities_Geo_Pts.shp",
                          "Cities", "ogr")
   ```

2. Next, get the map layer registry instance:

   ```
   registry = QgsMapLayerRegistry.instance()
   ```

3. Now, add the vector layers to the map:

   ```
   registry.addMapLayers([lyr_2, lyr_1])
   ```

4. Then, we retrieve the layers as an iterator:

   ```
   layers = registry.mapLayers()
   ```

5. Finally, we loop through the layers and print the titles:

```
for l in layers:
    print l.title()
```

6. Verify that you can read the layer titles in **Python Console**, similar to the following format. QGIS will assign a different unique ID for each layer each time you run this example:

```
Cities20140904160234792
Mississippi20140904160234635
```

How it works...

Layers in QGIS are independent of the map canvas until you add them to the map layers registry. They are assigned an ID as soon as they are created. When added to the map, they become part of the canvas, where they pick up titles, symbols, and many other attributes. In this case, you can use the map layers registry to iterate through them and access them in order to change the way they look, or to add and extract data.

Symbolizing a vector layer

The appearance of layers on a QGIS map is controlled by its symbology. A layer's symbology includes the renderer and one or more symbols. The renderer provides rules dictating the appearance of symbols. The symbols describe properties, including color, shape, size, and line width. In this recipe, we'll load a vector layer, change its symbology, and refresh the map.

Getting ready

Download the zipped shapefile and extract it to your `qgis_data` directory into a folder named `ms` from `https://github.com/GeospatialPython/Learn/raw/master/Mississippi.zip`.

How to do it...

We will load a layer, add it to the map layer registry, change the layer's color, and then refresh the map. To do this, perform the following steps:

1. First, using **Python Console**, we must import the `QtGui` library in order to access the `QColor` object, which is used to describe colors in the PyQGIS API:

   ```
   from PyQt4.QtGui import *
   ```

2. Next, we create our vector layer, as follows:

   ```
   lyr = QgsVectorLayer("/qgis_data/ms/mississippi.shp",
                        "Mississippi", "ogr")
   ```

3. Then, we add it to the map layer registry:

   ```
   QgsMapLayerRegistry.instance().addMapLayer(lyr)
   ```

4. Now, we access the layer's symbol list through the layer's renderer object:

   ```
   symbols = lyr.rendererV2().symbols()
   ```

5. Next, we reference the first symbol, represented by index 0, which, in this case, is the only symbol:

   ```
   sym = symbols[0]
   ```

6. Once we have the symbol, we can set its color to red:

   ```
   sym.setColor(QColor.fromRgb(255,0,0))
   ```

7. We must remember to repaint the layer in order to force the update. For efficiency, QGIS only updates layer rendering when triggered to do so, to save computing resources:

   ```
   lyr.triggerRepaint()
   ```

How it works...

Changing the color of a layer sounds simple, but remember that in QGIS, anything you see must be altered through the canvas API. Therefore, we add the layer to the map and access the layer's symbology through its renderer. The map canvas is rendered as a raster image. The renderer is responsible for turning the layer data into a bitmap image, so the presentation information for a layer is stored with its renderer.

Setting a transparent layer fill

Sometimes, you may just want to display the outline of a polygon in a layer and have the insides of the polygon render transparently, so you can see the other features and background layers inside that space. For example, this technique is common with political boundaries. In this recipe, we will load a polygon layer onto the map, and then interactively change it to just an outline of the polygon.

Getting ready

Download the zipped shapefile and extract it to your `qgis_data` directory into a folder named `ms` from

`https://github.com/GeospatialPython/Learn/raw/master/Mississippi.zip`.

How to do it...

In the following steps, we'll load a vector polygon layer, set up a properties dictionary to define the color and style, apply the properties to the layer's symbol, and repaint the layer. In **Python Console**, execute the following:

1. Create the polygon layer:

```
lyr = QgsVectorLayer("/qgis_data/ms/mississippi.shp",
                     "Mississippi", "ogr")
```

2. Load the layer onto the map:

```
QgsMapLayerRegistry.instance().addMapLayer(lyr)
```

3. Now, we'll create the properties dictionary:

```
properties = {}
```

4. Next, set each property for the fill color, border color, border width, and a style of no meaning no-brush or transparent fill. Note that we'll still set a fill color; we are just making it transparent:

```
properties["color"] = '#289e26'
properties["color_border"] = '#289e26'
properties["width_border"] = '2'
properties["style"] = 'no'
```

5. Now, we create a new symbol and set its properties:

```
sym = QgsFillSymbolV2.createSimple(properties)
```

6. Next, we access the layer's `renderer`:

```
renderer = lyr.rendererV2()
```

7. Then, we set the renderer's symbol to the new symbol we created:

```
renderer.setSymbol(sym)
```

8. Finally, we repaint the layer to show the style updates:

```
lyr.triggerRepaint()
```

How it works...

In the previous recipe, *Symbolizing a vector layer*, we used methods and objects to change the symbol. In this recipe, we used a simple dictionary to define our properties, combined with the `createSimple` method of the `QgsFillSymbolV2` class. Note that we could have changed the symbology of the layer before adding it to the canvas, but adding it first allows you to see the change take place interactively. You can get the full list of available properties by calling the `properties()` of the symbol layer. For example, at the Python console, you could enter the following:

```
q = QgsFillSymbolV2()
q.symbolLayers()[0].properties()
```

PyQGIS would return a dictionary with the following properties and values:

```
{u'outline_width': u'0.26', u'outline_color': u'0,0,0,255',
 u'offset_unit': u'MM', u'color': u'0,0,255,255',
 u'outline_style': u'solid', u'style': u'solid',
 u'joinstyle': u'bevel', u'outline_width_unit': u'MM',
 u'border_width_map_unit_scale': u'0,0,0,0,0,0', u'offset': u'0,0',
 u'offset_map_unit_scale': u'0,0,0,0,0,0'}
```

Using a filled marker symbol

A newer feature of QGIS is **filled marker symbols**. Filled marker symbols are powerful features that allow you to use other symbols such as point markers, lines, and shape bursts, as a fill pattern for a polygon. Filled marker symbols allow for an endless set of options for rendering a polygon. In this recipe, we'll do a very simple filled marker symbol that paints a polygon with stars.

Getting ready

Download the zipped shapefile and extract it to your `qgis_data` directory into a folder named `ms` from
`https://github.com/GeospatialPython/Learn/raw/master/Mississippi.zip`.

How to do it...

A filled marker symbol requires us to first create the representative star point marker symbol. Then, we'll add that symbol to the filled marker symbol and change it with the layer's default symbol. Finally, we'll repaint the layer to update the symbology:

1. First, create the layer with our polygon shapefile:

    ```
    lyr = QgsVectorLayer("/qgis_data/ms/mississippi.shp",
                         "Mississippi", "ogr")
    ```

2. Next, load the layer onto the map:

    ```
    QgsMapLayerRegistry.instance().addMapLayer(lyr)
    ```

3. Now, set up the dictionary with the properties of the star marker symbol:

```
marker_props = {}
marker_props["color"] = 'red'
marker_props["color_border"] = 'black'
marker_props["name"] = 'star'
marker_props["size"] = '3'
```

4. Now, create the star marker symbol:

```
marker = QgsMarkerSymbolV2.createSimple(marker_props)
```

5. Then, we create our filled marker symbol:

```
filled_marker = QgsPointPatternFillSymbolLayer()
```

6. We need to set the horizontal and vertical spacing of the filled markers in millimeters:

```
filled_marker.setDistanceX(4.0)
filled_marker.setDistanceY(4.0)
```

7. Now, we can add the simple star marker to the filled marker symbol:

```
filled_marker.setSubSymbol(marker)
```

8. Next, access the layer's renderer:

```
renderer = lyr.rendererV2()
```

9. Now, we swap the first symbol layer of the first symbol with our filled marker, using zero indexes to reference them:

```
renderer.symbols()[0].changeSymbolLayer(0, filled_marker)
```

10. Finally, we repaint the layer to see the changes:

```
lyr.triggerRepaint()
```

11. Verify that the result looks similar to the following screenshot:

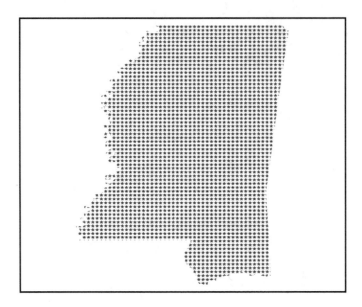

Rendering a single band raster using a color ramp algorithm

A color ramp allows you to render a raster using just a few colors to represent different ranges of cell values that have a similar meaning in order to group them. The approach that will be used in this recipe is the most common way to render elevation data.

Getting ready

You can download a sample DEM from https://github.com/GeospatialPython/Learn/raw/master/dem.zip, which you can unzip to a directory named rasters in your qgis_data directory.

How to do it...

In the following steps, we will set up objects to color a raster, create a list establishing the color ramp ranges, apply the ramp to the layer renderer, and finally, add the layer to the map. To do this, we need to perform the following:

1. First, we import the `QtGui` library for color objects in the **Python Console**:

   ```
   from PyQt4 import QtGui
   ```

2. Next, we load the raster layer, as follows:

   ```
   lyr = QgsRasterLayer("/qgis_data/rasters/dem.asc", "DEM")
   ```

3. Now, we create a generic raster shader object:

   ```
   s = QgsRasterShader()
   ```

4. Then, we instantiate the specialized ramp shader object:

   ```
   c = QgsColorRampShader()
   ```

5. We must name a type for the ramp shader. In this case, we use an INTERPOLATED shader:

   ```
   c.setColorRampType(QgsColorRampShader.INTERPOLATED)
   ```

6. Now, we'll create a list of our color ramp definitions:

   ```
   i = []
   ```

7. Then, we populate the list with the color ramp values that correspond to the elevation value ranges:

   ```
   i.append(c.ColorRampItem(400, QColor('#d7191c'), '400 meters'))
   i.append(c.ColorRampItem(900, QColor('#fdae61'), '900 meters'))
   i.append(c.ColorRampItem(1500, QColor('#ffffbf'), '1500 meters'))
   i.append(c.ColorRampItem(2000, QColor('#abdda4'), '2000 meters'))
   i.append(c.ColorRampItem(2500, QColor('#2b83ba'), '2500 meters'))
   ```

8. Now, we assign the color ramp to our shader:

   ```
   c.setColorRampItemList(i)
   ```

9. Now, we tell the generic raster shader to use the color ramp:

```
s.setRasterShaderFunction(c)
```

10. Next, we create a raster renderer object with the shader, specifying band number 1:

```
ps = QgsSingleBandPseudoColorRenderer(lyr.dataProvider(), 1, s)
```

11. We assign the renderer to the raster layer:

```
lyr.setRenderer(ps)
```

12. Finally, we add the layer to the canvas in order to view it:

```
QgsMapLayerRegistry.instance().addMapLayer(lyr)
```

How it works...

While it takes a stack of four objects to create a color ramp, this recipe demonstrates how flexible the PyQGIS API is. Typically, the more number of objects it takes to accomplish an operation in QGIS, the richer the API is, giving you the flexibility to make complex maps. Notice that, in each ColorRampItem object, you specify a starting elevation value, the color, and a label as the string. The range for the color ramp ends at any value less than the following item. So, in this case, the first color will be assigned to the cells with a value between 400 and 899. The following screenshot shows the applied color ramp:

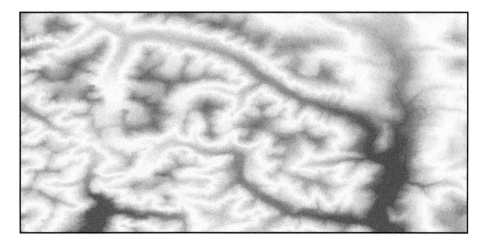

Setting a feature's color using a column in a CSV file

Comma Separated Value (**CSV**) files are an easy way to store basic geospatial information, but you can also store styling properties alongside the geospatial data for QGIS to use in order to dynamically style the feature data. In this recipe, we'll load some points into QGIS from a CSV file and use one of the columns to determine the color of each point. But note that you can define any property this way.

Getting ready

Download the sample zipped CSV file from the following URL:

```
https://github.com/GeospatialPython/Learn/raw/master/point_colors.csv.zip
```

Extract it and place it in your `qgis_data` directory in a directory named `shapes`.

How to do it...

We'll load the CSV file into QGIS as a vector layer and create a default point symbol. Then we'll specify the property and the CSV column we want to control. Finally, we'll assign the symbol to the layer and add the layer to the map:

1. First, create the URI string needed to load the CSV:

```
uri = "file:///qgis_data/shapes/point_colors.csv?"
uri += "type=csv&"
uri += "xField=X&yField=Y&"
uri += "spatialIndex=no&"
uri += "subsetIndex=no&"
uri += "watchFile=no&"
uri += "crs=epsg:4326"
```

2. Next, create the layer using the URI string:

```
lyr = QgsVectorLayer(uri,"Points","delimitedtext")
```

3. Now, create a default symbol for the layer's geometry type:

```
sym = QgsSymbolV2.defaultSymbol(lyr.geometryType())
```

4. Then, we access the layer's symbol layer:

```
symLyr = sym.symbolLayer(0)
```

5. Now, we perform the key step, which is to assign a symbol layer property to a CSV column:

```
symLyr.setDataDefinedProperty("color", '"COLOR"')
```

6. Then, we change the existing symbol layer with our data-driven symbol layer:

```
lyr.rendererV2().symbols()[0].changeSymbolLayer(0, symLyr)
```

7. Finally, we add the layer to the map and verify that each point has the correct color, as defined in the CSV:

```
QgsMapLayerRegistry.instance().addMapLayers([lyr])
```

How it works...

In this example, we pulled feature colors from the CSV, but you could control any symbol layer property in this manner. CSV files can be a simple alternative to databases for lightweight applications or for testing key parts of a large application before investing the overhead to set up a database.

Creating a complex vector layer symbol

The true power of QGIS symbology lies in its ability to stack multiple symbols in order to create a single complex symbol. This ability makes it possible to create virtually any type of map symbol you can imagine. In this recipe, we'll merge two symbols to create a single symbol and begin unlocking the potential of complex symbols.

Getting ready

For this recipe, we will need a line shapefile, which you can download and extract from https://github.com/GeospatialPython/Learn/raw/master/paths.zip.

Add this shapefile to a directory named shapes in your qgis_data directory.

How to do it...

Using **Python Console**, we will create a classic railroad line symbol by placing a series of short, rotated line markers along a regular line symbol. To do this, we need to perform the following steps:

1. First, we load our line shapefile:

   ```
   lyr = QgsVectorLayer("/qgis_data/shapes/paths.shp", "Route", "ogr")
   ```

2. Next, we get the symbol list and reference the default symbol:

   ```
   symbolList = lyr.rendererV2().symbols()
   symbol = symbolList[0]
   ```

3. Then, we create a shorter variable name for the symbol layer registry:

   ```
   symLyrReg = QgsSymbolLayerV2Registry
   ```

4. Now, we set up the line style for a simple line using a Python dictionary:

   ```
   lineStyle = {'width':'0.26', 'color':'0,0,0'}
   ```

5. Then, we create an abstract symbol layer for a simple line:

   ```
   symLyr1Meta = symLyrReg.instance()
                 .symbolLayerMetadata("SimpleLine")
   ```

6. We instantiate a symbol layer from the abstract layer using the line style properties:

   ```
   symLyr1 = symLyr1Meta.createSymbolLayer(lineStyle)
   ```

7. Now, we add the symbol layer to the layer's symbol:

   ```
   symbol.appendSymbolLayer(symLyr1)
   ```

8. Now, in order to create the rails on the railroad, we begin building a marker line style with another Python dictionary, as follows:

```
markerStyle = {}
markerStyle['width'] = '0.26'
markerStyle['color'] = '0,0,0'
markerStyle['interval'] = '3'
markerStyle['interval_unit'] = 'MM'
markerStyle['placement'] = 'interval'
markerStyle['rotate'] = '1'
```

9. Then, we create the marker line abstract symbol layer for the second symbol:

```
symLyr2Meta = symLyrReg.instance()
            .symbolLayerMetadata("MarkerLine")
```

10. We instantiate the symbol layer, as shown here:

```
symLyr2 = symLyr2Meta.createSymbolLayer(markerStyle)
```

11. Now, we must work with a `subSymbol` that defines the markers along the marker line:

```
sybSym = symLyr2.subSymbol()
```

12. We must delete the default subsymbol:

```
sybSym.deleteSymbolLayer(0)
```

13. Now, we set up the style for our rail marker using a dictionary:

```
railStyle = {'size':'2', 'color':'0,0,0', 'name':'line',
            'angle':'0'}
```

14. Now, we repeat the process of building a symbol layer, and add it to the subsymbol:

```
railMeta = symLyrReg.instance().symbolLayerMetadata("SimpleMarker")
rail = railMeta.createSymbolLayer(railStyle)
sybSym.appendSymbolLayer(rail)
```

15. Then, we add the subsymbol to the second symbol layer:

```
symbol.appendSymbolLayer(symLyr2)
```

16. Finally, we add the layer to the map:

```
QgsMapLayerRegistry.instance().addMapLayer(lyr)
```

How it works...

First, we must create a simple line symbol. The marker line, by itself, will render correctly, but the underlying simple line will be a randomly chosen color. We must also change the sub-symbol of the marker line because the default subsymbol is a simple circle.

Using icons as vector layer symbols

In addition to the default symbol types available in QGIS, you can also use **TrueType** fonts as map symbols. TrueType fonts are scalable vector graphics that can be used as point markers. In this recipe, we'll create a symbol of this type.

Getting ready

You can download the point shapefile used in this recipe from `https://github.com/GeospatialPython/Learn/raw/master/NYC_MUSEUMS_GEO.zip`.

Extract it to your `qgis_data` directory, in a folder named `nyc`.

How to do it...

We will load a point shapefile as a layer and then use the character G in a freely available font called `Webdings`, which is probably already on your system, to render a building icon on each point in the layer. To do this, we need to perform the following steps:

1. First, we'll define the path to our point shapefile:

   ```
   src = "/qgis_data/nyc/NYC_MUSEUMS_GEO.shp"
   ```

2. Then, we'll load the vector layer:

   ```
   lyr = QgsVectorLayer(src, "Museums", "ogr")
   ```

3. Now, we'll use a Python dictionary to define the font properties:

   ```
   fontStyle = {}
   fontStyle['color'] = '#000000'
   fontStyle['font'] = 'Webdings'
   fontStyle['chr'] = 'G'
   fontStyle['size'] = '6'
   ```

4. Now, we'll create a font symbol layer:

   ```
   symLyr1 = QgsFontMarkerSymbolLayerV2.create(fontStyle)
   ```

5. Then, we'll change the default symbol layer of the vector layer with our font's symbol information:

   ```
   lyr.rendererV2().symbols()[0].changeSymbolLayer(0, symLyr1)
   ```

6. Finally, we'll add the layer to the map:

   ```
   QgsMapLayerRegistry.instance().addMapLayer(lyr)
   ```

7. Verify that your map looks similar to the following screenshot:

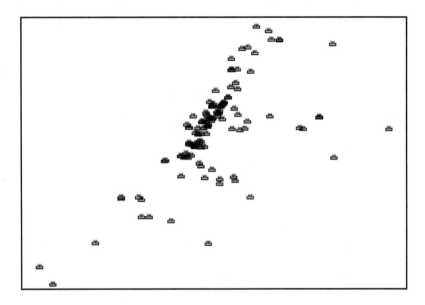

How it works...

The font marker symbol layer is just another type of marker layer; however, the range of possibilities with vector fonts is far broader than the built-in fonts in QGIS. Many industries define standard cartographic symbols using customized fonts as markers.

Using an outline for font markers

Font markers open up broad possibilities for icons, but a single-color shape can be hard to see across a varied map background. Recently, QGIS added the ability to place outlines around font marker symbols. In this recipe, we'll use font marker symbol methods to place an outline around the symbol to give it contrast and, therefore, visibility on any type of background.

Getting ready

Download the following zipped shapefile. Extract it and place it in a directory named `ms` in your `qgis_data` directory:

```
https://github.com/GeospatialPython/Learn/raw/master/tourism_points.zip
```

How to do it...

This recipe will load a layer from a shapefile, set up a font marker symbol, put an outline on it, and then add it to the layer. We'll use a simple text character, an @ sign, as our font marker to keep things simple:

1. First, we need to import the `QtGUI` library, so we can work with color objects:

   ```
   from PyQt4.QtGui import *
   ```

2. Now, we create a path string to our shapefile:

   ```
   src = "/qgis_data/ms/tourism_points.shp"
   ```

3. Next, we can create the layer:

   ```
   lyr = QgsVectorLayer(src, "Points of Interest", "ogr")
   ```

4. Then, we can create the font marker symbol, specifying the font size and color in the constructor:

   ```
   symLyr = QgsFontMarkerSymbolLayerV2(pointSize=16,
                                       color=QColor("cyan"))
   ```

5. Now, we can set the font family, character, outline width, and outline color:

   ```
   symLyr.setFontFamily("'Arial'")
   symLyr.setCharacter("@")
   symLyr.setOutlineWidth(.5)
   symLyr.setOutlineColor(QColor("black"))
   ```

6. We are now ready to assign the symbol to the layer:

   ```
   lyr.rendererV2().symbols()[0].changeSymbolLayer(0, symLyr)
   ```

7. Finally, we add the layer to the map:

   ```
   QgsMapLayerRegistry.instance().addMapLayer(lyr)
   ```

8. Verify that your map looks similar to the following screenshot:

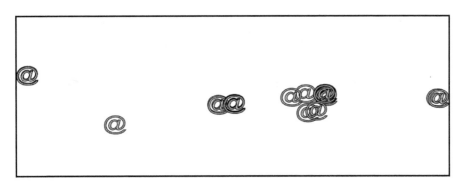

How it works...

We used class methods to set this symbol up, but we also could have used a property dictionary just as easily. Note that the font size and color were set in the object constructor for the font marker symbol instead of using `setter` methods. `QgsFontMarkerSymbolLayerV2` doesn't have methods for these two properties.

Using arrow symbols

Line features convey location, but sometimes you also need to convey a direction along a line. QGIS recently added a symbol that does just that by turning lines into arrows. In this recipe, we'll symbolize some line features showing historical human migration routes around the world. This data requires directional arrows for us to understand it.

Getting ready

We will use two shapefiles in this example. One is a world boundaries (countries) shapefile and the other is a route shapefile. You can download the countries shapefile here:

`https://github.com/GeospatialPython/Learn/raw/master/countries.zip`

You can download the routes shapefile here:

`https://github.com/GeospatialPython/Learn/raw/master/human_migration_routes.zip`

Download these ZIP files and unzip the shapefiles into your `qgis_data` directory.

How to do it...

We will load the countries shapefile as a background reference layer followed by the route shapefile. Before we display the layers on the map, we'll create the arrow symbol layer, configure it, and then add it to the routes layer. Finally, we'll add the layers to the map.

1. First, we'll create the URI strings for the paths to the two shapefiles:

    ```
    countries_shp = "/qgis_data/countries.shp"
    routes_shp = "/qgis_data/human_migration_routes.shp"
    ```

2. Next, we'll create our countries and routes layers:

    ```
    countries = QgsVectorLayer(countries_shp, "Countries", "ogr")
    routes = QgsVectorLayer(routes_shp, "Human Migration Routes",
                            "ogr")
    ```

3. Now, we'll create the arrow symbol layer:

    ```
    symLyr = QgsArrowSymbolLayer()
    ```

4. Then, we'll configure the layer. We'll use the default configuration except for two parameters–to curve the arrow and to not repeat the arrow symbol for each line segment:

    ```
    symLyr.setIsCurved(True)
    symLyr.setIsRepeated(False)
    ```

5. Next, we add the symbol layer to the map layer:

    ```
    routes.rendererV2().symbols()[0].changeSymbolLayer(0, symLyr)
    ```

6. Finally, we add the layers to the map:

    ```
    QgsMapLayerRegistry.instance().addMapLayers([routes,countries])
    ```

7. Verify that your map looks similar to the following screenshot:

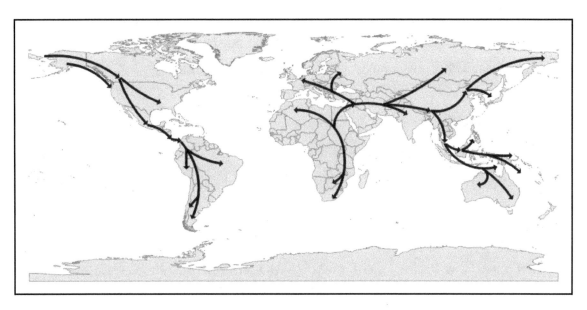

How it works...

The symbol calculates the arrow's direction based on the order of the geometry's nodes. You may find that you need to edit the underlying feature data to produce the desired visual effect, especially when using curved arrows. You have limited control over the arc of the curve using the end points plus an optional third vertex. This symbol is one of the several new powerful visual effects added to QGIS, which would have normally been done in a vector illustration program after you produced a map.

Creating a graduated vector layer symbol renderer

A graduated vector layer symbol renderer is the vector equivalent of a raster color ramp. You can group features into similar ranges and use a limited set of colors to visually identify these ranges. In this recipe, we'll render a graduated symbol using a polygon shapefile.

Getting ready

You can download a shapefile containing a set of urban area polygons from `https://github.com/GeospatialPython/Learn/raw/master/MS_UrbanAnC10.zip`.

Extract this file to a directory named `ms` in your `qgis_data` directory.

How to do it...

We will classify each urban area by population size using a graduated symbol, as follows:

1. First, we import the `QColor` object to build our color range:

   ```
   from PyQt4.QtGui import QColor
   ```

2. Next, we load our polygon shapefile as a vector layer:

   ```
   lyr = QgsVectorLayer("/qgis_data/ms/MS_UrbanAnC10.shp",
                        "Urban Areas", "ogr")
   ```

3. Now, we build some nested Python tuples that define the symbol graduation. Each item in the tuple contains a range label, range start value, range end value, and color name, as shown here:

   ```
   population = (("Village", 0.0, 3159.0, "cyan"),
                ("Small town", 3160.0, 4388.0, "blue"),
                ("Town", 43889.0, 6105.0, "green"),
                ("City", 6106.0, 10481.0, "yellow"),
                ("Large City", 10482.0, 27165, "orange"),
                ("Metropolis", 27165.0, 1060061.0, "red"))
   ```

4. Then, we establish a Python list to hold our QGIS renderer objects:

   ```
   ranges = []
   ```

5. Next, we loop through our range list, build the QGIS symbols, and add them to the renderer list:

   ```
   for label, lower, upper, color in population:
       sym = QgsSymbolV2.defaultSymbol(lyr.geometryType())
       sym.setColor(QColor(color))
       rng = QgsRendererRangeV2(lower, upper, sym, label)
       ranges.append(rng)
   ```

6. Now, reference the field name containing the population values in the shapefile attributes:

```
field = "POP"
```

7. Then, we create the renderer:

```
renderer = QgsGraduatedSymbolRendererV2(field, ranges)
```

8. We assign the renderer to the layer:

```
lyr.setRendererV2(renderer)
```

9. Finally, we add the map to the layer:

```
QgsMapLayerRegistry.instance().addMapLayer(lyr)
```

10. Verify that your map looks like the following screenshot:

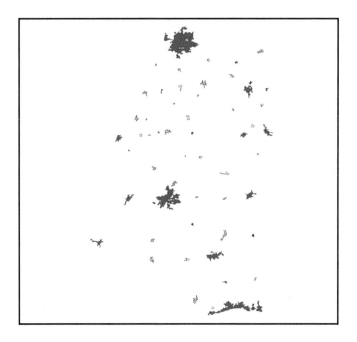

How it works...

The approach to using a graduated symbol for a vector layer is very similar to the color ramp shader for a raster layer. You can have as many ranges as you'd like by extending the Python tuple that is used to build the ranges. Of course, you can also build your own algorithms by programmatically examining the data fields first and then dividing up the values in equal intervals or some other scheme.

Creating a categorized vector layer symbol

A categorized vector layer symbol allows you to create distinct categories with colors and labels for unique features. This approach is typically used for datasets with a limited number of unique types of features. In this recipe, we'll categorize a vector layer into three different categories.

Getting ready

For this recipe, we'll use a land use shapefile, which you can download from
`https://github.com/GeospatialPython/Learn/raw/master/landuse_shp.zip`.

Extract it to a directory named `hancock` in your `qgis_data` directory.

How to do it...

We will load the vector layer, create three categories of land use, and render them as categorized symbols. To do this, we need to perform the following steps:

1. First, we need to import the `QColor` object for our category colors:

   ```
   from PyQt4.QtGui import QColor
   ```

2. Then, we load the vector layer:

```
lyr = QgsVectorLayer("Users/joellawhead/qgis_data
                    /hancock/landuse.shp", "Land Use", "ogr")
```

3. Next, we'll create our three land use categories using a Python dictionary with a field value as the key, color name, and label:

```
landuse = {
            "0":("yellow", "Developed"),
            "1":("darkcyan", "Water"),
            "2":("green", "Land")}
```

4. Now, we can build our categorized renderer items:

```
categories = []
for terrain, (color, label) in landuse.items():
    sym = QgsSymbolV2.defaultSymbol(lyr.geometryType())
    sym.setColor(QColor(color))
    category = QgsRendererCategoryV2(terrain, sym, label)
    categories.append(category)
```

5. We name the field containing the land use value:

```
field = "DN"
```

6. Next, we build the renderer:

```
renderer = QgsCategorizedSymbolRendererV2(field, categories)
```

7. We add the renderer to the layer:

```
lyr.setRendererV2(renderer)
```

8. Finally, we add the categorized layer to the map:

```
QgsMapLayerRegistry.instance().addMapLayer(lyr)
```

How it works…

There are only slight differences in the configurations of the various types of renderers in QGIS. Setting them up by first defining the properties of the renderer using native Python objects makes your code easier to read and, ultimately, manage. The following map image illustrates the categorized symbol in this recipe:

Using live layer effects

Live layer effects provide advanced cartographic effects for QGIS maps. These drawing effects go beyond the traditional GIS maps into the realm of map illustrations to add pleasing visualizations, including blur effects, inner and outer glows, and drop shadows. In this recipe, we'll add the inner glow and drop shadow live layer effects to a polygon layer.

Getting ready

Download the following zipped shapefile and extract it to a directory named `ms` in your `qgis_data` directory:

`https://github.com/GeospatialPython/Learn/raw/master/Mississippi.zip`

How to do it...

We will create a layer based on the shapefile. Then we'll build three symbol layers for the base fill color, the inner glow, and the drop shadow. We'll add those symbol layers to the layer's base symbol and finally, add the layer to the map:

1. First, we need to import the PyQt GUI library to handle color objects:

   ```
   from PyQt4.QtGui import *
   ```

2. Next, we'll create the shapefile layer:

   ```
   lyr = QgsVectorLayer("/qgis_data/ms/mississippi.shp",
                        "Mississippi", "ogr")
   ```

3. Then, we'll create a variable for the layer's symbol because we'll access it multiple times:

   ```
   sym = lyr.rendererV2().symbols()[0]
   ```

4. Now, we'll create the base fill symbol layer and set the fill color and outline colors using RGB values in `QColor` objects:

   ```
   fill = QgsSimpleFillSymbolLayerV2()
   fill.setFillColor(QColor.fromRgb(221,239,196))
   fill.setOutlineColor(QColor.fromRgb(63,122,17))
   ```

5. The second symbol layer is the inner glow, but before we create that we have to set up the live layer effect:

   ```
   inner_glow = QgsInnerGlowEffect()
   ```

6. We'll set the color of the inner glow to a darker color than the fill:

   ```
   inner_glow.setColor(QColor.fromRgb(46,129,4))
   ```

7. Then, we'll set the spread value to determine how far the color pushes from the edge toward the middle of the layer:

   ```
   inner_glow.setSpread(5.0)
   ```

8. Now that the effect is set up, we'll create another symbol layer:

   ```
   inner_glow_lyr = QgsSimpleFillSymbolLayerV2()
   ```

9. Then, we'll add the live layer effect to the symbol layer:

```
inner_glow_lyr.setPaintEffect(inner_glow)
```

10. Now, we're ready to set up the drop shadow effect using only the default configuration:

```
drop_shadow = QgsDropShadowEffect()
```

11. Then, we'll create a symbol layer for the drop shadow:

```
drop_shadow_lyr = QgsSimpleFillSymbolLayerV2()
drop_shadow_lyr.setPaintEffect(drop_shadow)
```

12. Next, we'll append the symbol layers to the symbol's symbol layer list:

```
sym.appendSymbolLayer(drop_shadow_lyr)
sym.appendSymbolLayer(fill)
sym.appendSymbolLayer(inner_glow_lyr)
```

13. Finally, we'll add the layer with all of its effects, to the map:

```
QgsMapLayerRegistry.instance().addMapLayer(lyr)
```

14. Verify that your map looks similar to the following screenshot:

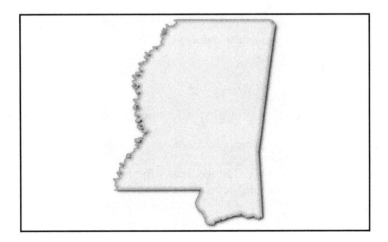

How it works...

A layer's symbol is just a container for symbol layers. Note that the order of the symbol layers is significant and is the same as the order in which they are rendered. That's why the shadow comes first and the glow comes last. Further more, as this recipe demonstrates, you can stack symbol layers indefinitely. Besides, beyond symbol layers, you can have multiple symbols per layer, but you can only have one effect per symbol layer.

Creating inverted polygon shapeburst fills

Shapeburst fills are a type of symbol layer that allows you to create buffered gradient fills. They are commonly used to shade water features in a realistic fashion, using different hues of blue to simulate water depth changes. In this recipe, we'll do exactly that. We'll use a land shapefile and a water shapefile, and in the water feature, we'll color it a darker blue toward the middle and lighter blue toward the edges to give the illusion of deeper water in the middle.

Getting ready

Download the following zipped set of shapefiles. Extract them into a directory named hancock in your qgis_data directory:

https://github.com/GeospatialPython/Learn/raw/master/hancock_land_water.zip.

How to do it...

We will create our layers for the land and water shapefiles. Then, we'll set up a fill symbol for the land layer. Next we'll set up the shapeburst fill for the water. Finally, we'll add those layers to the map to view them:

1. First, we need to import the PyQt GUI library to handle colors:

   ```
   from PyQt4.QtGui import *
   ```

2. Then, we create layers for the land and water shapefiles:

   ```
   land = QgsVectorLayer("/qgis_data/hancock/hancock_land.shp",
                 "Land", "ogr")
   water = QgsVectorLayer("/qgis_data/hancock/hancock_water.shp",
                 "Water", "ogr")
   ```

3. Now, we access the symbols for each layer:

```
land_sym = land.rendererV2().symbols()[0]
water_sym = water.rendererV2().symbols()[0]
```

4. Next, we create the fill symbol for the land layer, assigning it a fill color and outline color:

```
fill = QgsSimpleFillSymbolLayerV2()
fill.setFillColor(QColor.fromRgb(201,204,149))
fill.setOutlineColor(QColor.fromRgb(175,179,138))
```

5. Then, we change the default symbol layer for the land layer with our new fill symbol:

```
land_sym.changeSymbolLayer(0, fill)
```

6. Now, we need to create the two color objects for the shapeburst fill. They will be light blue and dark blue:

```
color1 = QColor.fromRgb(95,243,248)
color2 = QColor.fromRgb(51,44,247)
shapeburst = QgsShapeburstFillSymbolLayerV2(color=color1,
                                            color2=color2)
```

7. Now, we can set the shapeburst symbol layer to the water map layer:

```
water_sym.changeSymbolLayer(0, shapeburst)
```

8. Finally, we can add the layers to the map and see the result:

```
QgsMapLayerRegistry.instance().addMapLayers([land, water])
```

9. Ensure that your map looks similar to the following screenshot:

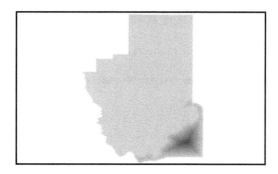

How it works...

The shapeburst fill shades each pixel in the polygon based on its distance to the nearest edge. As you get closer to the middle, the pixels get darker. This algorithm creates the darker-colored *veins* throughout the feature. There are additional settings that let you blur the separation between the colors or use a multi-colored gradient.

Creating a map bookmark

Map bookmarks allow you to save a location on a map in QGIS, so you can quickly jump to the points you need to view repeatedly without manually panning and zooming the map. PyQGIS does not contain API commands to read, write, and zoom to bookmarks. Fortunately, QGIS stores the bookmarks in an SQLite database. Python has a built-in SQLite library that we can use to manipulate bookmarks using the database API.

Getting ready

You can download a census tract polygon shapefile to use with this recipe from `https://github.com/GeospatialPython/Learn/raw/master/GIS_CensusTract.zip`.

Extract it to your `qgis_data` directory. We are going to create a bookmark that uses an area of interest within this shapefile. So, you can manually load the bookmark in order to test it out.

How to do it...

We will access the QGIS configuration variables to get the path of the user database, which stores the bookmarks. Then, we'll connect to this database and execute an SQL query that inserts a bookmark. Finally, we'll commit the changes to the database, as follows:

1. First, using **Python Console**, we must import Python's built-in SQLite library:

   ```
   import sqlite3
   ```

2. Next, get the path to the database:

   ```
   dbPath = QgsApplication.qgisUserDbFilePath()
   ```

3. Now, we connect to the database:

   ```
   db = sqlite3.connect(dbPath)
   ```

4. Then, we need a database cursor to manipulate the database:

   ```
   cursor = db.cursor()
   ```

5. Now, we can execute the SQL query, which is a string. In the VALUES portion of the query, we will leave the bookmark ID as NULL but give it a name; then, we leave the project name NULL and set the extents, as follows:

   ```
   cursor.execute("""INSERT INTO tbl_bookmarks
                  (bookmark_id, name, project_name,
                   xmin, ymin, xmax, ymax,
                   projection_srid)
                  VALUES(NULL, "BSL", NULL,
                      -89.51715550010032,
                      30.233838337125075,
                      -89.27257255649518,
                      30.381717490617945,
                      4269)""")
   ```

6. Then, we commit the changes:

   ```
   db.commit()
   ```

7. To test the map bookmark, load the census tract layer onto the map by dragging and dropping it from your filesystem into QGIS.
8. Next, click on the **View** menu in QGIS and select **Show Bookmarks**.
9. Then, select the **BSL** bookmark and click on the **ZoomTo** button.
10. Verify that the map snapped to an area of interest close to the polygons, with OBJECTIDs from `4625` to `4627`.

How it works...

Even when QGIS doesn't provide a high-level API, you can almost always use Python to dig deeper and access the information you want. QGIS is built on open source software; therefore, no part of the program is truly off-limits.

Navigating to a map bookmark

Map bookmarks store important locations on a map, so you can quickly find them later. You can programmatically navigate to bookmarks using the Python `sqlite3` library in order to access the bookmarks database table in the QGIS user database and then using the PyQGIS canvas API.

Getting ready

We will use a census tract layer to test out the bookmark navigation. You can download the zipped shapefile from
`https://github.com/GeospatialPython/Learn/raw/master/GIS_CensusTract.zip`.

Manually load this layer into QGIS after extracting it from the ZIP file. Also, make sure that you have completed the previous recipe, *Creating a map bookmark*. You will need a bookmark named BSL for an area of interest in this shapefile.

How to do it...

We will retrieve a bookmark from the QGIS user database and then set the map's extents to this bookmark. To do this, perform the following steps:

1. First, import the Python `sqlite3` library:

```
import sqlite3
```

2. Next, get the location of the user database from the QGIS data:

```
dbPath = QgsApplication.qgisUserDbFilePath()
```

3. Now, we connect to the database:

```
db = sqlite3.connect(dbPath)
```

4. Then, we need a database cursor to run queries:

```
cursor = db.cursor()
```

5. Now, we can get the bookmark information for the bookmark named **BSL**:

```
cursor.execute("""SELECT * FROM tbl_bookmarks WHERE name='BSL'""")
```

6. Now, we'll get the complete results from the query:

```
row = cursor.fetchone()
```

7. Then, we split the values of the result into multiple variables:

```
id,mark_name,project,xmin,ymin,xmax,ymax,srid = row
```

8. Now, we can use the extents of the bookmark to create a QGIS extent rectangle:

```
rect = QgsRectangle(xmin, ymin, xmax, ymax)
```

9. Next, we reference the map canvas:

```
canvas = qgis.utils.iface.mapCanvas()
```

10. Finally, we set the extent of the canvas to the rectangle and then refresh the canvas:

```
canvas.setExtent(rect)
canvas.refresh()
```

How it works...

Reading and writing bookmarks with SQLite is straightforward, even though it's not a part of the main PyQGIS API. Notice that bookmarks have a placeholder for a project name, which you can use to filter bookmarks by project if needed.

Setting scale-based visibility for a layer

Sometimes, a GIS layer only makes sense when it is displayed at a certain scale, for example, a complex road network. PyQGIS supports scale-based visibility to programmatically set the scale range, in which a layer is displayed. In this recipe, we'll investigate scale-dependent layers.

Getting ready

You will need the sample census tract shapefile, available as a ZIP file from
`https://github.com/GeospatialPython/Learn/raw/master/GIS_CensusTract.zip`.

Extract the zipped layer to a directory named `census` in your `qgis_data` directory.

How to do it...

We will load the vector layer, toggle scale-based visibility, set the visibility range, and then add the layer to the map. To do this, perform the following steps:

1. First, we load the layer:

```
lyr = QgsVectorLayer("/qgis_data/census/GIS_CensusTract_poly.shp",
                     "Census", "ogr")
```

2. Next, we toggle scale-based visibility:

```
lyr.toggleScaleBasedVisibility(True)
```

3. Then, we set the minimum and maximum map scales at which the layer is visible:

```
lyr.setMinimumScale(22945.0)
lyr.setMaximumScale(1000000.0)
```

4. Now, we add the layer to the map:

```
QgsMapLayerRegistry.instance().addMapLayer(lyr)
```

5. Finally, manually zoom in and out of the map to ensure that the layer disappears and reappears at the proper scales.

How it works...

The map scale is a ratio of map units to physical map size expressed as a floating-point number. You must remember to toggle scale-dependent visibility so that QGIS knows that it needs to check the range each time the map scale changes.

Using SVG for layer symbols

Scalable Vector Graphics (**SVG**) are an XML standard that defines vector graphics which can be scaled at any resolution. QGIS can use SVG files as markers for points. In this recipe, we'll use Python to apply one of the SVG symbols included with QGIS to a point layer.

Getting ready

For this recipe, download the following zipped point shapefile layer from
`https://github.com/GeospatialPython/Learn/raw/master/NYC_MUSEUMS_GEO.zip`.

Extract it to your `qgis_data` directory.

How to do it...

In the following steps, we'll load the vector layer, build a symbol layer and renderer, and add it to the layer, as follows:

1. First, we'll define the path to the shapefile:

```
src = "/qgis_data/NYC_MUSEUMS_GEO/NYC_MUSEUMS_GEO.shp"
```

2. Next, we'll load the layer:

```
lyr = QgsVectorLayer(src, "Museums", "ogr")
```

3. Now, we define the properties of the symbol, including the location of the SVG file as a Python dictionary:

```
svgStyle = {}
svgStyle['fill'] = '#0000ff'
svgStyle['name'] = 'landmark/tourism=museum.svg'
svgStyle['outline'] = '#000000'
svgStyle['outline-width'] = '6.8'
svgStyle['size'] = '6'
```

4. Then, we create an SVG symbol layer:

```
symLyr1 = QgsSvgMarkerSymbolLayerV2.create(svgStyle)
```

5. Now, we change the layer renderer's default symbol layer:

```
lyr.rendererV2().symbols()[0].changeSymbolLayer(0, symLyr1)
```

6. Finally, we add the layer to the map in order to view the SVG symbol:

```
QgsMapLayerRegistry.instance().addMapLayer(lyr)
```

How it works...

The default SVG layers are stored in the QGIS application directory. There are numerous graphics available, which cover many common uses. You can also add your own graphics as well. The following map image shows the recipe's output:

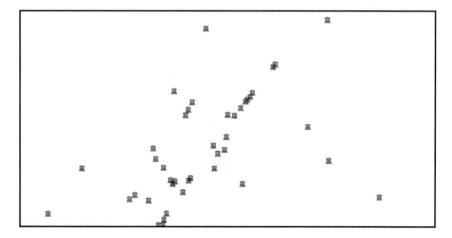

Using pie charts for symbols

QGIS has the ability to use dynamic pie charts as symbols describing the statistics in a given region. In this recipe, we'll use pie chart symbols on a polygon layer in QGIS.

Getting ready

For this recipe, download the following zipped shapefile and extract it to a directory named `ms` in your `qgis_data` directory from
`https://github.com/GeospatialPython/Learn/raw/master/County10PopnHou.zip`.

How to do it...

As with other renderers, we will build a symbol layer, add it to a renderer, and display the layer on the map. The pie chart diagram renderers are more complex than other renderers but have many more options. Perform the following steps to create a pie chart map:

1. First, we import the PyQt GUI library:

   ```
   from PyQt4.QtGui import *
   ```

2. Then, we load the layer:

   ```
   lyr = QgsVectorLayer("/qgis_data/ms/County10PopnHou.shp",
                        "Population", "ogr")
   ```

3. Next, we set up categories based on attribute names:

   ```
   categories = [u'PCT_WHT', u'PCT_BLK', u'PCT_AMIND', u'PCT_ASIAN',
                 u'PCT_HAW', u'PCT_ORA', u'PCT_MR', u'PCT_HISP']
   ```

4. Now, we set up a list of corresponding colors for each category:

   ```
   colors = ['#3727fa','#01daae','#f849a6','#268605','#6810ff',
             '#453990','#630f2f','#07dd45']
   ```

5. Next, we convert the hex color values to `QColor` objects:

   ```
   qcolors = map(QColor, colors)
   ```

6. Then, we create a pie diagram object:

```
diagram = QgsPieDiagram()
```

7. Then, we create a diagram settings object:

```
ds = QgsDiagramSettings()
```

8. Now, we define all the diagram settings that will be used for the renderer:

```
ds.font = QFont("Helvetica", 12)
ds.transparency = 0
ds.categoryColors = qcolors
ds.categoryAttributes = categories
ds.size = QSizeF(100.0, 100.0)
ds.sizeType = 0
ds.labelPlacementMethod = 1
ds.scaleByArea = True
ds.minimumSize = 0
ds.BackgroundColor = QColor(255,255,255,0)
ds.PenColor = QColor("black")
ds.penWidth = 0
```

9. Now, we can create our diagram renderer:

```
dr = QgsLinearlyInterpolatedDiagramRenderer()
```

10. We must set a few size parameters for our diagrams:

```
dr.setLowerValue(0.0)
dr.setLowerSize(QSizeF(0.0, 0.0))
dr.setUpperValue(2000000)
dr.setUpperSize(QSizeF(40,40))
dr.setClassificationAttribute(6)
```

11. Then, we can add our diagram to the renderer:

```
dr.setDiagram(diagram)
```

12. Next, we add the renderer to the layer:

```
lyr.setDiagramRenderer(dr)
```

13. Now, we apply some additional placement settings at the layer level:

```
dls = QgsDiagramLayerSettings()
dls.dist = 0
dls.priority = 0
dls.xPosColumn = -1
dls.yPosColumn = -1
dls.placement = 0
lyr.setDiagramLayerSettings(dls)
```

14. In QGIS 2.6, the diagram renderer is tied to the new PAL labeling engine, so we need to activate this engine:

```
label = QgsPalLayerSettings()
label.readFromLayer(lyr)
label.enabled = True
label.writeToLayer(lyr)
```

15. Next, we delete any cached images that are rendered and force the layer to repaint:

```
ifhasattr(lyr, "setCacheImage"):
lyr.setCacheImage(None)

lyr.triggerRepaint()
```

16. Finally, add our diagram layer to the map:

```
QgsMapLayerRegistry.instance().addMapLayer(lyr)
```

How it works...

The basics of pie chart diagram symbols are straightforward and work in a similar way to other types of symbols and renderers. However, it gets a little confusing, as we need to apply settings at three different levels – the diagram level, the render level, and the layer level. It turns out they are actually quite complex. Most of the settings are poorly documented, if at all. Fortunately, most of them are self-explanatory. The following screenshot shows an example of the completed pie chart diagram map:

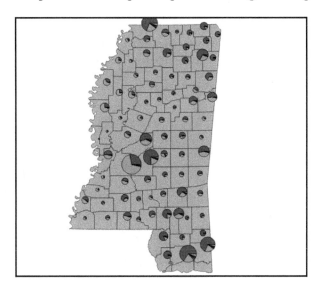

There's more...

To learn more about what is possible with pie chart diagram symbols, you can experiment with this recipe in the **Script Runner** plugin, where you can change or remove settings and quickly re-render the map. You can also manually change the settings using the QGIS dialogs, and then export the style to an XML file and see what settings are used. Most of them map well to the Python API.

Using the 2.5D renderer

The 2.5D renderer is a powerful new visualization for QGIS, which allows you to present buildings as three-dimensional shapes from a single angle. The locked viewpoint is why the developers named it 2.5D or 2 ½ D instead of full 3D. In this recipe, we'll render a small set of building footprints in 2.5D, with height values set as a shapefile attribute in the sample footprints.

Getting ready

Download the zipped building footprints shapefile from the following URL:

`https://github.com/GeospatialPython/Learn/raw/master/buildings.zip`

Extract it into a directory called `hancock` in your `qgis_data` directory.

How to do it...

We will create the vector layer, assign it the special renderer, configure the renderer, and finally add it to the map to see the result. We will be using a special set of properties that is normally reserved for labelling settings in QGIS:

1. First, create the layer from the building footprints shapefile:

```
lyr = QgsVectorLayer("/qgis_data/hancock/buildings.shp",
                     "Buildings", "ogr")
```

2. Next, we'll create the 2.5D renderer and set it as the layer renderer:

```
r = Qgs25DRenderer()
lyr.setRendererV2(r)
```

3. Then, we need to create the utility object for changing layer variables:

```
exp = QgsExpressionContextUtils()
```

4. Now, we will set the layer variable names and values that control the angle and height as custom properties:

```
exp.setLayerVariable(lyr, "qgis_25d_angle", 90)
exp.setLayerVariable(lyr, "qgis_25d_height", "HEIGHT")
```

5. Finally, we'll add the layer to the map:

```
QgsMapLayerRegistry.instance().addMapLayer(lyr)
```

6. Verify that your map looks similar to the following screenshot:

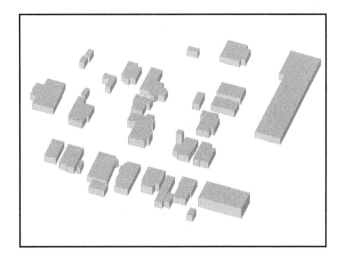

How it works...

This renderer is different from other renderers because it has methods for most of the renderer's properties, including roof color, wall color, and shadow information. The two most critical properties are stored in a generic collection of properties, called **custom properties**, which are mostly used for the newer labeling engine. But thanks to the QgsExpressionContextUtils object, we can easily change these variables in the context of the layer, to make a compelling map view.

Using XYZ tiled map services

A tiled map service allows you to efficiently display large raster data sets from web services. The raster dataset is broken into evenly-sized tiles at varying resolutions to create predictable naming conventions and bandwidth requirements for large datasets. QGIS now supports this standard as a part of the raster layer API. In this recipe, we'll load the **Open Street Map** tiled map service.

Getting ready

Open the QGIS Python console by selecting the **Plugins** menu and then clicking on **Python Console**.

How to do it...

We will quickly create a QGIS raster layer, and then we'll add it to the map:

1. Load the raster layer, specifying the type and the web service URL in the data source parameter. We'll also assign it the name **OSM** (**OpenStreetMap**):

```
rasterLyr = QgsRasterLayer("type=xyz&url=http://c.tile
                          .openstreetmap.org/{z}/{x}/{y}
                          .png", "OSM", "wms")
```

2. Then, the only remaining step is to add it to the map:

```
QgsMapLayerRegistry.instance().addMapLayer(rasterLyr)
```

3. Verify that the loaded map looks similar to the following screenshot:

How it works...

This feature is just an extension of the WMS data type for raster layers. The {z}/{x}/{y} portion of the URL provides a place holder for the naming conventions of each tile. In addition to just adding this to the API, this data type takes advantage of the multi-threaded capability added to QGIS, so tiles can be added to the map as soon as they are downloaded and while other tiles are still downloading. This makes QGIS feel much faster, and is technically faster than the third-party plugins that provided this capability previously.

Using Esri ArcGIS map services

Esri create its own version of the JSON format. QGIS now supports this special dialect of the JSON format Esri created for map services. It is almost similar to GeoJSON, but different enough to require special handling. There are two types of Esri services: **ArcGIS map services,** which provide tiled map layers, and **ArcGIS feature services,** which provide vector layers. In this recipe, we'll create a map with one of each type of service, including a world imagery basemap service and a 2011 worldwide earthquake point layer.

Getting Ready

For this example, it is important to ensure that the on-the-fly CRS transformation is turned off for your map project, because Esri services use a slightly different CRS **(EPSG:3857)**, and we don't want QGIS to automatically assume WGS 84. To verify this setting, perform the following steps:

1. Go to the QGIS **Project** menu and choose **Project Properties...**.
2. In the **Project Properties** dialog, choose the **CRS** panel on the left.
3. In the **CRS** panel at the very top, ensure that the **Enable 'on the fly' CRS transformation (OTF)** checkbox is unchecked, as shown in the following screenshot:

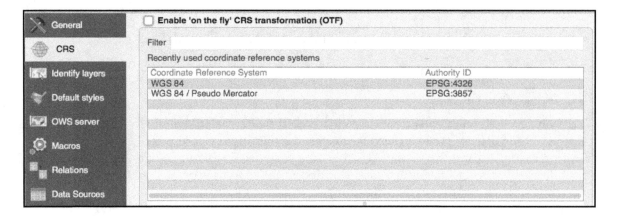

How to do it...

We will build the URI strings for each layer, then we'll create each layer, and finally, we'll add them to the map. The vector earthquake layer may take a few seconds to load as it consists of hundreds of points:

1. First, we'll build the URI string for the tiled imagery map service:

```
arc_map_server = "http://server.arcgisonline.com/"
arc_map_server += "ArcGIS/rest/services/World_Imagery
                  /MapServer?f=json"
```

2. Next, we'll build the much longer URI for the feature map service:

```
arc_feature_server = "https://services5.arcgis.com
                        /U8xJBTiAx2RGR2e2"
arc_feature_server += "/arcgis/rest/services/2011_Earthquakes
                        /FeatureServer/0/"
arc_feature_server += "query?outFields=*&
                        where=1%3D1&outSR=3857&f=json"
```

3. Then, we can create the imagery service as a standard raster layer:

```
basemap = QgsRasterLayer(arc_map_server, "World Imagery")
```

4. Now, we'll create the OGR-based vector layer:

```
earthquakes = QgsVectorLayer(arc_feature_server, "EarthQuakes",
                              "ogr")
```

5. Finally, we can add both the layers to the map:

```
QgsMapLayerRegistry.instance().addMapLayers([earthquakes, basemap])
```

6. Verify that your map looks similar to the following screenshot:

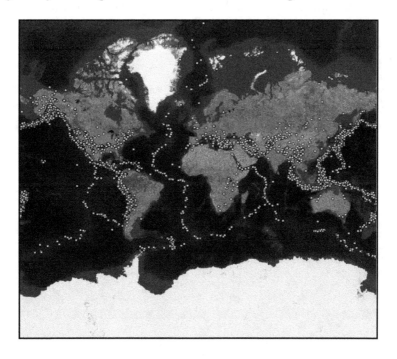

How it works...

Esri ArcGIS can also output Open GIS Consortium services, but JSON offers a lot of conveniences, including human readability, that you can test correctly in a browser. The query string at the end of the feature server URI is standard and can be used on any Esri feature service. It is a good idea to test these URLs in a browser because the service owners can disable JSON or query output if they desire.

Labeling a feature

Once your map layers are styled, the next step to creating a complete map is labeling features. We'll explore the basics of labeling in this recipe.

Getting ready

Download the following zipped shapefile from
`https://github.com/GeospatialPython/Learn/raw/master/MSCities_Geo_Pts.zip`.

Extract the shapefile to a directory named `ms` in your `qgis_data`directory.

How to do it...

We will load the point shapefile layer, create a label object, set its properties, apply it to the layer, and then add the layer to the map. To do this, we need to perform the following steps:

1. First, to save space, we'll specify the path to the shapefile:

```
src = "/qgis_data/ms/MSCities_Geo_Pts.shp"
```

2. Next, we'll load the layer:

```
lyr = QgsVectorLayer(src, "Cities", "ogr")
```

3. Then, we'll create the labeling object:

```
label = QgsPalLayerSettings()
```

4. Now, we'll configure the labels, starting with the current layer settings being read:

```
label.readFromLayer(lyr)
label.enabled = True
```

5. Then, we specify the attribute for the label data:

```
label.fieldName = 'NAME10'
```

6. Then, we can set the placement and size options:

```
label.placement= QgsPalLayerSettings.AroundPoint
label.setDataDefinedProperty(QgsPalLayerSettings
                       .Size,True,True,'8','')
```

7. Next, we commit the changes to the layer:

```
label.writeToLayer(lyr)
```

8. Finally, we can add the layer to the map to view the labels:

```
QgsMapLayerRegistry.instance().addMapLayers([lyr])
```

9. Verify that your map looks similar to the following screenshot:

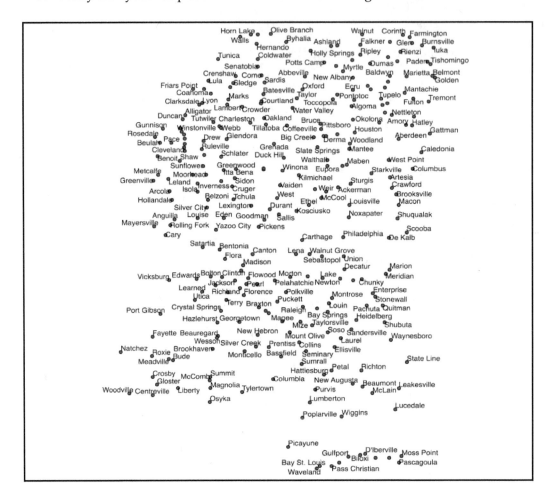

How it works...

An interesting part of labeling is the round trip read and write process to access the layer data and the assignment of the labeling properties. Labeling can be quite complex, but this recipe covers the basics needed to get started.

Using null symbols

Null symbols are a tool that allow you to have a layer without any symbology. Layers without symbology can be useful when you don't need to see a layer but need to interact with it in other ways, such as querying or specialized labeling. For example, if you have an imagery basemap, you may want to have labels on the map but no features. In this recipe, we'll load a point layer and label it, but use null symbology.

Getting ready

Download the zipped shapefile from
`https://github.com/GeospatialPython/Learn/raw/master/MSCities_Geo_Pts.zip`.

Extract the shapefile to a directory named `ms` in your `qgis_data` directory.

How to do it...

We will load the layer, set the renderer to the null symbol renderer, set up our labeling configuration, and then add it to the map. This recipe builds on the previous labeling recipe:

1. First, to save space, we'll specify the path to the shapefile:

    ```
    src = "/qgis_data/ms/MSCities_Geo_Pts.shp"
    ```

2. Next, we'll load the layer:

    ```
    lyr = QgsVectorLayer(src, "Cities", "ogr")
    ```

3. Now, we'll set the layer renderer as a null symbol renderer:

    ```
    lyr.setRendererV2(QgsNullSymbolRenderer())
    ```

4. Then, we'll create the labeling object:

    ```
    label = QgsPalLayerSettings()
    ```

5. Now, we'll configure the labels, starting with the current layer settings being read:

    ```
    label.readFromLayer(lyr)
    label.enabled = True
    ```

6. Then, we'll specify the attribute for the label data:

```
label.fieldName = 'NAME10'
```

7. Then, we can set the placement and size options:

```
label.placement= QgsPalLayerSettings.AroundPoint
label.textFont.setPointSize(12)
```

8. Next, we'll commit the changes to the layer:

```
label.writeToLayer(lyr)
```

9. Finally, we can add the layer to the map to view the labels:

```
QgsMapLayerRegistry.instance().addMapLayers([lyr])
```

10. Verify your map looks similar to the following screenshot:

How it works...

You could effectively accomplish the same effect by creating empty fill symbols with no outline. But that would require much more code and different code for different geometry types. The null symbol renderer is a simple way to accomplish the same thing.

Change map layer transparency

Map layer transparency allows you to change the opacity of a layer, so the items behind it are visible to some degree. A common technique is to make a vector layer polygon partially transparent in order to allow the underlying imagery or elevation data to add texture to the data.

Getting ready

In a directory called `ms`, in your `qgis_data` directory, download and extract the following shapefile from

https://github.com/GeospatialPython/Learn/raw/master/Mississippi.zip.

How to do it...

The process is extremely simple. Transparency is just a method:

1. First, we load the shapefile layer:

```
lyr = QgsVectorLayer("/qgis_data/ms/mississippi.shp",
                     "Mississippi", "ogr")
```

2. Next, we set the layer's transparency to 50 percent:

```
lyr.setLayerTransparency(50)
```

3. Finally, we add this layer to the map:

```
QgsMapLayerRegistry.instance().addMapLayer(lyr)
```

How it works...

If you set the transparency to 100 percent, the layer is completely opaque. If you set it to 0, the layer becomes completely invisible.

Adding standard map tools to the canvas

In this recipe, you'll learn how to add standard map navigation tools to a standalone map canvas. Creating the simplest possible interactive application provides a framework to begin building specialized geospatial applications using QGIS as a library.

Getting ready

Download the following zipped shapefile and extract it to your `qgis_data` directory into a folder named `ms` from

`https://github.com/GeospatialPython/Learn/raw/master/Mississippi.zip`.

How to do it...

We will walk you through the steps required to create a map canvas, add a layer to it, and then add some tools to zoom and pan the map, which are given as follows:

1. First, because we are working outside the QGIS Python interpreter, we need to import some QGIS and Qt libraries:

```
from qgis.gui import *
from qgis.core import *
from PyQt4.QtGui import *
from PyQt4.QtCore import SIGNAL, Qt
import sys, os
```

2. Then, we must set the location of our main QGIS application directory. This setting is platform-dependent:

```
# OSX:
    QgsApplication.setPrefixPath("/Applications/QGIS.app
                            /Contents/MacOS/", True)
# Windows:
    # app.setPrefixPath("C:/Program Files/QGIS Valmiera
                        /apps/qgis", True)
```

3. Next, we begin initializing the class:

```
class MyWnd(QMainWindow):
def __init__(self):
```

4. Now, we can initialize the application and create the map canvas:

```
QMainWindow.__init__(self)
QgsApplication.setPrefixPath("/Applications/QGIS.app
                        /Contents/MacOS/", True)
QgsApplication.initQgis()
self.canvas = QgsMapCanvas()
self.canvas.setCanvasColor(Qt.white)
```

5. Then, we can load the shapefile layer and add it to the canvas:

```
self.lyr = QgsVectorLayer("/qgis_data/ms/mississippi.shp",
                        "Mississippi", "ogr")
QgsMapLayerRegistry.instance().addMapLayer(self.lyr)
self.canvas.setExtent(self.lyr.extent())
self.canvas.setLayerSet([QgsMapCanvasLayer(self.lyr)])
self.setCentralWidget(self.canvas)
```

6. Next, we define the buttons that will be visible on the toolbar:

```
actionZoomIn = QAction("Zoom in", self)
actionZoomOut = QAction("Zoom out", self)
actionPan = QAction("Pan", self)
actionZoomIn.setCheckable(True)
actionZoomOut.setCheckable(True)
actionPan.setCheckable(True)
```

7. Now, we connect the signal created, when the buttons are clicked, to the Python methods that will provide each tool's functionality:

```
actionZoomIn.triggered.connect(self.zoomIn)
actionZoomOut.triggered.connect(self.zoomOut)
actionPan.triggered.connect(self.pan)
```

8. Next, we create our toolbar and add the buttons:

```
self.toolbar = self.addToolBar("Canvas actions")
self.toolbar.addAction(actionZoomIn)
self.toolbar.addAction(actionZoomOut)
self.toolbar.addAction(actionPan)
```

9. Then, we connect the buttons to the applications states:

```
self.toolPan = QgsMapToolPan(self.canvas)
self.toolPan.setAction(actionPan)
self.toolZoomIn = QgsMapToolZoom(self.canvas, False) # false = in
self.toolZoomIn.setAction(actionZoomIn)
self.toolZoomOut = QgsMapToolZoom(self.canvas, True) # true = out
self.toolZoomOut.setAction(actionZoomOut)
```

10. Then, we define which button will be selected when the application loads:

```
self.pan()
```

11. Now, we define the Python methods that control the application's behavior for each tool:

```
def zoomIn(self):
    self.canvas.setMapTool(self.toolZoomIn)
def zoomOut(self):
    self.canvas.setMapTool(self.toolZoomOut)
def pan(self):
    self.canvas.setMapTool(self.toolPan)
```

12. Then, we create a Qt application that uses our application's window class:

```
class MainApp(QApplication):
    def __init__(self):
        QApplication.__init__(self,[],True)
        wdg = MyWnd()
        wdg.show()
        self.exec_()
```

13. Finally, we enter the program's main loop:

```
if __name__ == "__main__":
    import sys
    app = MainApp()
```

How it works...

An application is a continuously running program loop that ends only when we quit the application. QGIS is based on the Qt windowing library, so our application class inherits from the main window class that provides the canvas and the ability to create toolbars and dialogs. This is a lot of setup, even for an extremely simple application, but once the framework for an application is complete, it becomes much easier to extend it.

Using a map tool to draw points on the canvas

QGIS contains a built-in functionality to zoom and pan the map in custom applications. It also contains the basic hooks to build your own interactive tools. In this recipe, we'll create an interactive point tool that lets you mark locations on the map by clicking on a point.

Getting ready

We will use the application framework from the previous *Adding standard map tools to the canvas* recipe, so complete that recipe. We will extend that application with a new tool. The complete version of this application is available in the code samples provided with this book.

How to do it...

We will set up the button, signal trigger, and actions as we do with all map tools. However, because we are building a new tool, we must also define a class to define exactly what the tool does. To do this, we need to perform the following screenshot:

1. First, we define our point tool's button in the actions portion of our application. Place this line after the `QAction("Pan")` method:

```
actionPoint = QAction("Point", self)
```

2. In the next section, we make sure that when we click on the button, it stays selected:

```
actionPoint.setCheckable(True)
```

3. In the section after that, we define the method that is used when the button is triggered:

```
self.connect(actionPoint, SIGNAL("triggered()"), self.point)
```

4. Now, we add the button to the toolbar along with the other buttons:

```
self.toolbar.addAction(actionPoint)
```

5. Then, we link the application to our specialized tool class:

```
self.toolPoint = PointMapTool(self.canvas)
self.toolPoint.setAction(actionPoint)
```

6. We set the point tool to be selected when the application loads:

```
self.point()
```

7. Now, we define the method in the main application class for our tool:

```
def point(self):
    self.canvas.setMapTool(self.toolPoint)
```

8. Now, we create a class that describes the type of tool we have and the output it provides. The output is a point on the canvas, defined in the `canvasPressEvent` method, that receives the button-click event. We will inherit from a generic tool in order to create points called the `QgsMapToolEmitPoint`:

```
class PointMapTool(QgsMapToolEmitPoint):
    def __init__(self, canvas):
        self.canvas = canvas
        QgsMapToolEmitPoint.__init__(self, self.canvas)
        self.point = None

    def canvasPressEvent(self, e):
        self.point = self.toMapCoordinates(e.pos())
        print self.point.x(), self.point.y()
        m = QgsVertexMarker(self.canvas)
        m.setCenter(self.point)
        m.setColor(QColor(0,255,0))
        m.setIconSize(5)
        m.setIconType(QgsVertexMarker.ICON_BOX) # or ICON_CROSS,
                                                #    ICON_X
        m.setPenWidth(3)
```

How it works...

For custom tools, PyQGIS provides a set of generic tools for the common functions that you can extend and piece together. In this case, the `EmitPoint` tool handles the details of the events and map functionality when you click on a location on the map.

Using a map tool to draw polygons or lines on the canvas

In this recipe, we'll create a tool to draw polygons on the canvas. This tool is an important tool because it opens the doors to even more advanced tools. Once you have a polygon on the canvas, you can do all sorts of operations that involve querying and geometry.

Getting ready

We will use the application framework from the *Adding standard map tools to the canvas* recipe, so complete that recipe. We will extend that application with a new tool. The complete version of this application is available in the code samples provided with this book.

How to do it...

We will add a new tool to the toolbar and also create a class that describes our polygon tool, as follows:

1. First, we define our polygon tool's button in the actions portion of our application. Place this line after the `QAction("Pan")` method:

   ```
   actionPoly = QAction("Polygon", self)
   ```

2. In the next section, we make sure that when we click on the button, it stays selected:

   ```
   actionPoly.setCheckable(True)
   ```

3. In the section after that, we define the method used when the button is triggered:

   ```
   self.connect(actionPoly, SIGNAL("triggered()"), self.poly)
   ```

4. Now, we add the button to the toolbar along with the other buttons:

   ```
   self.toolbar.addAction(actionPoly)
   ```

5. Then, we link the application to our specialized tool class:

   ```
   self.toolPoly = PolyMapTool(self.canvas)
   self.toolPoly.setAction(actionPoly)
   ```

6. We set the point tool to be selected when the application loads:

   ```
   self.poly()
   ```

7. Now, we define the method in the main application class for our tool:

   ```
   def poly(self):
       self.canvas.setMapTool(self.toolPoly)
   ```

8. Now, we create a class that describes the type of tool we have and the output it provides. The output is a point on the canvas defined in the `canvasPressEvent` method that receives the button-click event and the `showPoly` method. We will inherit from a generic tool in order to create points called the `QgsMapToolEmitPoint`; we will also use an object called `QgsRubberBand` for handling polygons:

```
class PolyMapTool(QgsMapToolEmitPoint):
    def __init__(self, canvas):
        self.canvas = canvas
        QgsMapToolEmitPoint.__init__(self, self.canvas)
        self.rubberband = QgsRubberBand(self.canvas, QGis.Polygon)
        self.rubberband.setColor(Qt.red)
        self.rubberband.setWidth(1)
        self.point = None
        self.points = []

    def canvasPressEvent(self, e):
        self.point = self.toMapCoordinates(e.pos())
        m = QgsVertexMarker(self.canvas)
        m.setCenter(self.point)
        m.setColor(QColor(0,255,0))
        m.setIconSize(5)
        m.setIconType(QgsVertexMarker.ICON_BOX)
        m.setPenWidth(3)
        self.points.append(self.point)
        self.isEmittingPoint = True
        self.showPoly()

    def showPoly(self):
        self.rubberband.reset(QGis.Polygon)
        for point in self.points[:-1]:
            self.rubberband.addPoint(point, False)
        self.rubberband.addPoint(self.points[-1], True)
        self.rubberband.show()
```

How it works...

All the settings for the polygon are contained in the custom class. There is a key property, called **EmittingPoint**, which we use to detect whether we are still adding points to the polygon. This value starts out as `false`. If this is the case, we reset our polygon object and begin drawing a new one. The following screenshot shows a polygon drawn with this tool on a map:

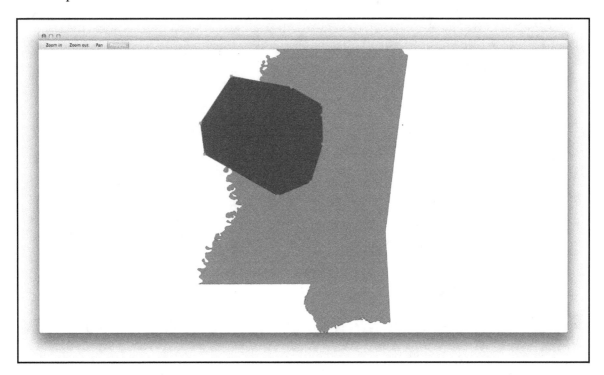

Building a custom selection tool

In this recipe, we will build a custom tool that both draws a shape on the map and interacts with other features on the map. These two basic functions are the basis for almost any map tool you would want to build in a standalone QGIS application such as this one or by extending the QGIS desktop application with a plugin.

Getting ready

We will use the application framework from the *Adding standard map tools to the canvas* recipe, so complete that recipe. We will extend that application with a new tool. The complete version of this application is available in the code samples provided with this book. It will also be beneficial to study the other two tool-related recipes, *Using a map tool to draw polygons or lines on the canvas* and *Using a map tool to draw points on the canvas*, as this recipe builds on them as well.

You will also need the following zipped shapefile from
`https://github.com/GeospatialPython/Learn/raw/master/NYC_MUSEUMS_GEO.zip`.

Download and extract it to your `qgis_data` directory.

How to do it...

We will add a new tool to the toolbar and also create a class describing our selection tool, including how to draw the selection polygon and how to select the features. To do this, we need to perform the following steps:

1. First, we define our polygon tool's button in the actions portion of our application. Place this line after the `QAction("Pan")` method:

    ```
    actionSelect = QAction("Select", self)
    ```

2. In the next section, we make sure that when we click on the button, it stays selected:

    ```
    actionSelect.setCheckable(True)
    ```

3. In the section after that, we define the method used when the button is triggered:

    ```
    self.connect(actionSelect, SIGNAL("triggered()"), self.select)
    ```

4. Now, we add the button to the toolbar along with the other buttons:

    ```
    self.toolbar.addAction(actionSelect)
    ```

5. Then, we link the application to our specialized tool class:

    ```
    self.toolSelect = SelectMapTool(self.canvas, self.lyr)
    self.toolSelect.setAction(actionSelect)
    ```

6. We set the point tool to be selected when the application loads:

```
self.select()
```

7. Now, we define the method in the main application class for our tool:

```
def select(self):
    self.canvas.setMapTool(self.toolSelect)
```

8. Next, we create a class that describes the type of tool we have and how it works. The output is a point on the canvas defined in the `canvasPressEvent` method that receives the button click-event and the `selectPoly` method. We will inherit from a generic tool to create points called the `QgsMapToolEmitPoint`; we will also use an object called `QgsRubberBand` to handle polygons. However, we must also perform the selection process to highlight the features that fall within our selection polygon:

```
class SelectMapTool(QgsMapToolEmitPoint):
    def __init__(self, canvas, lyr):
        self.canvas = canvas
        self.lyr = lyr
        QgsMapToolEmitPoint.__init__(self, self.canvas)
        self.rubberband = QgsRubberBand(self.canvas, QGis.Polygon)
        self.rubberband.setColor(QColor(255,255,0,50))
        self.rubberband.setWidth(1)
        self.point = None
        self.points = []

    def canvasPressEvent(self, e):
        self.point = self.toMapCoordinates(e.pos())
        m = QgsVertexMarker(self.canvas)
        m.setCenter(self.point)
        m.setColor(QColor(0,255,0))
        m.setIconSize(5)
        m.setIconType(QgsVertexMarker.ICON_BOX)
        m.setPenWidth(3)
        self.points.append(self.point)
        self.isEmittingPoint = True
        self.selectPoly()

    def selectPoly(self):
        self.rubberband.reset(QGis.Polygon)
        for point in self.points[:-1]:
            self.rubberband.addPoint(point, False)
        self.rubberband.addPoint(self.points[-1], True)
        self.rubberband.show()
```

```
if len(self.points) > 2:
    g = self.rubberband.asGeometry()
    featsPnt = self.lyr.getFeatures(QgsFeatureRequest()
                .setFilterRect(g.boundingBox()))
    for featPnt in featsPnt:
        if featPnt.geometry().within(g):
            self.lyr.select(featPnt.id())
```

How it works...

QGIS has a generic tool for highlighting features, but in this case, we can use the standard selection functionality, which simplifies our code. With the exception of a dialog to load new layers and the ability to show attributes, we have a very basic, but nearly complete standalone GIS application. The following screenshot shows the selection tool in action:

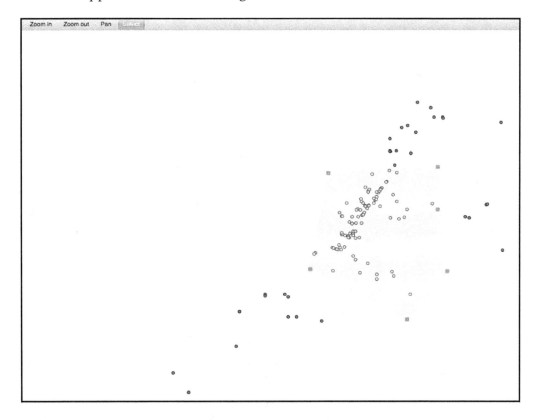

Creating a mouse coordinate tracking tool

In this recipe, we'll build a tool that tracks and displays the mouse coordinates in real time. This tool will also demonstrate how to interact with the status bar of a QGIS application.

Getting ready

We will use the application framework from the *Adding standard map tools to the* canvas recipe, so complete that recipe. We will extend that application with the coordinate tracking tool. A complete version of this application is available in the code samples provided with this book. It will also be beneficial to study the other two tool-related recipes in this chapter, *Using a map tool to draw polygons or lines on the canvas* and *Using a map tool to draw points on the canvas*, as this recipe builds on them as well.

How to do it...

We will add an event filter to the basic standalone QGIS application and use it to grab the current mouse coordinates as well as update the status bar. To do this, we need to perform the following steps:

1. At the last line of our application's __init__ method, insert the following line to create a default status bar message when the application loads:

   ```
   self.statusBar().showMessage(u"x: --, y: --")
   ```

2. Immediately after the application's __init__ method, we will add the following event filter method:

   ```
   def eventFilter(self, source, event):
       if event.type() == QEvent.MouseMove:
           if event.buttons() == Qt.NoButton:
               pos = event.pos()
               x = pos.x()
               y = pos.y()
               p = self.canvas.getCoordinateTransform()
                   .toMapCoordinates(x, y)
               self.statusBar().showMessage(u"x: %s, y: %s" %
                                       (p.x(), p.y()))
           else:
               pass
       return QMainWindow.eventFilter(self, source, event)
   ```

3. In the `MainApp` class, as the second-last line, we must install the event filter using the following code:

```
self.installEventFilter(wdg)
```

How it works...

In the Qt framework, in order to watch out for mouse events, we must insert an event filter that allows us to monitor all the events in the application. Within the default event filter method, we can then process any event we want. In this case, we watch for any movements of the mouse.

6
Composing Static Maps

In this chapter, we will cover the following recipes:

- Creating the simplest map renderer
- Using the Map Composer
- Adding labels to a map for printing
- Adding a scale bar to a map
- Adding a North arrow to the map
- Adding a logo to the map
- Adding a vertical legend to the map
- Adding a horizontal legend to the map
- Adding a custom shape to the map
- Adding a grid to the map
- Adding a table to the map
- Adding a world file to a map image
- Saving a map to a project
- Loading a map from a project

Introduction

In this chapter, we'll create maps using PyQGIS, Qt image objects, and QGIS Map Composer to create map layouts that can be exported as documents or images. The QGIS **Map Composer** is designed to create static map layouts with decorative and reference elements, for printing or inclusion in another document. We'll step through adding and configuring different elements on a map layout, which can be combined in different ways for different types of layouts.

Creating the simplest map renderer

In order to turn a dynamic GIS map into a static map image or document, you must create a renderer to **freeze** the map view and create a graphic version of it. In this recipe, we'll render a map to a JPEG image and save it.

Getting ready

You will need to download the following zipped shapefile and extract it to your `qgis_data` directory in a subdirectory named `hancock`:

`https://github.com/GeospatialPython/Learn/raw/master/hancock.zip`

You will also need to open the **Python Console** under the **Plugins** menu in QGIS. You can run these lines of code inside the console.

How to do it...

In this recipe, we will load our shapefile, add it to the map, create a blank image, set up the map view, render the map image, and save it. To do this, we need to perform the following steps:

1. First, we need to import the underlying Qt libraries required for image handling:

    ```
    from PyQt4.QtGui import *
    from PyQt4.QtCore import *
    ```

2. Next, we load the layer and add it to the map:

```
lyr = QgsVectorLayer("/qgis_data/hancock/hancock.shp",
                     "Hancock", "ogr")
reg = QgsMapLayerRegistry.instance()
reg.addMapLayer(lyr)
```

3. Now we create a blank image to accept the map image:

```
i = QImage(QSize(600,600), QImage.Format_ARGB32_Premultiplied)
c = QColor("white")
i.fill(c.rgb())
p = QPainter()
p.begin(i)
```

4. Then, we access the map renderer:

```
r = QgsMapRenderer()
```

5. Now, we get the IDs of the map layers:

```
lyrs = reg.mapLayers().keys()
```

6. Then, we tell the newly initialized renderer to use any layers in our map:

```
r.setLayerSet(lyrs)
```

7. Now, we get the full extent of the map as a rectangle:

```
rect = QgsRectangle(r.fullExtent())
```

8. Then, we set a scale for the renderer. Smaller numbers produce a larger scale, and larger numbers produce a smaller map scale. We can change the map scale to create a buffer around the map image:

```
rect.scale(1.1)
```

9. Next, we set the extent of the renderer to the rectangle:

```
r.setExtent(rect)
```

10. Now we set the output size and resolution of the image. The resolution is automatically calculated:

```
r.setOutputSize(i.size(), i.logicalDpiX())
```

11. Now, we can render the map and finalize the image:

```
r.render(p)
p.end()
```

12. Finally, we save the map image:

```
i.save("/qgis_data/map.jpg","jpg")
```

13. Verify that you have a map image in your `qgis_data` directory, similar to the map displayed in QGIS.

How it works...

QGIS uses the underlying `QtGui` library to create common image types. We haven't used any of the QGIS composer objects to render the image; however, this rendering technique is used to save maps created with the QGIS composer.

There's more...

The `QImage` object supports other image formats as well. To save a map image to a PNG, replace the last step in the *How to do it...* section with the following code:

```
i.save("/qgis_data/map.png","png")
```

Using the Map Composer

The QGIS Map Composer allows you to combine a map with nonspatial elements that enhance the understanding of the map. In this recipe, we'll create a basic map composition. A composition requires you to define a physical paper size and output format. Even a simple composition example such as this has over 20 lines of configuration options.

Getting ready

You will need to download the following zipped shapefile and extract it to your `qgis_data` directory in a subdirectory named `hancock`:

```
https://github.com/GeospatialPython/Learn/raw/master/hancock.zip
```

You will also need to open the **Python Console** under the **Plugins** menu in QGIS. You can run this recipe in the console, or wrap it in a script for the **Script Runner** plugin using the template provided with the plugin.

How to do it...

In this recipe, the major steps are to load the shapefile into a map, build the map composition, and render it to an image, as follows:

1. First, we need to import the Qt libraries for image handling:

    ```
    from PyQt4.QtGui import *
    from PyQt4.QtCore import *
    ```

2. Next, we load the layer and add it to the map:

    ```
    lyr = QgsVectorLayer("/qgis_data/hancock/hancock.shp",
                         "Hancock", "ogr")
    reg = QgsMapLayerRegistry.instance()
    reg.addMapLayer(lyr)
    ```

3. Now, we create a blank image to accept the map image:

    ```
    i = QImage(QSize(600,600), QImage.Format_ARGB32_Premultiplied)
    c = QColor("white")
    i.fill(c.rgb())
    p = QPainter()
    p.begin(i)
    ```

4. Next, we get the IDs of the map layers:

    ```
    lyrs = reg.mapLayers().keys()
    ```

5. Then, we access the map renderer:

    ```
    mr = iface.mapCanvas().mapRenderer()
    ```

6. We then tell the newly initialized renderer to use any layers in our map:

    ```
    mr.setLayerSet(lyrs)
    ```

7. Now, we get the full extent of the map as a rectangle:

    ```
    rect = QgsRectangle(lyr.extent())
    ```

8. Then, we set the scale for the renderer. Smaller numbers produce a larger scale, and larger numbers produce a smaller map scale to add an image buffer around the map:

```
rect.scale(1.2)
```

9. Now, we set the map renderer's extent to the full map's extent:

```
mr.setExtent(rect)
```

10. Next, we begin using the QGIS composer by creating a new composition and assigning it the map renderer:

```
c = QgsComposition(mr)
```

11. Then, we set the composition style. We will define it as `Print`, which will allow us to create both PDF documents and images. The alternative is to define it as a postscript, which is often used for direct output to printer devices:

```
c.setPlotStyle(QgsComposition.Print)
```

12. Now, we define our paper size, which is specified in millimeters. In this case, we use the equivalent of an `8.5x11` inch sheet of paper, which is the US letter size:

```
c.setPaperSize(215.9, 279.4)
```

13. Next, we'll calculate dimensions for the map so that it takes up approximately half the page and is centered:

```
w, h = c.paperWidth() * .50, c.paperHeight() * .50
x = (c.paperWidth() - w) / 2
y = ((c.paperHeight() - h)) / 2
```

14. Then, we create the Map Composer object and set its extent:

```
composerMap = QgsComposerMap(c,x,y,w,h)
composerMap.setNewExtent(rect)
```

15. Next, we give the map a frame around its border and add it to the page:

```
composerMap.setFrameEnabled(True)
c.addItem(composerMap)
```

16. Now, we ensure that the resolution of the composition is set. The resolution defines how much detail the output contains. Lower resolutions contain less detail and create smaller files. Higher resolutions provide more image detail but create larger files:

```
dpi = c.printResolution()
c.setPrintResolution(dpi)
```

17. We convert the dots-per-inch resolution to dots-per-millimeter:

```
mm_in_inch = 25.4
dpmm = dpi / mm_in_inch
width = int(dpmm * c.paperWidth())
height = int(dpmm * c.paperHeight())
```

18. Next, we initialize the image:

```
image = QImage(QSize(width, height), QImage.Format_ARGB32)
image.setDotsPerMeterX(dpmm * 1000)
image.setDotsPerMeterY(dpmm * 1000)
image.fill(0)
```

19. Now, we render the composition:

```
imagePainter = QPainter(image)
sourceArea = QRectF(0, 0, c.paperWidth(), c.paperHeight())
targetArea = QRectF(0, 0, width, height)
c.render(imagePainter, targetArea, sourceArea)
imagePainter.end()
```

20. Finally, we save the composition as a JPEG image:

```
image.save("/qgis_data/map.jpg", "jpg")
```

21. Verify that the output image resembles the following sample image:

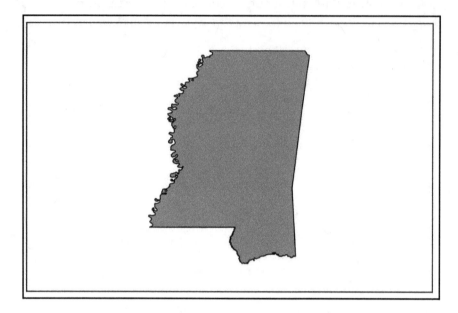

How it works...

Map compositions are very powerful, but they can also be quite complex. You are managing the composition that represents a virtual sheet of paper. On the composition, you place objects, such as the map. Then, you must also manage the rendering of the composition as an image. All these items are independently configurable, which can sometimes lead to unexpected results with sizing or visibility of items.

There's more...

In the upcoming versions of QGIS, the `MapComposer` class may be renamed to the `print layout` class. You can find out more information about this proposed change at
`https://github.com/qgis/QGIS-Enhancement-Proposals/pull/9`.

Adding labels to a map for printing

The `QgsComposition` object allows you to place arbitrary text anywhere in the composition. In this recipe, we'll demonstrate how to add a label to a map composition.

Getting ready

You will need to download the following zipped shapefile and extract it to your `qgis_data` directory in a subdirectory named `hancock`:

`https://github.com/GeospatialPython/Learn/raw/master/hancock.zip`

In addition to the shapefile, you will also need the `MapComposer` class. This class encapsulates the boilerplate composer code in a reusable way, to make adding other elements easier. You can download it from

`https://github.com/GeospatialPython/Learn/raw/master/MapComposer.py`.

This file must be accessible from the QGIS Python console by ensuring that it is in the Python path directory. Place the file in the `.qgis2/python` directory within your home directory.

How to do it...

To add a label to a composition, we'll first build the map composition, create a label, and then save the composition as an image. To do this, we need to perform the following steps:

1. First, we need to import the QtGUI libraries and the `MapComposer` class:

   ```
   from PyQt4.QtGui import *
   from PyQt4.QtCore import *
   import MapComposer
   ```

2. Next, we create a layer with the shapefile, setting the path to the shapefile in order to match your system:

   ```
   lyr = QgsVectorLayer("/qgis_data/hancock/hancock.shp",
                        "Hancock", "ogr")
   ```

3. Now, we add this layer to the map:

   ```
   reg = QgsMapLayerRegistry.instance()
   reg.addMapLayer(lyr)
   ```

4. Next, we access the map renderer:

```
mr = iface.mapCanvas().mapRenderer()
```

5. Then, we create a `MapComposer` object, passing in the map layer registry and the map renderer:

```
qc = MapComposer.MapComposer(qmlr=reg, qmr=mr)
```

6. Now, we create a new label object:

```
qc.label = QgsComposerLabel(qc.c)
```

7. We can set the label text to any string:

```
qc.label.setText("Hancock County")
```

8. We can automatically set the size of the label container to fit the string we used:

```
qc.label.adjustSizeToText()
```

9. Now, we add a frame around the label box:

```
qc.label.setFrameEnabled(True)
```

10. Then, we set the position of the label on the page, which is at the top-left corner of the map:

```
qc.label.setItemPosition(qc.x, qc.y-10)
```

11. Next, we add the label to the map composition, now that it is configured:

```
qc.c.addItem(qc.label)
```

12. Finally, we save the composition image:

```
qc.output("/qgis_data/map.jpg", "jpg")
```

13. Verify that your output image has a text label, in a frame at the top-left corner of the map, similar to the following image:

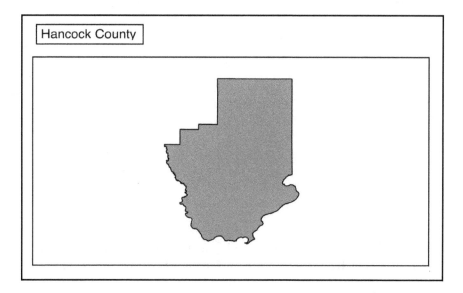

How it works...

In this case, we created a very simple label based on defaults. However, labels can be customized to change the font, size, color, and style for print quality compositions. Also, note that the *x*, *y* values used to place items in a composition start in the upper-left corner of the page. As you move an item down the page, the *y* value increases.

Adding a scale bar to a map

A scale bar is one of the most important elements of a map composition, as it defines the scale of the map to determine the ground distance on the map. The QGIS composer allows you to create several different types of scale bars from a simple text scale ratio to a graphical, double bar scale bar with two measurement systems. In this recipe, we'll create a scale bar that increments in kilometers.

Getting ready

You will need to download the following zipped shapefile and extract it to your `qgis_data` directory in a subdirectory named `ms`:

`https://github.com/GeospatialPython/Learn/raw/master/mississippi.zip`

`https://github.com/GeospatialPython/Learn/raw/master/Mississippi.zip`

In addition to the shapefile, you will also need the `MapComposer` class. This class encapsulates the boilerplate composer code in a reusable way, to make adding other elements easier. You can download it from
`https://github.com/GeospatialPython/Learn/raw/master/MapComposer.py`.

This file must be accessible from the QGIS Python console; ensure that it is in the Python path directory. Place the file in the `.qgis2/python` directory within your home directory.

For the scale bar to display correctly, you must ensure that QGIS is set to automatically reproject data on the fly. In QGIS, go to the **Settings** menu and select **Options...**. In the **Options** dialog, select the **CRS** panel. In the **Default CRS for new projects** section, check the **Enable 'on the fly' reprojection by default** radio button. Click on the **OK** button to confirm the setting.

How to do it...

First, we will generate the map, then we'll generate the composition, and finally, we'll create the scale bar and place it in the lower-right corner of the map. To do this, we need to perform the following steps:

1. First, we need to import the libraries we'll need:

```
from PyQt4.QtCore import *
from PyQt4.QtGui import *
from qgis.core import *
from qgis.gui import *
import MapComposer
```

2. Then, we'll build the map renderer using the shapefile:

```
lyr = QgsVectorLayer("/qgis_data/ms/mmississippi.shp",
                     "Mississippi", "ogr")
reg = QgsMapLayerRegistry.instance()
reg.addMapLayer(lyr)
mr = iface.mapCanvas().mapRenderer()
```

3. Next, we'll create the `MapComposer` object using the layer registry and map renderer:

```
qc = MapComposer.MapComposer(qmlr=reg, qmr=mr)
```

4. Now, we'll initialize the scale bar object:

```
qc.scalebar = QgsComposerScaleBar(qc.c)
```

5. Then, we define the scale bar type. The default is a text scale, but we'll create a more traditional box scale bar:

```
qc.scalebar.setStyle('Single Box')
```

6. Next, we apply the scale bar to the map and set the scale bar graphic to the default size:

```
qc.scalebar.setComposerMap(qc.composerMap)
qc.scalebar.applyDefaultSize()
```

7. We use the scale bar size, map size, and map position to calculate the desired position of the scale bar, in the lower-right corner of the map:

```
sbw = qc.scalebar.rect().width()
sbh = qc.scalebar.rect().height()
mcw = qc.composerMap.rect().width()
mch = qc.composerMap.rect().height()
sbx = qc.x + (mcw - sbw)
sby = qc.y + mch
```

8. Then, we set the calculated position of the scale bar and add it to the composition:

```
qc.scalebar.setItemPosition(sbx, sby)
qc.c.addItem(qc.scalebar)
```

9. Finally, we save the composition to an image:

```
qc.output("/qgis_data/map.jpg", "jpg")
```

10. Verify your map composition looks similar to the following image:

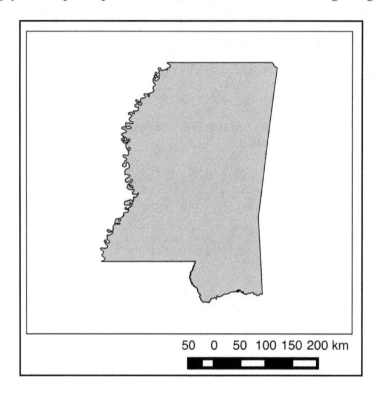

How it works...

The scale bar will display in kilometres if the map projection is set correctly, which is why it is important to have automatic reprojection enabled in the QGIS settings. The location of the scale bar within the composition is not important, as long as the `ComposerMap` object is applied to it.

Adding a North arrow to the map

North arrows are another common cartographic element, found even in ancient maps, which show the orientation of the map relative to either true, grid, or magnetic north. Sometimes, these symbols can be quite elaborate. However, QGIS provides a basic line arrow element that we will use in combination with a map label to make a basic North arrow.

Getting ready

You will need to download the following zipped shapefile and extract it to your `qgis_data` directory in a subdirectory named `ms`:

`https://github.com/GeospatialPython/Learn/raw/master/Mississippi.zip`

In addition to the shapefile, you will also need the `MapComposer` class, to simplify the code needed to add this one element. If you haven't already used it in a previous recipe, you can download it from
`https://github.com/GeospatialPython/Learn/raw/master/MapComposer.py`.

This file must be accessible from the QGIS Python console; for this, you need to ensure that it is in the Python path directory. Place the file in the `.qgis2/python` directory within your home directory.

How to do it...

In this recipe, we will create a map composition, draw an arrow to the right of the map, and then place a label with a capital letter N below the arrow. To do this, we need to perform the following steps:

1. First, we import the `Qt` and `MapComposer` Python libraries:

```
from PyQt4.QtCore import *
from PyQt4.QtGui import *
from qgis.core import *
from qgis.gui import *
import MapComposer
```

2. Next, we create the map composition object:

```
lyr = QgsVectorLayer("/qgis_data/ms/mississippi.shp",
                     "Mississippi", "ogr")
reg = QgsMapLayerRegistry.instance()
reg.addMapLayer(lyr)
mr = iface.mapCanvas().mapRenderer()
qc = MapComposer.MapComposer(qmlr=reg, qmr=mr)
```

3. Now, we calculate the position of the arrow along the right-hand side of the map, set its position, and then add it to the composition:

```
mcw = qc.composerMap.rect().width()
mch = qc.composerMap.rect().height()
ax =  qc.x + mcw + 10
ay =  (qc.y + mch) - 10
afy = ay - 20
qc.arrow = QgsComposerArrow(QPointF(ax, ay), QPointF(ax,afy), qc.c)
qc.c.addItem(qc.arrow)
```

4. Then, we create a capital letter N label and add it to the composition, just below the arrow:

```
f = QFont()
f.setBold(True)
f.setFamily("Times New Roman")
f.setPointSize(30)
qc.labelNorth = QgsComposerLabel(qc.c)
qc.labelNorth.setText("N")
qc.labelNorth.setFont(f)
qc.labelNorth.adjustSizeToText()
qc.labelNorth.setFrameEnabled(False)
qc.labelNorth.setItemPosition(ax - 5, ay)
qc.c.addItem(qc.labelNorth)
```

5. Finally, we save the composition to an image:

```
qc.output("/qgis_data/map.jpg", "jpg")
```

6. Verify that your output image looks similar to the following:

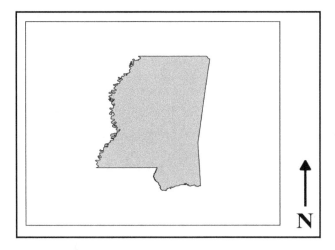

How it works...

The QGIS composer doesn't have a dedicated North arrow or compass rose object. However, it is quite simple to construct one, as demonstrated in the preceding section. The arrow is just a graphic. The direction of the arrow is controlled by the location of the start and end points listed, respectively, when you create the QgsComposerArrow object.

There's more...

You can extend this example to have an arrow point in multiple compass directions. You can also use an image of a more elaborate compass rose added to the composition. We'll demonstrate how to add images in the next recipe. Note that the arrow element can also be used to point to items on the map with an associated label.

Adding a logo to the map

An important part of customizing a map is to add your logo, or other graphics, to the composition. In this recipe, we'll add a simple logo to the map.

Getting ready

You will need to download the following zipped shapefile and extract it to your `qgis_data` directory in a subdirectory named `ms`:

`https://github.com/GeospatialPython/Learn/raw/master/Mississippi.zip`

You will also need a logo image, which you can download from
`https://github.com/GeospatialPython/Learn/raw/master/logo.png`.

Place the image in your `qgis_data/rasters` directory.

If you haven't already done so in the previous recipe, download the `MapComposer` library from `https://github.com/GeospatialPython/Learn/raw/master/MapComposer.py`, to simplify the creation of the map composition.

Place the file in the `.qgis2/python` directory within your home directory.

How to do it...

In this recipe, we will create the map composition, add the logo image, and save the map as an image. To do this, we need to perform the following steps:

1. First, we need to import the Qt GUI, core QGIS, QGIS GUI, and `MapComposer` libraries:

   ```
   from PyQt4.QtCore import *
   from PyQt4.QtGui import *
   from qgis.core import *
   from qgis.gui import *
   import MapComposer
   ```

2. Next, we will build a basic map composition using the shapefile:

   ```
   lyr = QgsVectorLayer("/qgis_data/ms/mississippi.shp",
                        "Mississippi", "ogr")
   reg = QgsMapLayerRegistry.instance()
   reg.addMapLayer(lyr)
   mr = iface.mapCanvas().mapRenderer()
   qc = MapComposer.MapComposer(qmlr=reg, qmr=mr)
   ```

3. Now, we initialize the picture object:

   ```
   qc.logo = QgsComposerPicture(qc.c)
   ```

4. Then, we set the path of the picture to our image file:

```
qc.logo.setPictureFile("/qgis_data/rasters/logo.png")
```

5. We must set the size of the box or scene rectangle such that it is large enough to contain the logo. Otherwise, the picture will appear cropped:

```
qc.logo.setSceneRect(QRectF(0,0,50,70))
```

6. Next, we calculate the position of the logo relative to the map image. We'll place the logo near the top-left corner of the map:

```
lx = qc.x + 50
ly = qc.y - 120
```

7. Now, we set the logo's position and add it to the map composition:

```
mcw = qc.composerMap.rect().width()
mch = qc.composerMap.rect().height()
lx =  qc.x
ly=  qc.y - 20
```

8. Finally, we save the composition as an image:

```
qc.output("/qgis_data/map.jpg", "jpg")
```

9. Verify your map composition looks similar to the following image:

How it works...

This recipe is very straightforward, as the `QgsComposerPicture` is an extremely simple object. You can use JPG, PNG, or SVG images. This technique can be used to add custom North arrows, or other cartographic elements, as well.

Adding a vertical legend to the map

A map legend decodes the symbology used in a thematic GIS map for the reader. Legends are tightly integrated into QGIS, and in this recipe, we'll add the default legend from the map to the print composition.

Getting ready

Download the shapefile for this map from `https://github.com/GeospatialPython/Learn/raw/master/Mississippi.zip` and extract it to your `qgis_data` directory in a subdirectory named `ms`.

As with the previous recipes in this chapter, we will use the `MapComposer` library from `https://github.com/GeospatialPython/Learn/raw/master/MapComposer.py`, to simplify the creation of the map composition.

Place the file in the `.qgis2/python` directory within your home directory.

How to do it...

This recipe is as simple as creating the map, adding the automatically generated legend, and saving the output to an image. To do this, we need to perform the following steps:

1. First, we will need to load the Qt and QGIS GUI libraries, followed by the `MapComposer` library:

```
from PyQt4.QtCore import *
from PyQt4.QtGui import *
from qgis.core import *
from qgis.gui import *
import MapComposer
```

2. Next, we will load the shapefile as a layer and create the map composition with the `MapComposer` library, passing it the map layer registry and map renderer:

```
lyr = QgsVectorLayer("/qgis_data/ms/mississippi.shp",
                     "Mississippi", "ogr")
reg = QgsMapLayerRegistry.instance()
reg.addMapLayer(lyr)
mr = iface.mapCanvas().mapRenderer()
qc = MapComposer.MapComposer(qmlr=reg, qmr=mr)
```

3. Now, we initialize the legend object:

```
qc.legend = QgsComposerLegend(qc.c)
```

4. We tell the legend which layer set we want to use:

```
qc.legend.model().setLayerSet(qc.qmr.layerSet())
```

5. Then, we set the legend's position to the left-hand side of the map and add it to the composition:

```
qc.legend.setItemPosition(5, qc.y)
qc.c.addItem(qc.legend)
```

6. Finally, we output the composition to the map:

```
qc.output("/qgis_data/map.jpg", "jpg")
```

7. Verify your map composition looks similar to the following image:

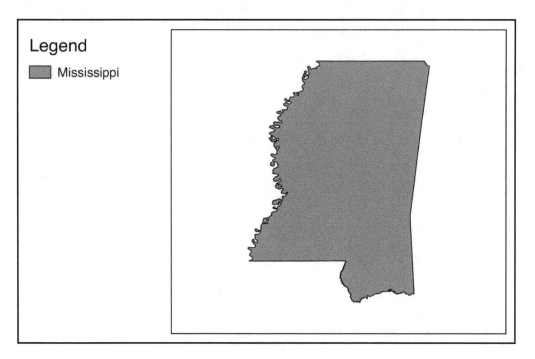

How it works...

Adding a legend is quite simple. QGIS will carry over the styling that is auto-generated when the layer is loaded or manually set by the user. Of course, you can also save layer styling, which is loaded with the layer and used by the legend. However, if you're generating a composition in the background, such as in a standalone application, for example, every aspect of the legend is customizable through the PyQGIS API.

Adding a horizontal legend

One of the map legend customization options is the direction. You can make an unusual horizontal legend just by changing the column count from the default of 1. In this recipe, we'll add two layers and set up the legend to run horizontally across the top of the map.

Getting ready

Download the first shapefile for this map from:

`https://github.com/GeospatialPython/Learn/raw/master/Mississippi.zip`

Download the second shapefile from here:

`https://github.com/GeospatialPython/Learn/raw/master/MSCities_Geo_Pts.zip`

Extract both zip files to your `qgis_data` directory, to a subdirectory named `ms`.

As with the previous recipes in this chapter, we will use the `MapComposer` library from `htt ps://github.com/GeospatialPython/Learn/raw/master/MapComposer.py.zip`.

This script will simplify a lot of the repetitive code needed for the creation of the map composition.

Extract the zip file and place the script in the `.qgis2/python` directory within your home directory.

How to do it...

We will set up our two layers, add them to the map, set up our composer, change the legend column count, and render the map image. Changing the column count will force the legend to spread horizontally.

1. First, we will need to load the Qt and QGIS GUI libraries, followed by the `MapComposer` library:

```
from PyQt4.QtCore import *
from PyQt4.QtGui import *
from qgis.core import *
from qgis.gui import *
import MapComposer
```

2. Next, we will load the shapefile as layers and create the map composition with the `MapComposer` library, passing it the map layer registry and map renderer:

```
lyr = QgsVectorLayer("/qgis_data/ms/mississippi.shp",
                     "Mississippi", "ogr")
lyr2 = QgsVectorLayer("/qgis_data/ms/MSCities_Geo_Pts.shp",
                      "Cities", "ogr")
reg = QgsMapLayerRegistry.instance()
reg.addMapLayers([lyr2, lyr])
mr = iface.mapCanvas().mapRenderer()
qc = MapComposer.MapComposer(qmlr=reg, qmr=mr)
```

3. Now, we initialize the legend object:

```
qc.legend = QgsComposerLegend(qc.c)
```

4. We tell the legend which layer set we want to use:

```
qc.legend.model().setLayerSet(qc.qmr.layerSet())
```

5. Then, we set the legend's position above the map, change the number of columns from one to two, and add it to the composition:

```
qc.legend.setItemPosition(50,50)
qc.legend.setColumnCount(2)
qc.c.addItem(qc.legend)
```

6. Finally, we output the composition to the map:

```
qc.output("/qgis_data/map.jpg", "jpg")
```

7. Verify your map composition looks similar to the following image:

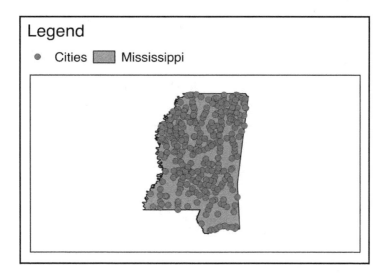

Adding a custom shape to the map

The QGIS composer has an object for drawing and styling nonspatial shapes, including rectangles, ellipses, and triangles. In this recipe, we'll add some rectangles filled with different colors, which resemble a simple bar chart, as an example of using shapes.

Getting ready

Download the zipped shapefile for this map from https://github.com/GeospatialPython/Learn/raw/master/Mississippi.zip and extract it to your qgis_data directory in a subdirectory named ms.

We will also use the MapComposer library from https://github.com/GeospatialPython/Learn/raw/master/MapComposer.py, to simplify the creation of the map composition.

Place the file in the .qgis2/python directory within your home directory.

How to do it...

First, we will create a simple map composition with the shapefile. Then, we will define the style properties for our rectangles. Next, we will draw the rectangles, apply the symbols, and render the composition. To do this, we need to perform the following steps:

1. First, we must import the PyQGIS and Qt GUI libraries, as well as the `MapComposer` library, as follows:

   ```
   from PyQt4.QtCore import *
   from PyQt4.QtGui import *
   from qgis.core import *
   from qgis.gui import *
   import MapComposer
   ```

2. Next, we create the map composition using the shapefile:

   ```
   lyr = QgsVectorLayer("/qgis_data/ms/mississippi.shp",
                        "Mississippi", "ogr")
   reg = QgsMapLayerRegistry.instance()
   reg.addMapLayer(lyr)
   mr = iface.mapCanvas().mapRenderer()
   qc = MapComposer.MapComposer(qmlr=reg, qmr=mr)
   ```

3. Now, we create three basic fill symbols by building Python dictionaries with color properties, and initialize the symbols with these dictionaries:

   ```
   red = {'color':'255,0,0,255','color_border':'0,0,0,255'}
   redsym = QgsFillSymbolV2.createSimple(red)
   blue = {'color':'0,0,255,255','color_border':'0,0,0,255'}
   bluesym = QgsFillSymbolV2.createSimple(blue)
   yellow = {'color':'255,255,0,255','color_border':'0,0,0,255'}
   yellowsym = QgsFillSymbolV2.createSimple(yellow)
   ```

4. Then we calculate the y position of the first shape relative to the map:

   ```
   mch = qc.composerMap.rect().height()
   sy = qc.y + mch
   ```

5. We create the first shape and set it to Type 1, which is a rectangle:

   ```
   qc.shape1 = QgsComposerShape(10,sy-25,10,25,qc.c)
   qc.shape1.setShapeType(1)
   ```

6. Next, we tell the shape to use a symbol, set the symbol for one of our three fill symbols, and add the shape to the composition:

```
qc.shape1.setUseSymbolV2(True)
qc.shape1.setShapeStyleSymbol(redsym)
qc.c.addItem(qc.shape1)
```

7. We repeat the process with two other shapes, changing their position, size, and symbols to make them look different:

```
qc.shape2 = QgsComposerShape(22,sy-18,10,18,qc.c)
qc.shape2.setShapeType(1)
qc.shape2.setUseSymbolV2(True)
qc.shape2.setShapeStyleSymbol(bluesym)
qc.c.addItem(qc.shape2)
qc.shape3 = QgsComposerShape(34,sy-12,10,12,qc.c)
qc.shape3.setShapeType(1)
qc.shape3.setUseSymbolV2(True)
qc.shape3.setShapeStyleSymbol(yellowsym)
qc.c.addItem(qc.shape3)
```

8. Finally, we output the composition as an image:

```
qc.output("/qgis_data/map.jpg", "jpg")
```

9. Verify that your output image looks similar to the following:

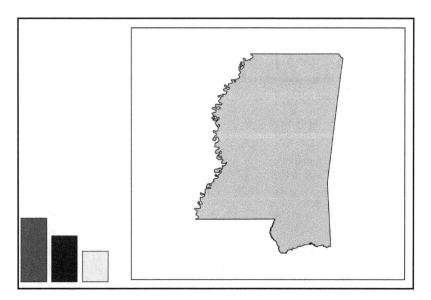

How it works...

This simple graphical output is nearly 40 lines of code. While there may be some limited uses for dealing with these shapes, in most cases, the simpler route will be to just import images. However, it provides a good foundation for a richer graphics API as QGIS continues to evolve.

There's more...

If you are using fill symbols within a Python plugin in a QGIS version earlier than 2.6, you must ensure that the symbols are defined in the global scope, or QGIS will crash due to a bug. The easiest way to include the variables in the global scope is to define them immediately after the import statements. It also affects scripts that are run in the **Script Runner** plugin. This bug has been fixed in version 2.6 and later.

Adding a grid to the map

An annotated reference grid is useful for map products used to locate features. This recipe teaches you how to add both reference lines on a map and annotations for the lines around the edges of the map.

Getting ready

You will need a shapefile for this map from
`https://github.com/GeospatialPython/Learn/raw/master/Mississippi.zip`, and you need to extract it to your `qgis_data` directory in a subdirectory named `ms`.

As with the previous recipes in this chapter, we will use the `MapComposer` library from `https://github.com/GeospatialPython/Learn/raw/master/MapComposer.py`, to simplify the creation of the map composition.

Place the file in the `.qgis2/python` directory within your home directory.

How to do it...

In this recipe, the general steps are to create the map composition, establish the overall grid parameters, define the grid line placement, and then style the grid and annotations. To do this, we need to perform the following steps:

1. First, we need to import all the GUI libraries and the `MapComposer` library:

   ```
   from PyQt4.QtCore import *
   from PyQt4.QtGui import *
   from qgis.core import *
   from qgis.gui import *
   import MapComposer
   ```

2. Next, we create the map composition using the shapefile:

   ```
   lyr = QgsVectorLayer("/qgis_data/ms/mmississippi.shp",
                        "Mississippi", "ogr")
   reg = QgsMapLayerRegistry.instance()
   reg.addMapLayer(lyr)
   mr = iface.mapCanvas().mapRenderer()
   qc = MapComposer.MapComposer(qmlr=reg, qmr=mr)
   ```

3. Now, we are going to create some variables to shorten some unusually long method and object names:

   ```
   setGridAnnoPos = qc.composerMap.setGridAnnotationPosition
   setGridAnnoDir = qc.composerMap.setGridAnnotationDirection
   qcm = QgsComposerMap
   ```

4. Then, we enable the grid, set the line spacing, and use solid lines for the grid:

   ```
   qc.composerMap.setGridEnabled(True)
   qc.composerMap.setGridIntervalX(.75)
   qc.composerMap.setGridIntervalY(.75)
   qc.composerMap.setGridStyle(qcm.Solid)
   ```

5. Next, we enable the annotation numbers for coordinates and set the decimal precision to 0 for whole numbers:

```
qc.composerMap.setShowGridAnnotation(True)
qc.composerMap.setGridAnnotationPrecision(0)
```

6. Now, we go around the map composition frame and define locations and directions for each set of grid lines using our shorter variable names from the previous steps:

```
setGridAnnoPos(qcm.OutsideMapFrame, qcm.Top)
setGridAnnoDir(qcm.Horizontal, qcm.Top)
setGridAnnoPos(qcm.OutsideMapFrame, qcm.Bottom)
setGridAnnoDir(qcm.Horizontal, qcm.Bottom)
setGridAnnoPos(qcm.OutsideMapFrame, qcm.Left)
setGridAnnoDir(qcm.Vertical, qcm.Left)
setGridAnnoPos(qcm.OutsideMapFrame, qcm.Right)
setGridAnnoDir(qcm.Vertical, qcm.Right)
```

7. Finally, we set some additional styling for the grid lines and annotations before adding the whole map to the overall composition:

```
qc.composerMap.setAnnotationFrameDistance(1)
qc.composerMap.setGridPenWidth(.2)
qc.composerMap.setGridPenColor(QColor(0, 0, 0))
qc.composerMap.setAnnotationFontColor(QColor(0, 0, 0))
qc.c.addComposerMap(qc.composerMap)
```

8. We output the composition to an image:

```
qc.output("/qgis_data/map.jpg", "jpg")
```

9. Verify that your output image looks similar to the following:

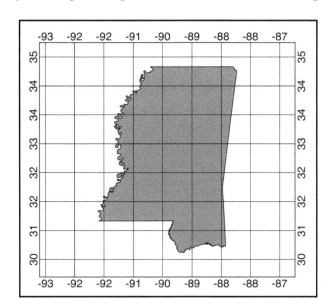

How it works...

This recipe has a lot of steps because the grids are customizable. The order of operations is important as well. Notice that we do not add the map to the composition until the very end. Often, you will make what seem to be minor changes and the grid may not render. Hence, modify this recipe carefully.

Adding a table to the map

The QGIS composer provides an object to add a table to a composition, representing either the attributes of a vector layer or an arbitrary text table you create. In this recipe, we'll add a table to the composition with the attributes of our map layer shapefile.

Getting ready

Download the shapefile for this map from
`https://github.com/GeospatialPython/Learn/raw/master/Mississippi.zip` and extract
it to your `qgis_data` directory in a subdirectory named `ms`.

As with the previous recipes in this chapter, we will use the `MapComposer` library from `htt`
`ps://github.com/GeospatialPython/Learn/raw/master/MapComposer.py`, to simplify
the creation of the map composition.

Place the file in the `.qgis2/python` directory within your home directory.

How to do it…

The following steps will create a map composition, add the table, and output the
composition to an image:

1. First, we import our GUI libraries and the `MapComposer` library:

   ```
   from PyQt4.QtCore import *
   from PyQt4.QtGui import *
   from qgisfromqgis.core import *
   from qgisfromqgis.gui import *
   import MapComposer
   ```

2. Next, we create the map composition:

   ```
   lyr = QgsVectorLayer("/qgis_data/ms/mississippi.shp",
                        "Mississippi", "ogr")
   reg = QgsMapLayerRegistry.instance()
   reg.addMapLayer(lyr)
   mr = iface.mapCanvas().mapRenderer()
   qc = MapComposer.MapComposer(qmlr=reg, qmr=mr)
   ```

3. Now, we can initialize the table object:

   ```
   qc.table = QgsComposerAttributeTable(qc.c)
   ```

4. Then, we reference the related map:

   ```
   qc.table.setComposerMap(qc.composerMap)
   ```

5. Next, we can specify the layer whose attributes we want to display in the table:

```
qc.table.setVectorLayer(lyr)
```

6. Now, we can position the table below the map and add it to the composition:

```
mch = qc.composerMap.rect().height()
qc.table.setItemPosition(qc.x, qc.y + mch + 20)
qc.c.addItem(qc.table)
```

7. Finally, we output the composition to an image:

```
qc.output("/qgis_data/map.jpg", "jpg")
```

How it works...

The table object is very straightforward. Using the attributes of a vector layer is automatic. You can also build the table cell by cell if you want to display customized information.

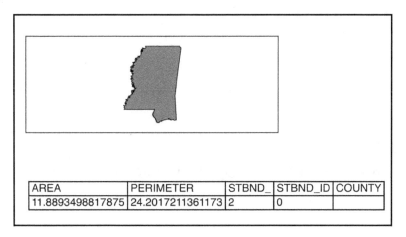

Adding a world file to a map image

Exporting a map as an image removes all of its spatial information. However, you can create an external text file, called a **world file**, which provides the georeferencing information for the raster image so that it can be used by GIS software, including QGIS, as a raster layer. In this recipe, we'll export a map composition as an image and create a world file along with it.

Getting ready

You will need to download the zipped shapefile from
`https://github.com/GeospatialPython/Learn/raw/master/Mississippi.zip` and extract
it to your `qgis_data` directory in a subdirectory named `ms`.

In addition to the shapefile, you will also need the `MapComposer` class, to simplify the code
needed to add this one element. If you have not already used it in a previous recipe, you
can download it from
`https://github.com/GeospatialPython/Learn/raw/master/MapComposer.py`.

This file must be accessible from the QGIS Python console; for this, you need to ensure that
it is in the Python path directory. Place the file in the `.qgis2/python` directory within your
home directory.

How to do it...

First, we'll create the map composition, then we'll save it as an image, and finally, we'll
generate the world file. To do this, we need to perform the following steps:

1. First, we need to import the GUI and `MapComposer` libraries:

```
from PyQt4.QtCore import *
from PyQt4.QtGui import *
from qgisfromqgis.core import *
from qgisfromqgis.gui import *
import MapComposer
```

2. Next, we'll create the map's composition using the `MapComposer` libraries:

```
lyr = QgsVectorLayer("/qgis_data/ms/mississippi.shp",
                     "Mississippi", "ogr")
reg = QgsMapLayerRegistry.instance()
reg.addMapLayer(lyr)
mr = iface.mapCanvas().mapRenderer()
qc = MapComposer.MapComposer(qmlr=reg, qmr=mr)
```

3. Now, we'll define the name of our output file:

```
output =  "/qgis_data/map"
```

4. Then, we can export the composition as an image:

```
qc.output(output + ".jpg", "jpg")
```

5. Now, we'll create an object that contains the world file's information:

```
qc.c.setWorldFileMap(qc.composerMap)
qc.c.setGenerateWorldFile(True)
wf = qc.c.computeWorldFileParameters()
```

6. Finally, we'll open a text file and write each line of the text file:

```
with open(output + ".jgw", "w") as f:
    f.write("%s\n" % wf[0])
    f.write("%s\n" % wf[1])
    f.write("%s\n" % wf[3])
    f.write("%s\n" % wf[4])
    f.write("%s\n" % wf[2])
    f.write("%s\n" % wf[5])
```

How it works...

The world file contains the ground distance per pixel and the upper-left coordinate of the map image. The QGIS composer automatically generates this information based on the referenced map. The world file's name must be the same as the image with an extension that uses the first and last letters of the image file extension plus the letter w. For example, a .tiff image file will have a world file with the extension .tfw. You can learn more about what the world file variables in each line mean at http://en.wikipedia.org/wiki/World_file.

Saving a map to a project

Saving a project automatically can be useful for auto save features, or as part of a process to auto-generate projects from dynamically updated data. In this recipe, we'll save a QGIS project to a .qgs project file.

Getting ready

You will need to download the following zipped shapefile and extract it to your qgis_data directory in a subdirectory named ms:

https://github.com/GeospatialPython/Learn/raw/master/Mississippi.zip

How to do it...

We will create a simple QGIS project by loading a shapefile layer, then we'll access the project object, and save the map project to a file, as follows:

1. First, we need the Qt core library in the QGIS Python console:

    ```
    from PyQt4.QtCore import *
    ```

2. Next, we load the shapefile and add it to the map:

    ```
    lyr = QgsVectorLayer("/qgis_data/ms/mississippi.shp",
                         "Mississippi", "ogr")
    reg = QgsMapLayerRegistry.instance()
    reg.addMapLayer(lyr)
    ```

3. Then, we create a `file` object to save our project:

    ```
    f = QFileInfo("/qgis_data/myProject.qgs")
    ```

4. Now, we can access the QGIS project object instance:

    ```
    p = QgsProject.instance()
    ```

5. Finally, we can save the project by writing it to the file object:

    ```
    p.write(f)
    ```

How it works...

QGIS simply creates an XML document with all the project settings and GIS map settings. You can read, and even modify, the XML output by hand.

Loading a map from a project

This recipe demonstrates how to load a project from a `.qgs` XML file. Loading a project will set up the map and project settings for a previously saved project within QGIS.

Getting ready

You will need to complete the previous recipe, *Saving a map to a project*, so that you have a project named `myProject.qgs` in your `qgis_data` directory.

How to do it...

For this recipe, you need to set up a file object, set a resource path, and then read the file object that references the project file. To do this, you need to perform the following steps:

1. First, we import the core `QtCore` library for the file object:

   ```
   from PyQt4.QtCore import *
   ```

2. Next, we initiate the file object with the path to the project file:

   ```
   f = QFileInfo("/qgis_data/myProject.qgs")
   ```

3. Now, we access the project object:

   ```
   p = QgsProject.instance()
   ```

4. Then, we set the resource path for QGIS to find data and other files, in case the project was saved with relative paths instead of absolute paths:

   ```
   p.readPath("/qgis_data/")
   ```

5. Finally, we tell the project object to read the project file in order to load the map:

   ```
   p.read(f)
   ```

How it works...

QGIS has a setting to save references to data and other files, either as relative paths, which are relative to the project file, or absolute paths, which contain the full path. If the saved paths are absolute, PyQGIS will be unable to locate data sources. Setting the read path to the full system path of the project file ensures that QGIS can find all the referenced files in the project file, if they are saved as relative paths.

7
Interacting with the User

In this chapter, we will cover the following recipes:

- Using log files
- Creating a simple message dialog
- Creating a warning dialog
- Creating an error dialog
- Displaying a progress bar
- Creating a simple text input dialog
- Creating a file input dialog
- Creating a combobox
- Creating radio buttons
- Creating checkboxes
- Creating a dock widget
- Displaying a message in the status bar
- Pushing a message to the message bar
- Pushing a widget to the message bar
- Creating tabs
- Stepping the user through a wizard
- Keeping dialogs on top

Introduction

QGIS has been built using the comprehensive graphical user interface framework called Qt. Both QGIS and Qt have Python APIs. In this chapter, we'll learn how to interact with the user in order to collect and display information outside the default QGIS interface. Qt has excellent documentation of its own. Since QGIS is built on top of Qt, all of this documentation applies to QGIS. Note that it is now possible to build QGIS with Qt version 5, which has a different API. Most packaged distributions of QGIS use Qt4, which is the focus of this book. You can find the Qt documentation at `https://www.qt.io/developers/`.

Using log files

Log files provide a way of tracking exactly what is going on in a Python plugin or script by creating messages that are available even if the script or QGIS crashes. These log messages make troubleshooting easier. In this recipe, we'll demonstrate two methods used for logging. One method is the actual log files on the filesystem, and the other is the QGIS Log Messages Panel window, which is available by clicking on the yellow triangle with an exclamation mark at the bottom-right corner of the QGIS application window, or by selecting the **View** menu, then clicking on **Panels**, and then checking **Log Messages Panel**.

Getting ready

To use log files, we must configure the `QGIS_LOG_FILE` environment variable by performing the following steps so that QGIS knows where to write log messages:

1. From the QGIS **Settings** menu, select **Options...**.
2. In the **Options** dialog, select **System** panel.
3. In the **System** panel, scroll down to the **Environment** section.
4. In the **Environment** section, check the **Use custom variables** checkbox.
5. Click on the **Add New Variable** button represented by a green plus icon.
6. Leave the first column, **Apply**, to the default setting of **Overwrite.**
7. In the **Variable** field, enter `QGIS_LOG_FILE`.

8. In the **Value** field, enter `/qgis_data/log.txt` or the path to another directory where you have write permissions.
9. Click on the **OK** button to close the **Options** dialog.
10. Restart QGIS for the environment variable to take effect.

How to do it...

We will write a message to our custom log file configured in the previous section, and then write a message to the tabbed QGIS **Log Messages Panel** window. To do this, we need to perform the following steps:

1. First,open the **Python Console** in QGIS.
2. Next, we'll write the following log file message:

```
QgsLogger.logMessageToFile("This is a message to a log file.")
```

3. Then, we'll write a message to the QGIS **Log Messages Panel** window, specifying the message as the first argument and a name for the tab in which the message will appear, and the message level:

```
QgsMessageLog.logMessage("This is a message from the Python
                         Console", "Python Console",
                         QgsMessageLog.INFO)
```

4. Now, open the log file and check whether the message has appeared.
5. Finally, open the QGIS **Log Messages Panel** window, click on the **Python Console** tab, and verify that the second log message appears.

How it works...

The traditional log file provides a simple and portable way to record information from QGIS using Python. The **Log Messages Panel** window is a more structured way to view information from many different sources, with a tabbed interface and a convenient timestamp on each message. In this example, we used the simple `INFO` level. Other levels include `ALL`, `WARNING`, `CRITICAL`, and `NONE`. In most cases, you'll probably want to use the **Log Messages Panel** window because QGIS users are familiar with it. However, use it sparingly. It's OK to log lots of messages when testing code, but restrict the logging for plugins or applications to serious errors only. Heavy logging, for example, logging messages while looping over every feature in a layer, can slow down QGIS or even cause it to crash. The following screenshot shows the **Log Messages Panel** window with our test message:

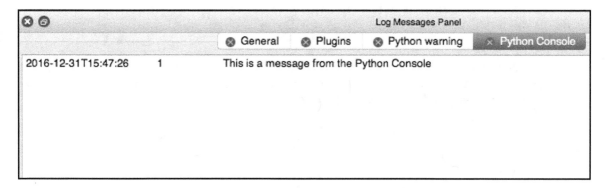

There's more...

Instead of explicitly specifying the logging panel directly as we do above, you can store the name in a variable and place that in the logging statement. That way, if you need to change the panel name, you can change the variable value instead of changing potentially hundreds of logging message statements.

Creating a simple message dialog

Message dialogs pop up to grab the user's attention and to display important information. In this recipe, we'll create a simple information dialog.

Getting ready

Open the QGIS Python console by going to the **Plugins** menu and selecting **Python Console**.

How to do it...

We will create a message dialog and display some text in it, as follows:

1. First, we need to import the GUI library:

   ```
   from PyQt4.QtGui import *
   ```

2. Then,we'll create the message dialog:

   ```
   msg = QMessageBox()
   ```

3. Next, we'll set the message we want to display:

   ```
   msg.setText("This is a simple information message.")
   ```

4. Finally,we'll call the `show` method to display the message dialog:

   ```
   msg.show()
   ```

How it works...

Note that we are directly using the underlying Qt framework from which QGIS is built. QGIS API's objects begin with `Qgs`, while `Qt` objects begin with just the letter `Q`.The following screenshot shows the message dialog:

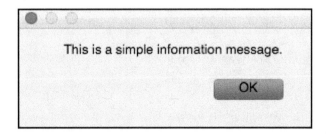

There's more...

A message dialog box should also be used sparingly, because it is a popup that can become annoying to the user or can get lost in the array of open windows and dialogs on a user's desktop. You can also set the title of the message box; however, you can't see the title in OSX. The preferred method for QGIS information messages is to use the `QgsMessageBar()` method. You can see how to use it later in this chapter in the recipe *Pushing messages to the message bar*. It is also well-documented in the PyQGIS Developer Cookbook found at `http://docs.qgis.org/testing/en/docs/pyqgis_developer_cookbook/communicating.html`.

Creating a warning dialog

Sometimes, you need to notify a user when an issue is detected, which might lead to problems if the user continues. This situation calls for a warning dialog, which we will demonstrate in this recipe.

Getting ready

Open the QGIS Python console by going to the **Plugins** menu and selecting **Python Console**.

How to do it...

In this recipe, we will create a dialog, set the warning message and a warning icon, and display the dialog, as follows:

1. First, we import the GUI library:

   ```
   from PyQt4.QtGui import *
   ```

2. Next, we initialize the warning dialog:

   ```
   msg = QMessageBox()
   ```

3. Then, we set the warning message:

   ```
   msg.setText("This is a warning...")
   ```

4. Now, add a warning icon to the dialog that has an enumeration index of 2:

```
msg.setIcon(QMessageBox.Warning)
```

5. Finally, we call the `show` method to display the dialog:

```
msg.show()
```

How it works...

Message dialogs should be used sparingly because they interrupt the user experience and can easily become annoying. However, sometimes it is important to prevent a user from taking an action, which may cause data corruption or a program to crash. The following screenshot shows the warning dialog:

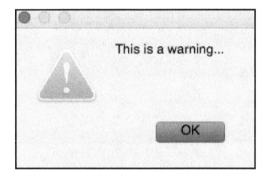

Creating an error dialog

You can issue an error dialog box when you need to end a process due to a serious error. In this recipe, we'll create an example of an error dialog.

Getting ready

Open the QGIS Python console by selecting the **Plugins** menu and then clicking on **Python Console**.

How to do it...

In this recipe, we will create a dialog, assign an error message, set an error icon, and display the dialog, as follows:

1. First, we need to import the GUI library:

   ```
   from PyQt4.QtGui import *
   ```

2. Next, we initialize the dialog:

   ```
   msg = QMessageBox()
   ```

3. Then, we set the error message:

   ```
   msg.setText("This is an error!")
   ```

4. Subsequently, we set an icon number for the error icon:

   ```
   msg.setIcon(QMessageBox.Critical)
   ```

5. Finally; we execute the error dialog:

   ```
   msg.show()
   ```

How it works...

An important feature of modal windows is that they always stay on top of the application, regardless of whether the user changes the window's focus. This feature ensures that the user addresses the dialog before they proceed. The following screenshot shows the error dialog:

Displaying a progress bar

A progress bar is a dynamic dialog that displays the percentage of completion bar for a running process that the user must wait for before continuing. A progress bar is more advanced than a simple dialog, because it needs to be updated continuously. In this recipe, we'll create a simple progress dialog based on a timer.

Getting ready

Open the QGIS Python console by selecting the **Plugins** menu and then clicking on **Python Console**.

How to do it...

The steps for this recipe include creating a custom class based on the QProgressBar, initializing the dialog and setting its size and title, creating a timer, connecting the progress bar to the timer, starting the time, and displaying the progress. To do this, we need to perform the following steps:

1. First, we must import both the GUI and QGIS core libraries:

```
from PyQt4.QtGui import *
from PyQt4.QtCore import *
```

2. Next, we create a custom class for our progress bar, including a method to increase the value of the progress bar:

```
class Bar(QProgressBar):
    value = 0
    def increaseValue(self):
        self.setValue(self.value)
        self.value = self.value+1
```

3. Now, we set the progress bar:

```
bar = Bar()
```

4. Next, we set the progress bar's size and title:

```
bar.resize(300,40)
bar.setWindowTitle('Working...')
```

5. Then, we initialize the timer, which will serve as the process we monitor:

```
timer = QTimer()
```

6. Now, we connect the the timer's `timeout` signal to the `increaseValue` method that we created earlier. Whenever the timer finishes its countdown, it will emit the `timeout` signal and notify the `increaseValue` method:

```
timer.timeout.connect(bar.increaseValue)
```

7. Now, we will start the timer, specifying an interval of 500 milliseconds. The timer will call its `timeout()` signal every 0.5 seconds:

```
timer.start(500)
```

8. Finally, we show the progress bar and start the progress meter:

```
bar.show()
```

How it works...

The progress bar will stop when its value reaches 100, but our timer will continue to run until the `stop()` method is called. In a more realistic implementation, you will need a way to determine whether the monitored process is complete. The indicator might be the creation of a file or even better, a signal. The Qt framework uses the concept of signals and slots to connect GUI elements. A GUI is event-based, with multiple events occurring at different times, including user actions and other triggers. The signal/slot system allows you to define reactions to events when they occur, without writing code to continuously monitor changes. In this recipe, we used a predefined signal from the timer and create our own slot. A slot is just a method identified as a slot by passing it to a signal's `connect()` method. The following screenshot shows an example of the progress bar:

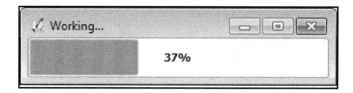

There's more...

In a complex GUI application such as QGIS, you will end up with multiple signals that trigger multiple slots simultaneously. You must take care that a rapidly updating element such as a progress bar doesn't slow down the application. Using a thread to only update the progress bar when something has truly changed is more efficient. For an example of this technique, take a look at `https://snorfalorpagus.net/blog/2013/12/07/multithreading-in-qgis-python-plugins/`.

Using the `QgsMessageBar` object is preferred to display informative messages, but it can also accept widgets such as the progress bar. The PyQGIS Developer Cookbook has an example that shows how to place the progress bar in the `QgsMessageBar` object (`http://docs.qgis.org/testing/en/docs/pyqgis_developer_cookbook/communicating.html`).

Creating a simple text input dialog

In this recipe, we'll demonstrate one of the simplest methods used for accepting input from a user: a text input dialog.

Getting ready

Open the QGIS Python console by selecting the **Plugins** menu and then clicking on **Python Console**.

How to do it...

In this recipe, we will initialize the dialog and then configure its title and label. We'll set the editing mode and the default text. When you click on the **OK** button, the text will be printed to the **Python Console**. To do this, we need to perform the following steps:

1. First, we need to import the GUI library:

   ```
   from PyQt4.QtGui import *
   ```

2. Next, we initialize the dialog:

   ```
   qid = QInputDialog()
   ```

3. Now, we set the window's title, label text, editing mode, and default text:

```
title = "Enter Your Name"
label = "Name: "
mode = QLineEdit.Normal
default = "<your name here>"
```

4. We configure the dialog while capturing the user input and the return code in variables:

```
text, ok = QInputDialog.getText(qid, title, label, mode, default)
```

5. When the dialog appears, type in some text and click on the **OK** button.
6. Now, we print the user input to the console:

```
print text
```

7. Finally, verify that the correct text is printed to the **Python Console**.

How it works...

The editing mode differentiates between normal, which we used here, and password, to obscure typed passwords. Although we haven't used it in this example, the return code is a Boolean, which can be used to verify that the user input occurred. The following screenshot shows the text input dialog:

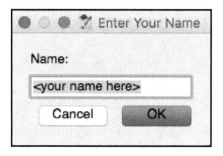

Creating a file input dialog

The best way to get a filename from the user is to have them browse to the file using a dialog. You can have the user type in a filename using the text input dialog, but this method is prone to errors. In this recipe, we'll create a file dialog and print the chosen filename to the console.

Getting ready

Open the QGIS Python console by selecting the **Plugins** menu and then clicking on **Python Console**.

How to do it...

In this recipe, we will create and configure the dialog, browse to a file, and print the chosen filename, as follows:

1. First, we import the GUI library:

   ```
   from PyQt4.QtGui import *
   ```

2. Next, we initialize the file dialog and specify its window title:

   ```
   qfd = QFileDialog()
   title = 'Open File'
   ```

3. Now, we specify a path to the directory we want the file dialog to start in:

   ```
   path = "/Users/joellawhead/qgis_data"
   ```

4. Then, we configure the file dialog with the preceding parameters and assign the output to a variable:

   ```
   f = QFileDialog.getOpenFileName(qfd, title, path)
   ```

5. When the dialog appears, browse to a file, select it, and click on the **OK** button.
6. Finally, we print the chosen filename to the console:

   ```
   print f
   ```

How it works...

The file dialog simply provides a filename. After the user selects the file, you must open it or perform some other operation on it. If the user cancels the file dialog, the file variable is just an empty string. You can use the `QFileInfo` object to get the path of the selected file:

```
from PyQt4.QtCore import *
path = QFileInfo(f).path()
```

Then, you can save this path in the project settings, as demonstrated in `Chapter 1`, *Automating QGIS*. This way, the next time you open a file dialog, you will start in the same directory location as the previous file, which is usually more convenient. The following screenshot shows what the file dialog looks like on MacOS:

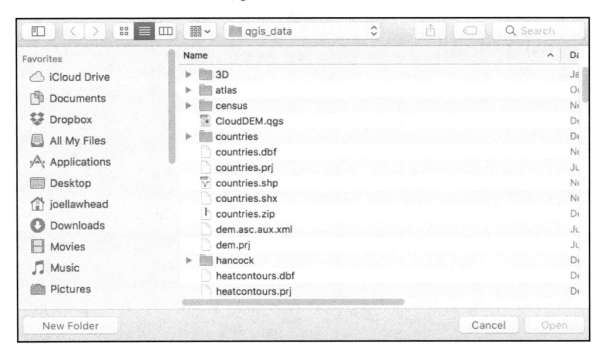

There's more…

You can also use the `QFileDialog.getOpenFileNames()` method to get the filenames to be saved. You can also use the `QFileDialog.selectNameFilter()` and `QFileDialog.selectNameFilter()` methods to filter files by type. You can use the `FileMode` enumeration to restrict the user to selecting directories as well. For more detailed documentation, visit: `http://pyqt.sourceforge.net/Docs/PyQt4/qfiledialog.html`

Creating a combobox

A combobox provides a drop-down list to limit the user's selection to a defined set of choices. In this recipe, we'll create a simple combobox.

Getting ready

Open the QGIS Python console by selecting the **Plugins** menu and then clicking on **Python Console**.

How to do it…

In this recipe, we will initialize the combobox widget, add choices to it, resize it, display it, and then capture the user input in a variable for printing to the console. To do this, we need to perform the following steps:

1. First, we import the GUI library:

    ```
    from PyQt4.QtGui import *
    ```

2. Now, we create our combobox object:

    ```
    cb = QComboBox()
    ```

3. Next, we add the items that we want the user to choose from:

    ```
    cb.addItems(["North", "South", "West", "East"])
    ```

4. Then, we resize the widget:

    ```
    cb.resize(200,35)
    ```

5. Now, we can display the widget to the user:

```
cb.show()
```

6. Next, choose an item from the list to change it from the default.
7. Finally, we print the choice to the console by accessing the current value:

```
print cb.currentText()
```

8. Verify that the selection is printed to the console.

How it works...

Items added to the combobox are a Python list. This feature makes it easy to dynamically generate choices using Python as the result of a database query or other dynamic data. You may also want the index of the object in the list, which you can access with the `currentIndex` method. The following screenshot shows the combobox widget:

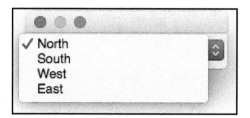

Creating radio buttons

Radio buttons are good for user input when you want the user to select an exclusive choice from a list of options, as opposed to checkboxes, which let a user select many or all the options available. For a longer list of choices, a combobox is a better option. Once a radio button is selected, you can unselect it only by choosing another radio button.

Getting ready

Open the QGIS Python console by selecting the **Plugins** menu and then clicking on **Python Console**.

How to do it...

Radio buttons are easier to manage as part of a class, so we'll create a custom class that also includes a textbox to view which radio button is selected. To do this, perform the following steps:

1. First, we'll import both the GUI and the core QGIS libraries:

```
from PyQt4.QtCore import *
from PyQt4.QtGui import *
```

2. Next, we'll create the RadioButton class and set up the radio buttons and the textbox:

```
class RadioButton(QWidget):
    def __init__(self, parent=None):
        QWidget.__init__(self, parent)
```

3. We must also define a layout to manage the placement of the widgets, as follows:

```
self.layout = QVBoxLayout()
self.rb1 = QRadioButton('Option 1')
self.rb2 = QRadioButton('Option 2')
self.rb3 = QRadioButton('Option 3')
self.textbox = QLineEdit()
```

4. Now, we'll connect the toggled signal of each radio button to the methods we'll define in just a moment, in order to detect when a radio button is selected:

```
self.rb1.toggled.connect(self.rb1_active)
self.rb2.toggled.connect(self.rb2_active)
self.rb3.toggled.connect(self.rb3_active)
```

5. Then, we'll add the radio buttons and the textbox to the layout:

```
self.layout.addWidget(self.rb1)
self.layout.addWidget(self.rb2)
self.layout.addWidget(self.rb3)
self.layout.addWidget(self.textbox)
```

6. Now, we can define the layout for the custom widget we are building:

```
self.setLayout(self.layout)
```

7. Next, we can define the methods to indicate which radio button is selected. You can also define these options in a single method, but for better understanding, three methods are easier:

```
def rb1_active(self, on):
    if on:
        self.textbox.setText('Option 1 selected')
def rb2_active(self, on):
    if on:
        self.textbox.setText('Option 2 selected')
def rb3_active(self, on):
    if on:
        self.textbox.setText('Option 3 selected')
```

8. We are now ready to initialize our class and display the radio buttons:

```
buttons = RadioButton()
buttons.show()
```

9. Finally, click on each of the three radio buttons and verify that the text in the textbox changes to indicate that the radio button you clicked on is selected.

How it works...

Radio buttons are almost always grouped together as a single object because they are related options. Many GUI frameworks expose them as a single object in the API; however, Qt keeps them as separate objects for maximum control. The following screenshot shows the checkbox dialog in action:

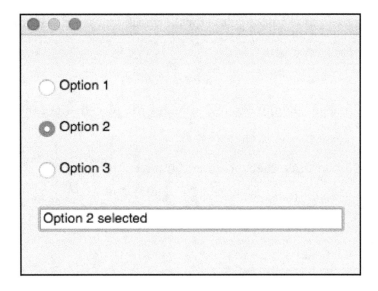

Creating checkboxes

Checkboxes are closely related to radio buttons, in that they offer options around a single theme. However, unlike radio buttons, checkboxes can be selected or unselected. You can also select more than one checkbox at a time. In this recipe, we'll create a dialog with checkboxes and some textboxes to programmatically track which checkboxes are selected.

Getting ready

Open the QGIS Python console by selecting the **Plugins** menu and then clicking on **Python Console**.

How to do it...

In this recipe, we'll use a class to manage the checkboxes and the textbox widgets, as follows:

1. First, we import the GUI and QGIS core libraries:

```
from PyQt4.QtCore import *
from PyQt4.QtGui import *
```

2. Next, we create our custom class for the checkboxes and textboxes:

```
class CheckBox(QWidget):
    def __init__(self, parent=None):
        QWidget.__init__(self, parent)
```

3. Next, we'll need a layout object to manage the placement of the widgets:

```
self.layout = QVBoxLayout()
```

4. Now, we'll add three checkboxes and three textboxes:

```
self.cb1 = QCheckBox('Option 1')
self.cb2 = QCheckBox('Option 2')
self.cb3 = QCheckBox('Option 3')
self.textbox1 = QLineEdit()
self.textbox2 = QLineEdit()
self.textbox3 = QLineEdit()
```

5. Then, we'll connect the status signals of the checkboxes to the methods that we'll define later:

```
self.cb1.toggled.connect(self.cb1_active)
self.cb2.toggled.connect(self.cb2_active)
self.cb3.toggled.connect(self.cb3_active)
```

6. Next, we must add the widgets to the layout:

```
self.layout.addWidget(self.cb1)
self.layout.addWidget(self.cb2)
self.layout.addWidget(self.cb3)
self.layout.addWidget(self.textbox1)
self.layout.addWidget(self.textbox2)
self.layout.addWidget(self.textbox3)
```

7. Now, we set our custom class's layout to the layout we created:

```
self.setLayout(self.layout)
```

8. We then create the methods that change the textboxes each time a checkbox is toggled:

```
# First checkbox
def cb1_active(self, on):
    if on:
        self.textbox1.setText('Option 1 selected')
    else: self.textbox1.setText('')
```

```
# Second checkbox
def cb2_active(self, on):
    if on:
        self.textbox2.setText('Option 2 selected')
    else: self.textbox2.setText('')
# Third checkbox
def cb3_active(self, on):
    if on:
        self.textbox3.setText('Option 3 selected')
    else: self.textbox3.setText('')
```

9. Now, we are ready to initialize our custom class and display the dialog:

```
buttons = CheckBox()
buttons.show()
```

10. Toggle the checkboxes separately and simultaneously, and then verify that the textboxes reflect the changes.

How it works...

Textboxes allow you to verify that you are programmatically catching the signal from the checkboxes as they are toggled. You can also use a single checkbox as a Boolean for an option with only two choices. When you run this recipe, the result should look similar to the following screenshot:

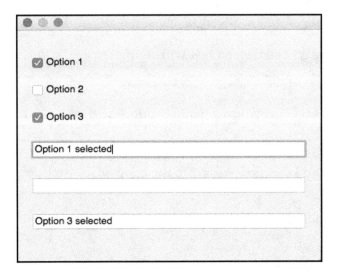

Creating a dock widget

All the panels in QGIS are dock widgets. These widgets can attach to a side of the main window or float freely in a separate window. These panels can contain any other type of widget, which is why they are usually the interface for QGIS plugins. In this recipe, we'll create a dock widget with a text editor widget inside.

Getting ready

Open the QGIS Python console by selecting the **Plugins** menu and then clicking on **Python Console**.

How to do it...

We'll create a **QTextEdit** widget. Then we'll create a **QDockWidget** and place the QTextEdit widget inside it. Finally we'll display the dock widget in the main window:

1. First, we import the Qt libraries, which contain all the widgets:

   ```
   from PyQt4.QtCore import *
   from PyQt4.QtGui import *
   ```

2. Next, we create the text edit widget with a default message:

   ```
   te = QTextEdit("<b>Project notes:</b>")
   ```

3. Now, we create the dock widget with a title:

   ```
   dw = QDockWidget("QGIS Sticky Notes")
   ```

4. Now, we set the text edit widget to the dock widget:

   ```
   dw.setWidget(te)
   ```

5. Finally, we add the dock widget to the main QGIS window, specifying the right side:

   ```
   iface.addDockWidget(Qt.RightDockWidgetArea, dw)
   ```

How it works...

The combination of these two widgets creates a simple sticky-notes tool that keeps project notes in an easy to access place. The panel can sit attached with the main window and share space with the other panels such as the Processing Toolbox. It can also detach and float wherever you want. If you close it, you'll notice it appears in the **View** menu under **Panels** as QGIS Sticky Notes in Windows and OSX and under **Settings/View** on Linux. And if you open it, any text you typed in the box will persist. The following screenshot shows the dock widget in action:

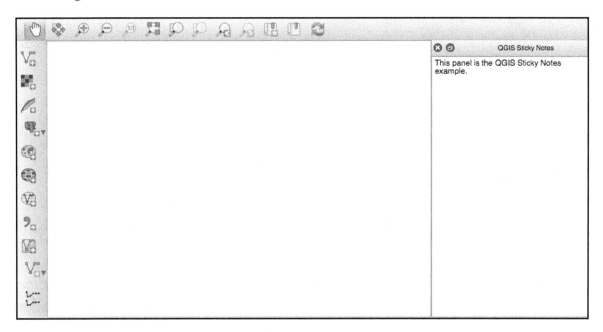

Displaying a message in the status bar

The status bar in QGIS displays a variety of information in all sorts of contexts. It can be used for static information such as the current project projection or for real-time scrolling information such as the mouse coordinates. In this recipe, we'll print the current time to the status bar.

Getting ready

Open the QGIS Python console by selecting the **Plugins** menu and then clicking on **Python Console**.

How to do it...

All we need to do is call the status bar message method with the current time:

1. First, we import the time module:

   ```
   import time
   ```

2. Then, we call the showMessage() method of the status bar with the current time and date:

   ```
   iface.mainWindow().statusBar().showMessage(time.asctime())
   ```

How it works...

QGIS automatically places the message in an open space on the status bar. We placed a simple message in the status bar, but you can also add pretty much any other widget as well. The following screenshot shows the timestamp on the bottom-left of the QGIS status bar:

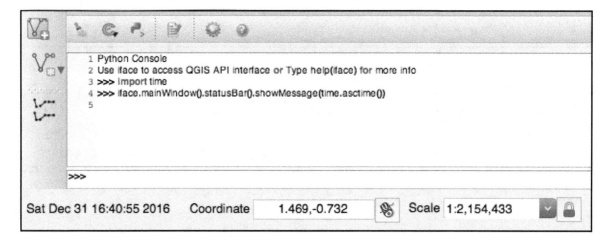

Pushing messages to the message bar

The QGIS message bar provides an unobtrusive way to display messages to the user. It displays on the top of the map window on a timer, so it automatically goes away without any required interaction from the user. In this recipe, we'll push a simple message to the status bar.

Getting ready

Open the QGIS Python console by selecting the **Plugins** menu and then clicking on **Python Console**.

How to do it...

This recipe is a simple one-liner because using the message bar is really easy. We just call the message bar API with a header text message, which will be displayed in bold and another message, which will be displayed without any formatting.

All we do is push two strings to the message bar. The first string will be displayed in bold:

```
iface.messageBar().pushInfo(u'Time is running out', u'Read this
quickly!')
```

How it works...

The message bar lasts for about five seconds and has a button to pause the timer if needed. The message bar is now the primary user communication widget in QGIS. It allows developers to display messages to the user without interrupting the user experience. The user can ignore the message and it will go away on its own. The following screenshot shows the message bar portion of the QGIS main window:

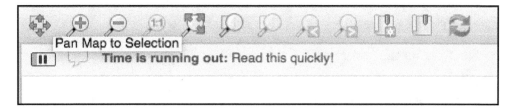

Pushing widgets to the message bar

Just like the status bar, the message bar can contain any type of widget, not just text. Although it is primarily intended for simple text messages, sometimes you may want to add items such as a progress bar to track processing. In this recipe, we'll display a progress bar in the message bar.

Getting ready

Open the QGIS Python console by selecting the **Plugins** menu and then clicking on **Python Console**.

How to do it...

First we'll build out our progress bar as we did earlier in this chapter. It will simply run on a timer. Then we'll add it to the message bar and we'll tell the message bar to stay visible for 10 seconds instead of the usual five seconds, so we can see the progress bar finish:

1. First, we must import both the GUI and QGIS core libraries:

   ```
   from PyQt4.QtGui import *
   from PyQt4.QtCore import *
   ```

2. Next, we create a custom class for our progress bar, including a method to increase the value of the progress bar:

   ```
   class Bar(QProgressBar):
       value = 0
       def increaseValue(self):
           self.setValue(self.value)
           self.value = self.value+1
   ```

3. Now, we set the progress bar:

   ```
   bar = Bar()
   ```

4. Next, we set the progress bar's size and title:

   ```
   bar.resize(300,40)
   bar.setWindowTitle('Working...')
   ```

5. Then, we initialize the timer, which will serve as the process we monitor:

```
timer = QTimer()
```

6. Now, we'll connect the timer's `timeout` signal to the `increaseValue` method, which we created earlier. Whenever the timer finishes its countdown, it will emit the `timeout` signal and notify the `increaseValue` method:

```
timer.timeout.connect(bar.increaseValue)
```

7. Now, we will start the timer, specifying an interval of `100` milliseconds. The timer will call its `timeout()` signal every `0.1` seconds, so it will move fairly quickly:

```
timer.start(100)
```

8. Finally, we have the progress bar built, so we can push it to the message bar specifying a 10-second delay before it closes:

```
iface.messageBar().pushWidget(bar, QgsMessageBar.INFO, 10)
```

How it works...

This recipe is an edge case as far as typical GIS workflows go, but it does show how easily you can combine widgets in PyQt. These principles make the software easier to learn and easier to use. In addition to the **INFO** option for the message level, you can also use **WARNING**, **CRITICAL**, or **SUCCESS**.

The following screenshot shows the progress bar in the message bar at the top of the window:

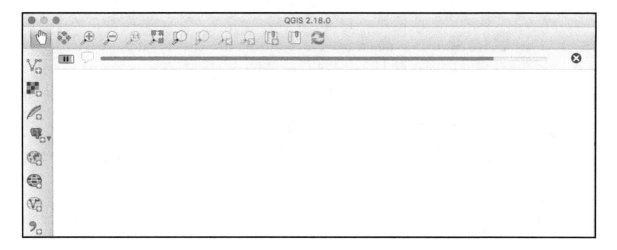

Creating tabs

Tabs allow you to condense the information from several screens into a relatively small place. Tabs provide titles at the top of the window, which present an individual widget layout for each title when clicked. In this recipe, we'll create a simple tabbed interface.

Getting ready

Open the QGIS Python console by selecting the **Plugins** menu and then clicking on **Python Console**.

How to do it...

We will create an overarching tab widget. Then, we'll create three generic widgets to represent our tabs. We'll set up layouts with three different GUI widgets and assign each layout to our tab widgets. Finally, we'll add our tabs to the tab widget and display it. To do this, we need to perform the following steps:

1. First, we need to import the GUI and QGIS core libraries:

    ```
    from PyQt4.QtCore import *
    from PyQt4.QtGui import *
    ```

2. Next, we create our tab and configure its title and size:

    ```
    qtw = QTabWidget()
    qtw.setWindowTitle("PyQGIS Tab Example")
    qtw.resize(400,300)
    ```

3. Now, we initialize our tab widgets:

    ```
    tab1 = QWidget()
    tab2 = QWidget()
    tab3 = QWidget()
    ```

4. Then, we'll set up a widget and a layout with a rich text input box, using HTML tags for bold text for our first tab:

    ```
    layout1 = QVBoxLayout()
    layout1.addWidget(QTextEdit("<b>Type text here</b>"))
    tab1.setLayout(layout1)
    ```

5. Now, we'll set up a simple button for our second tab, following the same format as the first tab:

    ```
    layout2 = QVBoxLayout()
    layout2.addWidget(QPushButton("Button"))
    tab2.setLayout(layout2)
    ```

6. Next, we'll create the widget and the layout for our third tab with a simple text label:

    ```
    layout3 = QVBoxLayout()
    layout3.addWidget(QLabel("Label text example"))
    tab3.setLayout(layout3)
    ```

7. Then, we'll add the tabs to the tab window:

```
qtw.addTab(tab1, "First Tab")
qtw.addTab(tab2, "Second Tab")
qtw.addTab(tab3, "Third Tab")
```

8. Finally, we'll display the tab window:

```
qtw.show()
```

9. Verify that you can click on each tab and interact with the widgets.

How it works...

The key to this recipe is the `QTabWidget()` method. Everything else is just arbitrary layouts and widgets, which are ultimately contained in the tab widget.

The general rule of thumb for tabs is to keep the information on them independently.

There is no way to predict how the user will interact with a tabbed interface, and if the information across tabs is dependent, problems will arise. The following screenshot shows the tab dialog with the first tab selected:

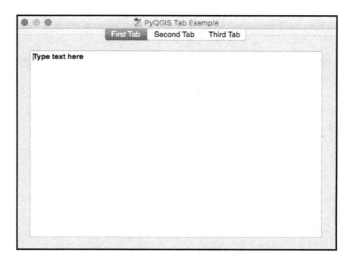

Stepping the user through a wizard

A wizard is a series of dialogs that lead the user through a sequence of steps. The information on each page of a wizard might relate in some way to the information on other pages. In this recipe, we'll create a simple three-page wizard to collect some information from the user and display it back to them.

Getting ready

Open the QGIS Python console by selecting the **Plugins** menu and then clicking on **Python Console**.

How to do it...

We will create three classes, each representing a page of our wizard. The first two pages will collect information, and the third page will display it back to the user. We will create a QWizard object to tie the page classes together. We will also use the concept of wizard fields to pass information among the pages. To do this, we need to perform the following steps:

1. First, we import the GUI and QGIS core libraries:

    ```
    from PyQt4.QtCore import *
    from PyQt4.QtGui import *
    ```

2. Next, we create the class for the first page of our wizard and add a textbox to collect the user's name as the uname variable:

    ```
    class Page1(QWizardPage):
        def __init__(self, parent=None):
            super(Page1, self).__init__(parent)
            self.setTitle("What's Your Name?")
            self.setSubTitle("Please enter your name.")
            self.label = QLabel("Name:")
            self.uname = QLineEdit("<enter your name>")
    ```

3. Now, we register the `uname` field, so that we'll be able to access the entered value later on without having to keep track of the variable itself:

```
self.registerField("uname", self.uname)
```

4. Then, we set up the layout for the page:

```
layout = QVBoxLayout()
layout.addWidget(self.label)
layout.addWidget(self.uname)
self.setLayout(layout)
```

5. Next, we'll set the class for our second page:

```
class Page2(QWizardPage):
    def __init__(self, parent=None):
        super(Page2, self).__init__(parent)
        self.setTitle("When's Your Birthday?")
        self.setSubTitle("Select Your Birthday.")
```

6. Then, we'll add a calendar widget to get the user's birthday:

```
self.cal = QCalendarWidget()
```

7. We'll register the selected date as a `field` to be accessed later on:

```
self.registerField("cal", self.cal, "selectedDate")
```

8. Then, we'll set up the layout for this page:

```
layout = QVBoxLayout()
layout.addWidget(self.cal)
self.setLayout(layout)
```

9. We are now ready to set up the third page, which will display the user's information. We'll use simple labels, which are dynamically populated in the next step:

```
class Page3(QWizardPage):
    def __init__(self, parent=None):
        super(Page3, self).__init__(parent)
        self.setTitle("About You")
        self.setSubTitle("Here is Your Information:")
        self.name_lbl = QLabel()
        self.date_lbl = QLabel()
        layout = QVBoxLayout()
        layout.addWidget(self.name_lbl)
```

```
layout.addWidget(self.date_lbl)
self.setLayout(layout)
```

10. Now, we set up the initialization of the page. We will first access the fields registered from the previous pages to grab the user input:

```
def initializePage(self):
    uname = self.field("uname")
    date = self.field("cal").toString()
```

11. Then, all we have to do is set those values to the text for the labels, using Python string formatting:

```
self.name_lbl.setText("Your name is %s" % uname)
self.date_lbl.setText("Your birthday is %s" % date)
```

12. Finally, we create our wizard widget, add pages, and display the wizard:

```
wiz = QWizard()
wiz.addPage(Page1())
wiz.addPage(Page2())
wiz.addPage(Page3())
wiz.show()
```

How it works...

The wizard interface shares many traits of the tab widget, with some important differences. The wizard only allows the user to move back and forth in a linear progression based on the page order. It can share information among pages if it is registered as a field, which then makes them global to the scope of the wizard. However, the `field()` method is a protected method, so your pages must be defined as classes inherited from the `QWizardPage` object, for the registered fields to work as expected.

The following screenshot shows the calendar screen of the wizard:

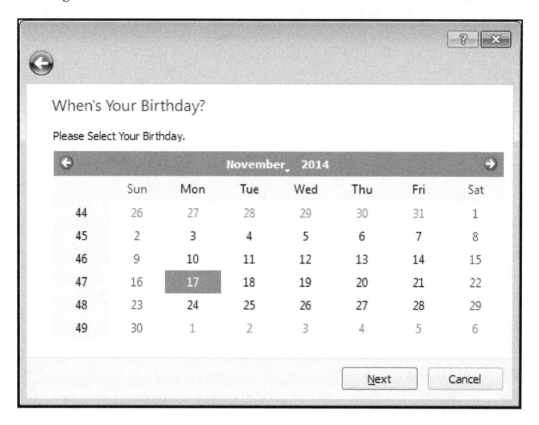

Keeping dialogs on top

It's easy to lose track of windows that pop up in front of QGIS. As soon as the user changes focus to move the main QGIS application window, your dialog can disappear behind it, forcing the user to rearrange their whole desktop to find the smaller window again. Fortunately, Qt has a window setting called hint, which allows you to force a window to stay on top. This type of dialog is called a modal dialog. In this recipe, we'll create a message dialog using hint.

Getting ready

Open the QGIS Python console by selecting the **Plugins** menu and then clicking on **Python Console**.

How to do it...

In this recipe, we will create a simple message dialog and set it to stay on top, as follows:

1. First, we import the Qt GUI and QGIS core libraries:

```
from PyQt4.QtGui import *
from PyQt4.QtCore import *
```

2. Next, we create the text for our message:

```
msg = "This window will always stay on top."
```

3. Now, we create our dialog and specify the message and hint:

```
lbl = QLabel(msg, None, Qt.WindowStaysOnTopHint)
```

4. We can resize and show the dialog:

```
lbl.resize(400,400)
lbl.show()
```

5. Click on the main QGIS application window to change the window focus and verify that the dialog stays on top of QGIS.

How it works...

This simple technique can help us ensure that a user addresses an important dialog before moving on. The following screenshot shows the dialog box on top of the QGIS window:

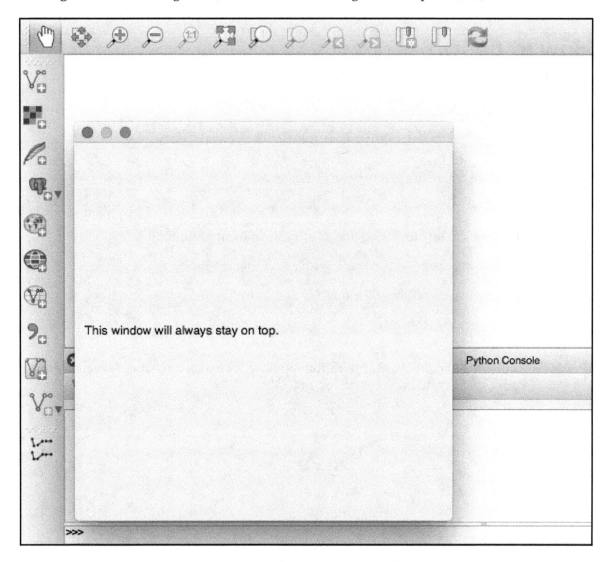

8
QGIS Workflows

In this chapter, we will cover the following recipes:

- Creating an NDVI
- Geocoding addresses
- Creating raster footprints.
- Performing network analysis
- Routing along streets
- Tracking a GPS
- Creating a mapbook
- Finding the least cost path
- Performing nearest neighbor analysis
- Creating a DEM from LiDAR data
- Creating a heat map
- Creating a dot density map
- Collecting field data
- Computing road slope using elevation data
- Geolocating photos on the map
- Image change detection
- Adjusting imprecise building footprints
- Visualizing multi-temporal data

Introduction

In this chapter, we'll use Python to perform a variety of common geospatial tasks in QGIS, which may be complete workflows in themselves or a key piece of a larger workflow. In previous chapters, the recipes were usually related to a common theme. In this chapter we'll cover different topics which are loosely related or unrelated to cover as many different types of workflows as possible including both geospatial tasks and different aspects of the PyQGIS API.

Creating an NDVI

A **Normalized Difference Vegetation Index** (**NDVI**) is one of the oldest remote sensing algorithms used to detect green vegetation in an area of interest, using the red and near-infrared bands of an image. The chlorophyll in plants absorbs visible light, including the red band, while the cell structures of plants reflect near-infrared light. The NDVI formula provides a ratio of near-infrared light to the total incoming radiation, which serves as an indicator of vegetation density. This recipe will use Python to control the QGIS raster calculator in order to create an NDVI using a multispectral image of a farm field.

Getting ready

Download the image from `https://github.com/GeospatialPython/Learn/raw/master/farm-field.tif` and place it in your `qgis_data` in a directory named `rasters`.

How to do it...

We will load the raster as a QGIS raster layer, perform the NDVI algorithm, and finally apply a color ramp to the raster so that we can easily visualize the greener vegetation in the image. To do this, we need to perform the following steps:

1. In the QGIS **Python Console**, import the following libraries:

```
from PyQt4.QtGui import *
from PyQt4.QtCore import *
from qgis.analysis import *
```

2. Now, load the raster image as a layer using the following code:

```
rasterName = "farm"
raster = QgsRasterLayer("/qgis_data/qgis_data/rasters/
                        farm-field.tif", rasterName)
```

3. Then, create entries in the QGIS raster calculator for the two bands using the following code:

```
ir = QgsRasterCalculatorEntry()
r = QgsRasterCalculatorEntry()
```

4. Now, using the following lines of code, assign the raster layer as the raster component of each calculator entry:

```
ir.raster = raster
r.raster = raster
```

5. Select the appropriate band for each entry, so the calculator will use the data we need for the NDVI. The red and infrared band numbers are typically listed in the raster's metadata:

```
ir.bandNumber = 2
r.bandNumber = 1
```

6. Next, assign a reference ID to each entry using the special QGIS naming convention, as shown here, with the name of the layer as a prefix followed by an @ symbol and the band number as a suffix:

```
ir.ref = rasterName + "@2"
r.ref = rasterName + "@1"
```

7. Build the raster calculator expression with the following code:

```
references = (ir.ref, r.ref, ir.ref, r.ref)
exp = "1.0 * (%s - %s) / 1.0 + (%s + %s)" % references
```

8. Then, specify the output name of the NDVI image:

```
output = "/qgis_data/qgis_data/rasters/ndvi.tif"
```

9. Set up the variables for the rest of the raster calculator call by defining the raster's extent, its width and height in columns and rows, and the raster entries we defined in the previous steps:

```
e = raster.extent()
w = raster.width()
h = raster.height()
entries = [ir,r]
```

10. Now, create the NDVI using our expression:

```
ndvi = QgsRasterCalculator(exp, output, "GTiff", e, w, h,
                           entries)
ndvi.processCalculation()
```

11. Next, load the NDVI output as a raster layer:

```
lyr = QgsRasterLayer(output, "NDVI")
```

12. We must perform a histogram stretch on the image, otherwise the differences in values will be difficult to see. A stretch is performed using a QGIS contrast enhancement algorithm:

```
algorithm = QgsContrastEnhancement.StretchToMinimumMaximum
limits = QgsRaster.ContrastEnhancementMinMax
lyr.setContrastEnhancement(algorithm, limits)
```

13. Next, build a color ramp shader to colorize the NDVI, as follows:

```
s = QgsRasterShader()
c = QgsColorRampShader()
c.setColorRampType(QgsColorRampShader.INTERPOLATED)
```

14. Then, add entries for each color in the image. Each entry consists of a lower value range, a color, and a label. The color in an entry will continue from the lower value until it encounters a higher value or the maximum value. Note that we will use a variable alias for the extremely long name of the QGIS `ColorRampItem` object:

```
i = []
qri = QgsColorRampShader.ColorRampItem
i.append(qri(0, QColor(0,0,0,0), 'NODATA'))
i.append(qri(214, QColor(120,69,25,255), 'Lowest Biomass'))
i.append(qri(236, QColor(255,178,74,255), 'Lower Biomass'))
i.append(qri(258, QColor(255,237,166,255), 'Low Biomass'))
i.append(qri(280, QColor(173,232,94,255), 'Moderate Biomass'))
i.append(qri(303, QColor(135,181,64,255), 'High Biomass'))
i.append(qri(325, QColor(3,156,0,255), 'Higher Biomass'))
i.append(qri(400, QColor(1,100,0,255), 'Highest Biomass'))
```

15. Now, we can add the entries to the shader and apply it to the image:

```
c.setColorRampItemList(i)
s.setRasterShaderFunction(c)
ps = QgsSingleBandPseudoColorRenderer(lyr.dataProvider(), 1, s)
lyr.setRenderer(ps)
```

16. Finally, add the classified NDVI image to the map in order to visualize it:

```
QgsMapLayerRegistry.instance().addMapLayer(lyr)
```

How it works...

The QGIS raster calculator is exactly what its name implies. It allows you to perform an array math on images. Both the QGIS raster menu and the Processing Toolbox have several raster processing tools, but the raster calculator can perform custom analysis that can be defined in a single mathematical equation. The NDVI algorithm is the infrared band minus the red band divided by the infrared band plus the red band, or *(IR-R)/(IR+R)*. In our calculator expression, we multiply each side of the equation by 1.0 to avoid division-by-zero errors. Your output should look similar to the following image if you load the result into QGIS. In this screenshot, NODATA values are represented as black; however, your QGIS installation may default to using white:

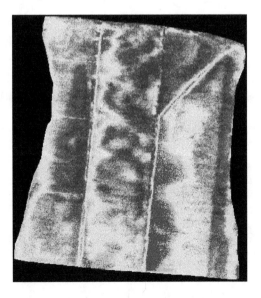

Geocoding addresses

Geocoding is the process of turning an address into earth coordinates. Geocoding requires a comprehensive dataset that ties zip codes, cities, streets, and street numbers (or street number ranges) to the coordinates. In order to have a geocoder that works for any address in the world with reasonable accuracy, you need to use a cloud service because geocoding datasets are very dense and can be quite large. Creating a geocoding dataset for any area beyond a few square miles requires a significant amount of resources. There are several services available, including Google and MapQuest. In QGIS, the easiest way to access these services is through the QGIS Python **GeoCoding** plugin. In this recipe, we'll use this plugin to programmatically geocode an address.

Getting ready

You will need to install the QGIS Python GeoCoding plugin by Alessandro Pasotti for this exercise, as follows:

1. From the QGIS **Plugins** menu, select **Manage and Install Plugins...**.
2. In the **Plugins** dialog search box, search for **Geocoding**.
3. Select **GeoCoding** plugin and click on the **Install plugin button**.

How to do it...

In this recipe, we will access the GeoCoding plugin methods using Python, feed the plugin an address, and print the resulting coordinates. To do this, we need to perform the following steps:

1. In the QGIS **Python Console**, import the OpenStreetMap `GeoCoding` object using the following code:

```
from GeoCoding import GeoCoding
```

2. Next, we'll initialize the plugin:

```
init = GeoCoding.GeoCoding(iface)
```

3. Now we can load our OpenStreetMap geocoder:

```
from geopy.geocoders import Nominatim
```

4. Then we can create the geocoder:

```
geocoder = Nominatim()
```

5. Then, using the following code, we'll geocode an address:

```
location = geocoder.geocode("The Ugly Pirate, Bay Saint Louis,
                 MS 39520")
```

6. Finally, we'll print the results to see the coordinates:

```
print location
```

7. Check whether you have received the following output printed to the console:

```
(u'The Ugly Pirate, 144, Demontluzin Street, Bay St. Louis,
    Hancock County, Mississippi, 39520,
    United States of America', (30.3124059, -89.3281418))
```

How it works...

The **GeoCoding** plugin is designed to be used with the QGIS GUI interface. However, like most QGIS plugins, it is written in Python and we can access it through the Python console.

> This trick doesn't work with every plugin. Sometimes, the user interface is too intertwined with the plugin's GUI that you can't programmatically use the plugin's methods without triggering the GUI.

However, in most cases, you can use the plugins to not only extend QGIS but also for its powerful Python API. If you write a plugin yourself, consider making it accessible to the QGIS Python console in order to make it even more useful.

Creating raster footprints

A common way to catalog the raster datasets that consist of a large number of files is by creating a vector dataset with polygon footprints of the extent of each raster file. The vector footprint files can be easily loaded in QGIS or served over the Web. This recipe demonstrates a method to create a footprint vector from a directory full of raster files. We will build this program as a Processing Toolbox script, which is easier to build than a QGIS plugin and provides both a GUI and a clean programming API.

Getting ready

Download the sample raster image scenes from `https://github.com/GeospatialPython/Learn/raw/master/scenes.zip`. Unzip the `scenes` directory into a directory named `rasters` in your `qgis_data` directory.

For this recipe, we will create a new Processing Toolbox script using the following steps:

1. In the QGIS Processing Toolbox, expand the **Scripts** tree menu.
2. Next, expand the **Tools** tree menu.
3. Finally, double-click on the **Create new script** item to bring up the processing script editor.

How to do it...

First, we will use the Processing Toolbox header naming conventions, which will simultaneously define our GUI and the input and output variables. Then, we'll create the logic, which processes a raster directory and calculates the image extents, and finally we'll create the vector file. To do this, we need to perform the following steps:

1. First, we define our input variables using comments to tell the Processing Toolbox to add these to the GUI when the script is invoked by a user. The first item defines the script's group menu to place our script in the toolbox. The second item defines the directory containing the rasters, and the third item is the output name of our shapefile. The script must start with these comments. Each item also declares a type allowed by the Processing Toolbox API. The names of the variables in these comments become available to the script:

   ```
   ##Vector=group
   ##Input_Raster_Directory=folder
   ##Output_Footprints_Vector=output vector
   ```

2. Next, we import the Python libraries we will need using the following commands:

```
import os
from qgis.core import *
```

3. Now, we get a list of files in the raster directory. The following script makes no attempt to filter the files by type. If there are other types of data in the directory that are not raster files, they will be included as well:

```
files = os.listdir(Input_Raster_Directory)
```

4. Then, we declare a couple of variables, which will hold our raster extents and the coordinate reference string, as shown here:

```
footprints = []
crs = ""
```

5. Now, we loop through the rasters, load them as a raster layer to grab their extents, store them as point data in Python dictionaries, and add them to our list of footprints for temporary storage. If the raster can't be processed, a warning is issued using the Processing Toolbox progress object:

```
for f in files:
    try:
        fn = os.path.join(Input_Raster_Directory, f)
        lyr = QgsRasterLayer(fn, "Input Raster")
        crs = lyr.crs()
        e = lyr.extent()
        ulx = e.xMinimum()
        uly = e.yMaximum()
        lrx = e.xMaximum()
        lry = e.yMinimum()
        ul = (ulx, uly)
        ur = (lrx, uly)
        lr = (lrx, lry)
        ll = (ulx, lry)
        fp = {}
        points = []
        points.append(QgsPoint(*ul))
        points.append(QgsPoint(*ur))
        points.append(QgsPoint(*lr))
        points.append(QgsPoint(*ll))
        points.append(QgsPoint(*ul))
        fp["points"] = points
        fp["raster"] = fn
        footprints.append(fp)
```

```
except:
    progress.setInfo("Warning: The file %s does not appear
                      to be a valid raster file." % f)
```

6. Using the following code, we will create a memory vector layer to build the footprint vector before writing it to a shapefile:

```
vectorLyr = QgsVectorLayer("Polygon?crs=%s&field=raster:
                           string(100)"% crs,
                           "Footprints" ,"memory")
vpr = vectorLyr.dataProvider()
```

7. Now, we'll turn our list of extents into features:

```
features = []
for fp in footprints:
    poly = QgsGeometry.fromPolygon([fp["points"]])
    f = QgsFeature()
    f.setGeometry(poly)
    f.setAttributes([fp["raster"]])
    features.append(f)
vpr.addFeatures(features)
vectorLyr.updateExtents()
```

8. We'll then set up the file driver and the CRS for the shapefile:

```
driver = "Esri Shapefile"
ct = QgsCoordinateTransform(crs, crs)
```

9. Finally, we'll write the selected output file, specifying the layer we are saving to disk, the name of the output file, the file encoding, which might change depending on the input, the coordinate reference system, and the driver for the output file type, which in this case is a shapefile:

```
error = QgsVectorFileWriter.writeAsVectorFormat(vectorLyr,
                Output_Footprints_Vector, "utf-8", srs, driver)
if not QgsVectorFileWriter.NoError:
    progress.setInfo("Unable to output footprints.")
```

How it works...

It is important to remember that a Processing Toolbox script can be run in several different contexts. You can run them as a GUI process such as a plugin or using the Processing Toolbox GUI interface. You can run them as a programmatic script from the Python console or you can use them in the **Graphical Modeler framework** built into the Processing Toolbox. Therefore, it is important to follow the documented Processing Toolbox API so that it can work as expected in all of these contexts. This includes defining clear inputs and outputs and using the progress object. The progress object is the proper way to provide feedback to the user for both progress bars as well as messages. Although the API allows you to define outputs that let the user select different OGR and GDAL outputs, only shapefiles and GeoTIFFs seem to be supported currently.

There's more...

The Graphical Modeler tool within the Processing Toolbox let's you visually chain different processing algorithms together to create complex workflows. Another interesting plugin is the Processing Workflows plugin, which not only allows you to chain algorithms together but also provides a nice tabbed interface with instructions for the end user to help beginners through complicated geospatial workflows.

The following screenshot shows the raster footprints over an OpenStreetMap basemap:

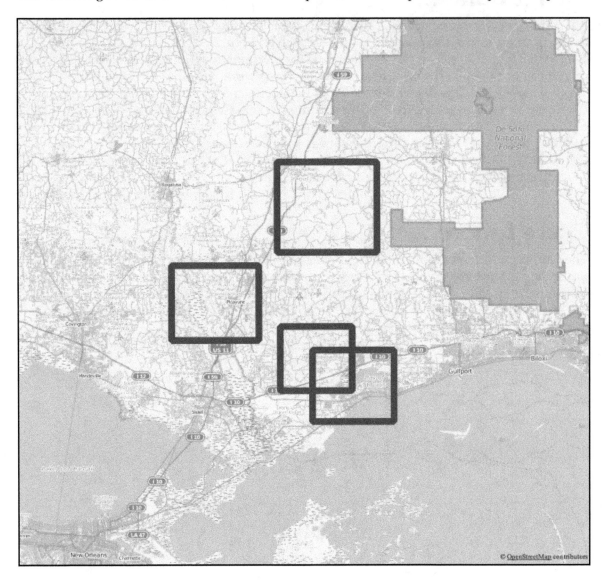

Performing network analysis

Network analysis allows you to find the most efficient route between two points along a
defined network of connected lines. These lines might represent streets, pipes in a water
system, the Internet, or any number of connected systems. Network analysis abstracts this
common problem so that the same techniques and algorithms can be applied across a wide
variety of applications. In this recipe, we'll use a generic line network to perform analysis
using the Dijkstra algorithm, which is one of the oldest algorithms used to find the shortest
path. QGIS has all of this functionality built-in.

Getting ready

First, download the vector dataset from the following link, which includes two shapefiles,
and unzip it to a directory named shapes in your qgis_data directory:

https://github.com/GeospatialPython/Learn/raw/master/network.zip

How to do it...

We will create a network graph by defining the beginning and end of our network of lines
and then use this graph to determine the shortest route along the line network between our
two points. To do this, we need to perform the following steps:

1. In the QGIS **Python Console**, we'll first import the libraries we'll need including
   the QGIS Network Analyzer:

   ```
   from qgis.core import *
   from qgis.gui import *
   from qgis.networkanalysis import *
   from PyQt4.QtCore import *
   ```

2. Next, we'll load our line network shapefile and the shapefile containing the
   points along the network we want the Network Analyzer to consider when
   selecting a route:

   ```
   network = QgsVectorLayer("/qgis_data/qgis_data/shapes/
                            Network.shp","Network Layer","ogr")
   waypoints = QgsVectorLayer("/qgis_data/qgis_data/shapes/
                              NetworkPoints.shp","Waypoints",
                              "ogr")
   ```

3. Now, we will create a graph director to define the properties of the graph. The `director` object accepts our line shapfile, a field ID for direction information, and some other documented integer codes involving direction properties in the network. In our example, we're going to tell the director to ignore directions. The `properter` object is a basic algorithm for a routing strategy that gets added to the network graph and considers line length:

```
director = QgsLineVectorLayerDirector(network, -1, '', '',
                                      '', 3)
properter = QgsDistanceArcProperter()
director.addProperter(properter)
crs = network.crs()
```

4. Now, we create the `GraphBuilder` object to actually convert the line network into a graph:

```
builder = QgsGraphBuilder(crs)
```

5. We define the two points that are the start and end of our route:

```
ptStart = QgsPoint(-0.8095638694, -0.1578175511)
ptStop = QgsPoint(0.8907435677, 0.4430834924)
```

6. Then, we tell the director to turn our point layer into tie points in our network, which define the way points along our network and can also optionally provide resistance values:

```
tiePoints = director.makeGraph(builder, [ptStart, ptStop])
```

7. Now, we can use the following code to build the graph:

```
graph = builder.graph()
```

8. We now locate our start and end points as tie points in the graph:

```
tStart = tiePoints[0]
tStop = tiePoints[1]
idStart = graph.findVertex(tStart)
idStop = graph.findVertex(tStop)
```

9. Then, we can tell the analyzer to use our start point in order to find the shortest route through the network:

```
(tree, cost) = QgsGraphAnalyzer.dijkstra(graph, idStart, 0)
```

10. Next, we loop through the resulting tree and grab the points along the output route:

```
p = []
curPos = idStop
while curPos != idStart:
    p.append(graph.vertex(graph.arc(tree[curPos]).inVertex())
             .point())
    curPos = graph.arc(tree[curPos]).outVertex()
p.append(tStart)
```

11. Now, we'll load our two input shapefiles onto the map and create a rubber band in order to visualize the route:

```
QgsMapLayerRegistry.instance().addMapLayers([network,waypoints])
rb = QgsRubberBand(iface.mapCanvas())
rb.setColor(Qt.red)
```

12. Finally, we'll add the route points to the rubber band in order to see the output of the Network Analyzer:

```
for pnt in p:
    rb.addPoint(pnt)
```

How it works...

This recipe is an extremely simple example to be used as a starting point for the investigation of a very complex and powerful tool. The line network shapefiles can have a field defining each line as unidirectional or bi-directional. The point shapefile provides waypoints along the network as well as resistance values, which might represent elevation, traffic density, or other factors that will make a route less desirable.

The output will look similar to the following image:

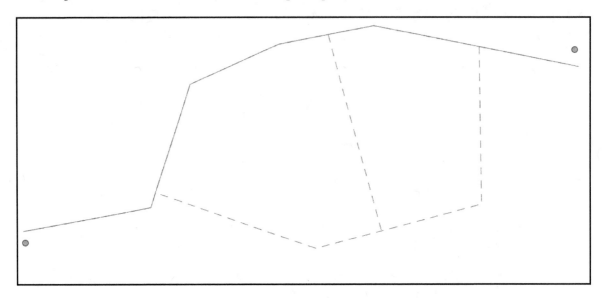

We also use a `QgsRubberBand` object in this example. This object is used for building temporary lines and polygons on a map. Rubber bands are the traditional nickname for polygons or polylines snapped around an area of interest on a map the same way you would snap a rubber band around your fingers. We also use rubber bands in *Building a custom selection tool* recipe, from `Chapter 5`, *Creating Dynamic Maps*.

More information and examples of the network analysis tool are available in the QGIS documentation at
`http://docs.qgis.org/testing/en/docs/pyqgis_developer_cookbook/network_analysis.html`.

There's more...

You can read more about the Dijkstra Algorithm here:
`https://en.wikipedia.org/wiki/Dijkstra%27s_algorithm`

You can also use the `NetworkX` library to do this exercise as it is compatible with Python and QGIS. Learn more about it here:

`http://networkx.github.io/`

Routing along streets

Sometimes, you may want to find the best driving route between two addresses. Street routing has now become so commonplace that we take it for granted. However, if you explore the recipes on geocoding and network analysis in this book, you will begin to see what a complex challenge street routing truly is. To perform routing operations in QGIS, we'll use the QGIS **GeoSearch** plugin, which is written in Python, so that we can access it from the console.

Getting ready

You will need to install the QGIS Python GeoSearch plugin for this exercise in order to do the routing as well as the QGIS OpenLayers plugin to overlay the result on a Google map, as follows:

1. From the QGIS **Plugins** menu, select **Manage and Install Plugins...**.
2. If you have the QGIS GeoCoding plugin installed, then you must uninstall it, as sometimes it conflicts with the GeoSearch plugin. So, select this in the plugins' list and click on the **Uninstall plugin** button.
3. In the **Plugins** dialog search box, search for **GeoSearch**.
4. Select the **GeoSearch** plugin and click on the **Install plugin** button.
5. Next, in the **Plugins** search dialog, search for **OpenLayers**.
6. Select the **OpenLayers Plugin** and click on the **Install plugin** button.

How to do it...

We will invoke the GeoSearch plugin's routing function, which uses Google's routing engine, and display the result over a Google map from the OpenLayers plugin. To do this, we need to perform the following steps:

1. In the QGIS **Python Console**, we first import the QGIS `utils` library as well as the required portions of the GeoSearch plugin:

   ```
   import qgis.utils
   from GeoSearch import geosearchdialog, GoogleMapsApi
   ```

2. Next, we'll use the QGIS `utils` library to access the OpenLayers plugin:

   ```
   openLyrs = qgis.utils.plugins['openlayers_plugin']
   ```

3. The GeoSearch plugin isn't really designed for programmatic use; so, in order to invoke this plugin, we must invoke it through the GUI interface, but then we need to pass blank values so that it doesn't trigger the GUI plugin interface:

```
g = geosearchdialog.GeoSearchDialog(iface)
g.SearchRoute([])
```

4. Now, using the following code, we can safely create our routing engine object:

```
d = GoogleMapsApi.directions.Directions()
```

5. Next, we create our origin and destination addresses.

```
origin = "Boston, MA"
dest = "2517 Main Rd, Dedham, ME 04429"
```

6. Then, we can calculate the route using the simplest possible options, as shown here:

```
route = d.GetDirections(origin, dest, mode = "driving",
                        waypoints=None, avoid=None,
                        units="imperial")
```

7. Now, we use the OpenLayers plugin to add Google map's base map to the QGIS map:

```
layerType = openLyrs._olLayerTypeRegistry.getById(4)
openLyrs.addLayer(layerType)
```

8. Finally, we use the `GeoSearch` plugin to create a QGIS layer on top of the base map for our route:

```
g.CreateVectorLayerGeoSearch_Route(route)
```

How it works...

Even though they are built in Python, neither the GeoSearch nor OpenLayers plugins are designed to be used from Python by a programmer. However, we are still able to use the tools in a script without much trouble. To take advantage of some of the routing options available with the GeoSearch plugin, you can use its GUI to see what is available and then add those options to your script. Be aware that most plugins don't have a true API, so a slight change to the plugin in a future version can break your script.

Tracking a GPS

QGIS has the ability to connect to a GPS that uses the **National Marine Electronics Association** (**NMEA**) standard. QGIS can use a serial connection to the GPS or communicate with it through the open source software called **gpsd** using the QGIS GPS information panel. The location information from the GPS can be displayed on the QGIS map, and QGIS can even automatically pan the map to follow the GPS point. In this recipe, we'll use the QGIS API to process NMEA sentences and update a point on a global map. The information needed to connect to different GPS units can vary widely, so we'll use an online NMEA sentence generator to get some simulated GPS information.

Getting ready

This recipe doesn't require any preparation.

How to do it...

We'll grab a batch of NMEA GPS sentences from a free online generator, create a worldwide basemap using online GeoJSON data, create a vector point layer to represent the GPS, and finally loop through the sentences and make our track point move around the map. To do this, we need to perform the following steps:

1. First, we need to import some standard Python libraries using the QGIS Python console:

   ```
   import urllib
   import urllib2
   import time
   ```

2. Next, we'll connect to the online NMEA generator, download a batch of sentences, and turn them into a list, as follows:

   ```
   url = 'http://freenmea.net/api/emitnmea'
   values = {'types' :'default'}
   data = urllib.urlencode(values)
   req = urllib2.Request(url, data)
   results = []for i in range(10):
       response = urllib2.urlopen(req)
       results.extend(response.read().split("\n"))
   ```

3. Next, we can add our world countries basemap using a GeoJSON service:

```
wb = "https://raw.githubusercontent.com/johan/world.geo.json/
    master/countries.geo.json"
basemap = QgsVectorLayer(wb, "Countries", "ogr")
qmr = QgsMapLayerRegistry.instance()
qmr.addMapLayer(basemap)
```

4. Now, we can create our GPS Point layer and access its data provider:

```
vectorLyr = QgsVectorLayer('Point?crs=epsg:4326', GPS Point',
                           "memory")
vpr = vectorLyr.dataProvider()
```

5. Then, we need some variables to hold the current coordinates as we loop through the locations, and we'll also access the mapCanvas object:

```
cLat = None
cLon = None
canvas = iface.mapCanvas()
```

6. Next, we'll create a GPS connection object for data processing. If we are using a live GPS object, we will use this line to enter the device's information:

```
c = QgsNMEAConnection(None)
```

7. Now, we set up a flag to determine whether we are processing the first point or not:

```
firstPt = True
```

8. We can loop through the NMEA sentences now, but we must check the sentence type to see which type of information we are using. In a live GPS connection, QGIS handles this part automatically and this part of the code will be unnecessary:

```
for r in results:
    l = len(r)
    if "GGA" in r:
        c.processGGASentence(r,l)
    elif "RMC" in r:
        c.processRMCSentence(r,l)
    elif "GSV" in r:
        c.processGSVSentence(r,l)
    elif "VTG" in r:
        c.processVTGSentence(r,l)
```

```
elif "GSA" in r:
    c.processGSASentence(r,l)
```

9. Then, we can get the current GPS information:

```
i=c.currentGPSInformation()
```

10. Now, we will check this information to make sure that the GPS location has actually changed since the previous loop before we try to update the map:

```
if i.latitude and i.longitude:
    lat = float(i.latitude)
    lon = float(i.longitude)
if cLat is None:
    cLat = float(i.latitude)
    cLon = float(i.longitude)
elif round(lat, 2)==round(cLat, 2) and
     round(lon, 2)==round(cLon, 2):
    continue
else:
    cLat = lat
    cLon = lon
pnt = QgsGeometry.fromPoint(QgsPoint(lon,lat))
```

11. Now that we have a new point, we check whether this is the first point and add the whole layer to the map, if it is. Otherwise, we edit the layer and add a new feature, as follows:

```
if firstPt:
    firstPt = False
    f = QgsFeature()
    f.setGeometry(pnt)
    vpr.addFeatures([f])
    qmr.addMapLayer(vectorLyr)
else:
    print lon, lat
    vectorLyr.startEditing()
    vectorLyr.changeGeometry(1,pnt)
    vectorLyr.commitChanges()
```

12. Finally, we refresh the map and watch the tracking point jump to a new location:

```
vectorLyr.setCacheImage(None)
vectorLyr.updateExtents()
vectorLyr.triggerRepaint()
time.sleep(2)
```

How it works...

A live GPS will move in a linear, incremental path across the map. In this recipe, we used randomly generated points that leap around the world, but the concept is the same. To connect a live GPS, you will need to use QGIS's GPS information GUI first to establish a connection or at least get the correct connection information and then use Python to automate things from there. Once you have the location information, you can easily manipulate the QGIS map using Python.

There's more...

The NMEA standard is old and widely used, but it is a poorly-designed protocol by modern standards. Nearly every smartphone has a GPS now; however, they do not use the NMEA protocol. There are, however, several apps available for nearly every smartphone platform which will output the phone's GPS as NMEA sentences, which can be used by QGIS. Later in this chapter, in the *Collecting field data* recipe, we'll demonstrate another method for tracking a cell phone, GPS, or even estimated locations for digital devices, which is much simpler and much more modern.

Creating a mapbook

A mapbook is an automatically generated document, which can also be called an **atlas**. A mapbook takes a dataset and breaks it down into smaller, detailed maps based on a coverage layer that zooms the larger map to each feature in the coverage in order to make a page of the mapbook. The coverage layer may or may not be the same as the map layer featured on each page of the mapbook. In this recipe, we'll create a mapbook that features all the countries in the world.

Getting ready

For this recipe, you need to download the world countries dataset and put it in a directory named shapes within your qgis_data directory from
https://github.com/GeospatialPython/Learn/raw/master/countries.zip.

Next, you'll need to install the PyPDF2 library. On Linux or OSX, just open a console and run the following command:

```
sudo easy_install PyPDF2
```

On Windows, open the **OSGeo4W** console from your start menu and run this:

```
easy_install PyPDF2
```

Finally, in your `qgis_data` directory, create a folder called `atlas` to store the mapbook's output.

How to do it...

We will build a QGIS composition and set it to atlas mode. Then, we'll add a composer map, where each country will be featured, and an overview map. Next, we'll run the atlas process to produce each page of the mapbook as separate PDF files. Finally, we'll combine the individual PDFs into a single PDF file. To do this, we need to perform the following steps:

1. First, import all the libraries that are needed:

   ```
   from PyQt4.QtCore import *
   from PyQt4.QtGui import *
   from qgis.core import *
   import PyPDF2
   import os
   ```

2. Next, create variables related to the output files, including the mapbook's name, the coverage layer, and the naming pattern for the individual PDF files:

   ```
   filenames = []
   mapbook = "/qgis_data/qgis_data/atlas/mapbook.pdf"
   coverage = "/qgis_data/qgis_data/shapes/countries.shp"
   atlasPattern = "/qgis_data/qgis_data/atlas/output_"
   ```

3. Now, add the coverage layer to the map using the following code:

   ```
   vlyr = QgsVectorLayer(coverage, "Countries", "ogr")
   QgsMapLayerRegistry.instance().addMapLayer(vlyr)
   ```

4. Next, establish the map renderer:

   ```
   mr = QgsMapRenderer()
   mr.setLayerSet([vlyr.id()])
   mr.setProjectionsEnabled(True)
   mr.setMapUnits(QGis.DecimalDegrees)
   crs = QgsCoordinateReferenceSystem()
   crs.createFromSrid(4326)
   mr.setDestinationCrs(crs)
   ```

5. Then, set up the composition:

```
c = QgsComposition(mr)
c.setPaperSize(297, 210)
```

6. Create a symbol for the coverage layer:

```
gray = {"color": "155,155,155"}
mapSym = QgsFillSymbolV2.createSimple(gray)
renderer = QgsSingleSymbolRendererV2(mapSym)
vlyr.setRendererV2(renderer)
```

7. Now, add the first composer map to the composition, as shown here:

```
atlasMap = QgsComposerMap(c, 20, 20, 130, 130)
atlasMap.setFrameEnabled(True)
c.addComposerMap(atlasMap)
```

8. Then, create the `atlas` framework:

```
atlas = c.atlasComposition()
atlas.setCoverageLayer(vlyr)
atlas.setHideCoverage(False)
atlas.setEnabled(True)
c.setAtlasMode(QgsComposition.ExportAtlas)
```

9. Next, establish the overview map:

```
ov = QgsComposerMap(c, 180, 20, 50, 50)
ov.setFrameEnabled(True)
ov.setOverviewFrameMap(atlasMap.id())
c.addComposerMap(ov)
rect = QgsRectangle(vlyr.extent())
ov.setNewExtent(rect)
```

10. Then, create the overview map symbol:

```
yellow = {"color": "255,255,0,255"}
ovSym = QgsFillSymbolV2.createSimple(yellow)
ov.setOverviewFrameMapSymbol(ovSym)
```

11. Next, you need to label each page with the name of the country, which is stored in the CNTRY_NAME field of the shapefile:

```
lbl = QgsComposerLabel(c)
c.addComposerLabel(lbl)
lbl.setText('[% "CNTRY_NAME" %]')
lbl.setFont(QgsFontUtils.getStandardTestFont())
lbl.adjustSizeToText()
lbl.setSceneRect(QRectF(150, 5, 60, 15))
```

12. Now, we'll tell the atlas to use automatic scaling for each country in order to best fit each map in the window:

```
atlasMap.setAtlasDriven(True)
atlasMap.setAtlasScalingMode(QgsComposerMap.Auto)
atlasMap.setAtlasMargin(0.10)
```

13. Now we tell the atlas to loop through all the features and create PDF maps, as follows:

```
atlas.setFilenamePattern("'%s' || $feature" % atlasPattern)
atlas.beginRender()
for i in range(0, atlas.numFeatures()):
    atlas.prepareForFeature(i)
    filename = atlas.currentFilename() + ".pdf"
    print "Writing file %s" % filename
    filenames.append(filename)
    c.exportAsPDF(filename)
atlas.endRender()
```

14. Finally, we will use the PyPDF2 library to combine the individual PDF files into a single PDF file, as shown here:

```
output = PyPDF2.PdfFileWriter()
for f in filenames:
    pdf = open(f, "rb")
    page = PyPDF2.PdfFileReader(pdf)
    output.addPage(page.getPage(0))
    os.remove(f)
print "Writing final mapbook..."
book = open(mapbook, "wb")
output.write(book)
with open(mapbook, 'wb') as book:
    output.write(book)
```

How it works...

You can customize the template that creates the individual pages as much as you want. The GUI atlas tool can export the atlas to a single file, but this functionality is not available in PyQGIS, so we use the pure Python PyPDF2 library. You can also create a template in the GUI, save it, and load it with Python; but it is often easier to make changes if you have the layout available in the code. You should also know that the PDF pages are just images. The maps are exported as rasters, so the mapbook will not be searchable and the file size can be large.

Finding the least cost path

Least cost path (LCP) analysis is the raster equivalent of network analysis, which is used to find the optimal path between two points in a raster. In this recipe, we'll perform LCP analysis on a **Digital Elevation Model (DEM)**.

Getting ready

You need to download the following DEM and extract the ZIP file to your `qgis_data/rasters` directory: `https://github.com/GeospatialPython/LeaYou`must also have a verison of QGIS which includes GRASS and SAGA. For more information, see the *Installing QGIS for development* recipe from `Chapter 1`, *Automating QGIS*.

How to do it...

We will load our DEM and two shapefiles consisting of start and end points. Then, we'll use GRASS through the Processing Toolbox to create a cumulative cost layer that assigns a cost to each cell in a raster based on its elevation, the value of the other cells around it, and its distance to and from the end points.

Then, we'll use a SAGA processing algorithm to find the least cost path between two points. Finally, we'll load the output onto the map. To do this, we need to perform the following steps:

1. First, we'll import the QGIS processing Python library:

   ```
   import processing
   ```

2. Now, we'll set the paths to the layers, as follows:

   ```
   path = "/qgis_data/rasters/lcp/"
   dem = path + "dem.asc"
   start = path + "start-point.shp"
   finish = path + "end-point.shp"
   ```

3. We need the DEM's extent as a string for the algorithms:

   ```
   demLyr = QgsRasterLayer(dem, "DEM")
   ext = demLyr.extent()
   xmin = ext.xMinimum()
   ymin = ext.yMinimum()
   xmax = ext.xMaximum()
   ymax = ext.xMaximum()
   box = "%s,%s,%s,%s".format(xmin,xmax,ymin,ymax)
   ```

4. Using the following code, we will establish the end points as layers:

   ```
   a = QgsVectorLayer(start, "Start", "ogr")
   b = QgsVectorLayer(finish, "End", "ogr")
   ```

5. Then, we'll create the cumulative cost raster, specifying the algorithm name, cost layer (DEM), start point layer, end point layer, speed or accuracy option, keep null values option, extent of interest, cell size (0 for default), and some additional defaults:

   ```
   cost = path + "cost.tif"
   tmpCost = processing.runalg("grass7:r.cost.points",dem,a,None,
                           False,False,box,0,-1,0.0001,cost)
   ```

6. We also need to combine the points into a single layer for the SAGA algorithm:

   ```
   merge = path + "merge.shp"
   tmpMerge = processing.runalg("qgis:mergevectorlayers","{};{}"
                           .format(start,finish),merge)
   ```

7. Next, we set up the inputs and outputs for the LCP algorithm:

```
vLyr = QgsVectorLayer(merge, "Destination Points", "ogr")
rLyr = QgsRasterLayer(cost, "Accumulated Cost")
line = path + "path.shp"
points = path + "profilePts.shp"
```

8. Then, we run the LCP analysis using the following code:

```
results = processing.runalg("saga:leastcostpaths",vLyr,rLyr,
                            dem,points,line)
```

9. Finally, we can load the path to view it:

```
lcp = QgsVectorLayer(line, "Least Cost Path", "ogr")
QgsMapLayerRegistry.instance().addMapLayers([vLyr, lcp,
                                            demLyr])
```

10. Verify your path looks similar to the following image:

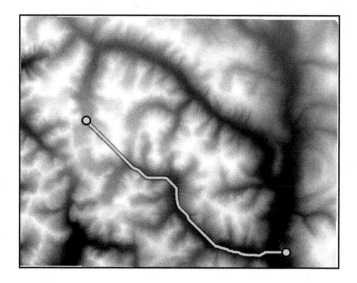

How it works...

GRASS has an LCP algorithm too, but the SAGA algorithm is easier to use. GRASS does a great job of creating the cost grid. Processing Toolbox algorithms allow you to create temporary files that are deleted when QGIS closes. So, we use temporary files for the intermediate products, including the cost grid and the merged shapefile. The preceding image shows the path through the DEM with darker portions of the image showing lower elevation and lighter areas higher elevation.

The algorithm uses a combination of distance and slope to calculate the cost of moving over the terrain. So we don't get the complete picture looking at the just elevation. If we look at the path over the cost grid, we can see the path moves through the lighter areas of least resistance and get a better idea of what QGIS and SAGA see when creating the path:

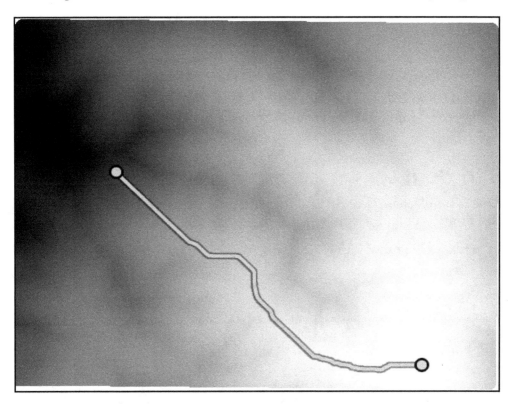

Performing nearest neighbor analysis

Nearest neighbor analysis relates one point to the nearest point in one or more datasets. In this recipe, we'll relate one set of points to the closest point from another dataset. In this case, we'll find the closest major city for each entry in a catalog of **unidentified flying object (UFO)** sightings from the National UFO reporting center. This analysis will tell you which major cities have the most UFO activity. The UFO catalog data just contains latitude and longitude points, so we'll use nearest neighbor analysis to assign names to places.

Getting ready

Download the following ZIP file and extract it to a directory named `ufo` in your `qgis_data` directory:

`https://github.com/GeospatialPython/Learn/raw/master/ufo.zip`

You will also need the mmqgis plugin:

1. From the QGIS **Plugins** menu, select **Manage and Install Plugins...**.
2. In the **Plugins** dialog search box, search for `mmqgis`.
3. Select the **mmqgis** plugin and click on the **Install plugin** button.

How to do it...

This recipe is simple; here, we will load the layers and run the nearest neighbor algorithm within the mmqgis plugin, as follows:

1. First, we'll import the `mmqgis` plugin:

   ```
   from mmqgis import mmqgis_library as mmqgis
   ```

2. Next, as shown here, we'll load all our datasets:

   ```
   srcPath = "/qgis_data/ufo/ufo-sightings.shp"
   dstPath = "/qgis_data/ufo/major-cities.shp"
   usPth = "/qgis_data/ufo/continental-us.shp"
   output = "/qgis_data/ufo/alien_invasion.shp"
   srcName = "UFO Sightings"
   dstName = "Major Cities"
   usName = "Continental US"
   source = QgsVector(srcPath, srcName, "ogr")
   dest = QgsVector(dstPath, dstName, "ogr")
   us = QgsVector(usPath, usName, "ogr")
   QgsMapLayerRegistry.instance().addMapLayers([source, dest, us])
   ```

3. Finally, we'll run and load the algorithm, which will draw lines from each UFO sighting point to the nearest city:

   ```
   mmqgis.mmqgis_hub_distance(iface, srcName, dstName, "NAME",
                              "Miles", True, output, False, True)
   ```

How it works...

There are a couple of different nearest neighbor algorithms in QGIS, but the MMQGIS version is an excellent implementation and has the best visualization. Like the other recipes in this chapter, the plugin doesn't have an intentional Python API, so a good way to explore its functionality is to use the GUI interface before taking a look at the Python code. The following image shows the output, with UFO sightings represented by smaller points and hub lines leading to the which are represented by larger, darker points.

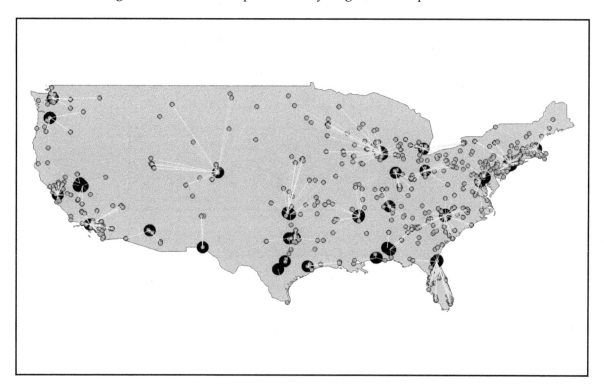

Creating a DEM from LIDAR

Recent versions of QGIS include the ability to integrate a package named LAStools, which processes **Light Detection and Ranging** (**LIDAR**) data. LIDAR data is stored as a point cloud in the LAS format which stores x, y, z laser returns; however, this format isn't good for most GIS map visualizations. In this recipe, we'll convert a LAS point cloud file to a **Digital Elevation Model** (**DEM**) in GeoTIFF format used in other examples throughout this book. The DEM can then be used as a raster layer in QGIS.

Getting ready

If your QGIS installation isn't already configured for LAStools, you'll need to do so. You can find instructions for Windows in the official QGIS documentation here:

`https://docs.qgis.org/testing/en/docs/training_manual/forestry/basic_lidar.html`

For OSX, you must use Wine. Instructions for configuring LAStools and Wine for OSX can be found here:

`https://rapidlasso.com/2014/10/04/using-lastools-on-mac-os-x-with-wine/`

Once you have LAStools configured in OSX and it is working on the command line, the instructions for QGIS are the same except you also add the path to Wine. The following screenshot shows the correct settings on an OSX QGIS installation; however, the prefix for the path to LAStools and Wine may vary slightly on your system:

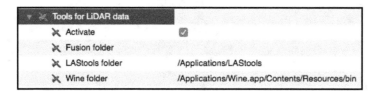

When LAStools is configured correctly, you should see over 70 algorithms in the Processing Toolbox under the **Tools for LiDAR data** menu. If you see less than 70, try restarting QGIS.

For other versions of Linux, instructions for compiling LAStools from source can be found here:

`http://blog.samuelphillips.net/2015/05/compiling-laszip-on-linux.html`

Next you'll need to download our sample zipped LAS file from the following URL:

```
https://github.com/GeospatialPython/Learn/raw/master/lidar.zip
```

Extract the LAS file into a directory named `rasters` into your `qgis_data` directory.

The following screenshot shows what the point cloud in the LAS file looks like rotated at an oblique angle before we convert it to a continuous raster as a DEM:

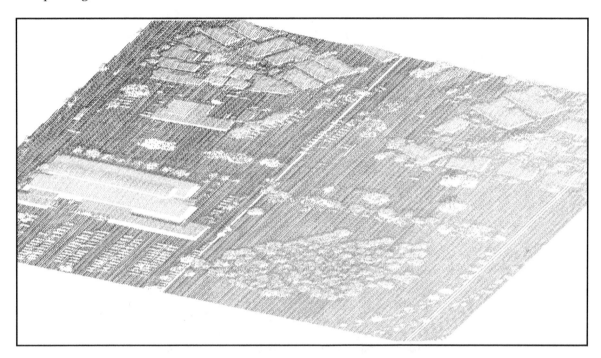

How to do it...

To convert the LAS file to a DEM, we'll run it through the LAStools las2dem algorithm and output it to a GeoTIFF. Then we will load the DEM into QGIS as a raster layer.

1. First we import the processing module:

    ```
    import processing
    ```

2. Next we'll create a variable with the path to the LAS file:

    ```
    lidar = "/qgis_data/rasters/lidar.las"
    ```

3. We'll also need a variable with our output path and file name in the same directory:

```
output = "/qgis_data/rasters/lidar.tif"
```

4. Now we can run the las2dem processing algorithm specifying the input and output parameters:

```
processing.runalg("lidartools:las2dem",False,False,lidar,
                  0,1,0,0,False,"",output)
```

5. Then we can load the layer as a raster layer:

```
lyr = QgsRasterLayer(output, "DEM")
```

6. Finally, we can load the raster DEM onto the map:

```
QgsMapLayerRegistry.instance().addMapLayer(lyr)
```

7. Verify that your DEM looks similar to the following image:

How it works...

A raster is a seamless dataset with pixels on an *x, y* grid while the LAS file has *x, y, z* laser returns which are not evenly spaced. LAStools must do some interpolation in order to convert the erratic LIDAR data into a DEM. While it is often useful to convert a LAS to a DEM for mapping and analysis, different information can be gleaned from each format. They are not equivalent. There are many uses for LIDAR independent of elevation analysis and all of them are accessible through Python via LAStools.

Creating a heat map

A **heat map** is used to show the geographic clustering of data using a raster image that shows density. The clustering can also be weighed using a field in the data to not only show geographic density but also an intensity factor. In this recipe, we'll use earthquake point data to create a heat map of the impact of an earthquake and weigh the clustering by the earthquake's magnitude.

Getting ready

This recipe requires no preparation; however, make sure your installation of QGIS includes SAGA. For more information, see the *Installing QGIS for development* recipe from Chapter 1, *Automating QGIS*.

How to do it...

We will build a map with a worldwide base layer of countries and earthquake locations, both in GeoJSON. Next, we'll run the SAGA kernel density estimation algorithm to produce the heat map image. We'll create a layer from the output, add a color shader to it, and add it to the map. To do this, we need to perform the following steps:

1. First, we'll import the Python libraries that we'll need in the Python console:

```
from PyQt4.QtCore import *
from PyQt4.QtGui import *
import processing
```

2. Next, using the following code, we'll define our map layers and the output raster name:

```
countries = "https://raw.githubusercontent.com/johan/
            world.geo.json/"
countries += "master/countries.geo.json"
quakes = "https://github.com/GeospatialPython/Learn/"
quakes += "raw/master/quakes2014.geojson"
output = "/qgis_data/qgis_data/rasters/heat.tif"
output = "/qgis_data/rasters/heat.tif"
```

3. Now we'll add the layers to the map:

```
basemap = QgsVectorLayer(countries, "World", "ogr")
quakeLyr = QgsVectorLayer(quakes, "2014 Earthquakes", "ogr")
QgsMapLayerRegistry.instance().addMapLayers([quakeLyr,
                                             basemap])
```

4. We need to get the extent of the earthquake layer for the Processing Toolbox algorithm to use:

```
ext = quakeLyr.extent()
xmin = ext.xMinimum()
ymin = ext.yMinimum()
xmax = ext.xMaximum()
ymax = ext.xMaximum()
box = "%s,%s,%s,%s".format(xmin,xmax,ymin,ymax)
```

5. Now, we can run the kernel density estimation algorithm by specifying the `mag` or magnitude field as our weighting factor:

```
processing.runalg("saga:kerneldensityestimation",quakeLyr,
              "mag",10,1,box,1,0,output)
```

6. Next, we load the output as a layer:

```
heat = QgsRasterLayer(output, "Earthquake Heatmap")
```

7. Then, we create the color ramp shader and apply it to the layer:

```
algorithm = QgsContrastEnhancement.StretchToMinimumMaximum
limits = QgsRaster.ContrastEnhancementMinMax
heat.setContrastEnhancement(algorithm, limits)
s = QgsRasterShader()
c = QgsColorRampShader()
c.setColorRampType(QgsColorRampShader.INTERPOLATED)
i = []
```

```
qri = QgsColorRampShader.ColorRampItem
i.append(qri(0, QColor(255,255,178,255),
            'Lowest Earthquake Impact'))
i.append(qri(0.106023, QColor(254,204,92,255),
            'Lower Earthquake Impact'))
i.append(qri(0.212045, QColor(253,141,60,255),
            'Moderate Earthquake Impact'))
i.append(qri(0.318068, QColor(240,59,32,255),
            'Higher Earthquake Impact'))
i.append(qri(0.42409, QColor(189,0,38,255),
            'Highest Earthquake Impact'))
c.setColorRampItemList(i)
s.setRasterShaderFunction(c)
ps = QgsSingleBandPseudoColorRenderer(heat.dataProvider(),
                                      1, s)
heat.setRenderer(ps)
```

8. Finally, we add the `Heatmap` to our map:

```
QgsMapLayerRegistry.instance().addMapLayers([heat])
```

How it works...

The kernel density estimation algorithm looks at the point dataset and forms clusters. The higher the value, the denser is the cluster. The algorithm then increases values based on the weighting factor, which is the earthquake's magnitude. The output image is, of course, a grayscale GeoTIFF, but we use the color ramp shader to make the visualization easier to understand. The following screenshot shows the expected output:

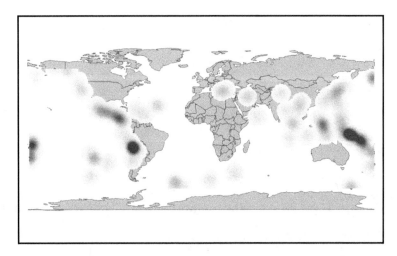

Creating a dot density map

A dot density map uses point density to illustrate a field value within a polygon. We'll use this technique to illustrate population density in some US census bureau tracts.

Getting ready

You will need to download the census tract layer and extract it to a directory named census in your qgis_data directory from
https://github.com/GeospatialPython/Learn/raw/master/GIS_CensusTract.zip.

How to do it...

We will load the census layer, create a memory layer, loop through the features in the census layer, calculate a random point within the feature for every 100 people, and finally add the point to the memory layer. To do this, we need to perform the following steps:

1. In the QGIS Python console, we'll import the random module:

   ```
   import random
   ```

2. Next, we'll load the census layer:

   ```
   src = "/qgis_data/qgis_data/census/GIS_CensusTract_poly.shp"
   tractLyr = QgsVectorLayer(src, "Census Tracts", "ogr")
   ```

3. Then, we'll create our memory layer:

   ```
   popLyr =  QgsVectorLayer('Point?crs=epsg:4326', "Population" ,
                            "memory")
   ```

4. We need the index for the population value:

   ```
   i = tractLyr.fieldNameIndex('POPULAT11')
   ```

5. Now, we get our census layer's features as an iterator:

   ```
   features = tractLyr.getFeatures()
   ```

6. We need a data provider for the memory layer so that we can edit it:

   ```
   vpr = popLyr.dataProvider()
   ```

7. We'll create a list to store our random points:

```
dotFeatures = []
```

8. Then, we can loop through the features and calculate the density points:

```
for feature in features:
    pop = feature.attributes()[i]
    density = pop / 100
    found = 0
    dots = []
    g = feature.geometry()
    minx =  g.boundingBox().xMinimum()
    miny =  g.boundingBox().yMinimum()
    maxx =  g.boundingBox().xMaximum()
    maxy =  g.boundingBox().yMaximum()
    while found < density:
        x = random.uniform(minx,maxx)
        y = random.uniform(miny,maxy)
        pnt = QgsPoint(x,y)
        if g.contains(pnt):
            dots.append(pnt)
            found += 1
        geom = QgsGeometry.fromMultiPoint(dots)
        f = QgsFeature()
        f.setGeometry(geom)
        dotFeatures.append(f)
```

9. Now, we can add our features to the memory layer using the following code and add them to the map in order to see the result:

```
vpr.addFeatures(dotFeatures)
popLyr.updateExtents()
QgsMapLayerRegistry.instance().addMapLayers([popLyr,tractLyr])
```

How it works...

This approach is slightly inefficient; it uses a brute-force approach that can place randomly generated points outside irregular polygons. We use the feature's extents to contain the random points as close as possible and then use the geometry objects `contains()` method to verify that the point is inside the polygon. The following screenshot shows a sample of the output:

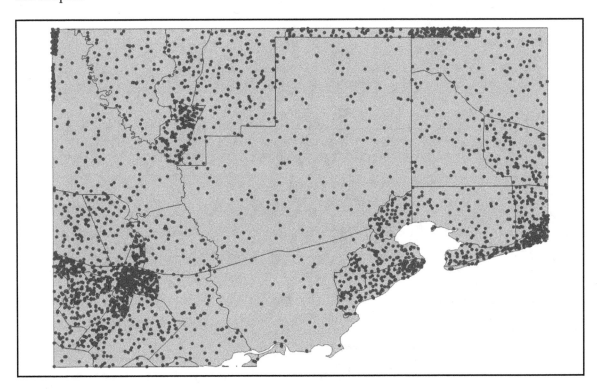

Collecting field data

For decades, collecting field observation data from the field into a GIS required hours of manual data entry or, at best, loading data after a trip. Smartphones and laptops with cellular connections have revolutionized this process. In this recipe, we'll use a simple but interesting GeoJSON-based framework to enter information and a map location from any Internet-connected device with a web browser to update a map in QGIS. Note that this example will post the location of the device you are using to a publicly visible website. The information is anonymous but it is visible to anyone.

Getting ready

There is no preparation required for this recipe.

How to do it...

We will load a world boundaries layer and the field data layer onto a QGIS map. Go to the field data mobile website and create an entry, and then refresh the QGIS map to see the update. To do this, we need to perform the following steps:

1. In the QGIS Python console, add the following GeoJSON layers:

```
wb = "https://raw.githubusercontent.com/johan/world.geo.json/
        master/countries.geo.json"
basemap = QgsVectorLayer(wb, "Countries", "ogr")
observations = QgsVectorLayer("http://bit.ly/QGISFieldApp",
                             "Field Observations", "ogr")
QgsMapLayerRegistry.instance().addMapLayers([observations,
                                            basemap])
```

2. Now, in a browser on your computer or preferably on a mobile device with a data connection, go to
   `http://geospatialpython.github.io/qgis/fieldwork.html`. The application will ask you for permission to use your location, which you should temporarily allow for the program to work.
3. Enter information in the form and click on the **Send** button.
4. Verify that you can see the GeoJSON data, including your submission, at
   `https://api.myjson.com/bins/3ztvz`.
5. Finally, update the map in QGIS by zooming or panning and locate your record.

How it works...

The simple mobile-friendly web page uses the `Leaflet.js` library for mapping and HTML5 for the form submission. The data is stored as a snippet on the `MyJSON.com` service. This approach serves our examples and demonstrates the client-server model. However, it is not very robust because users working concurrently can easily overwrite each other's data. So, if you don't see your update, try it again once or twice and it will probably work. Sample observations are reset from time to time in order to keep the site lightweight. Note that it's important to refresh the map either manually or programmatically to force QGIS to refresh the network link. You can get the source code for the mobile page on GitHub (`https://github.com/GeospatialPython/qgis`).

The following image shows the mobile field application on an iPhone:

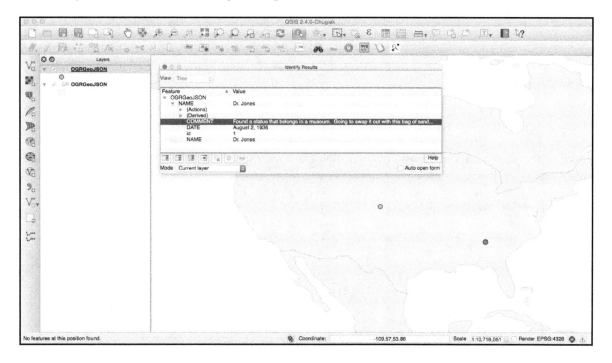

Computing road slope using elevation data

A common geospatial workflow is to assign raster values to a coincident vector layer so that you can style or perform further analysis on the vector layer. This recipe will use this concept to illustrate the steepness of a road using color by mapping values to the road vector from a slope raster.

Getting ready

You will need to download a zipped directory from
`https://github.com/GeospatialPython/Learn/raw/master/road.zip` and place the directory, named `road`, in your `qgis_data` directory.

You must also have a verison of QGIS which includes GRASS and SAGA. For more information, see the *Installing QGIS for development* recipe from `Chapter 1`, *Automating QGIS,*

How to do it...

We'll start with a DEM and compute its slope. Then, we'll load a road vector layer and break it into interval lengths of 500 meters. Next, we'll load the layer and style it using green, yellow, and red values for each segment to show the range of steepness. We'll overlay this layer on a hillshade of the DEM for a nice visualization. To do this, we need to perform the following steps:

1. First, we need to import the libraries we'll need:

   ```
   from PyQt4.QtCore import *
   from PyQt4.QtGui import *
   import processing
   ```

2. Next we need to set up all of the path strings for our inputs and outputs:

   ```
   dem = "/qgis_data/road/dem.asc"
   road = "/qgis_data/road/road.shp"
   slope = "/qgis_data/road/slope.tif"
   segRoad = "/qgis_data/road/segRoad.shp"
   steepness = "/qgis_data/road/steepness.shp"
   hillshade = "/qgis_data/road/hillshade.tif"
   ```

3. Now we can load our layers:

   ```
   demLyr = QgsRasterLayer(dem, "DEM")
   roadLyr = QgsVectorLayer(road, "Road", "ogr")
   ```

4. Then we need the bounding box of our DEM for the processing algorithms:

   ```
   ext = demLyr.extent()
   xmin = ext.xMinimum()
   ymin = ext.yMinimum()
   xmax = ext.xMaximum()
   ymax = ext.yMaximum()
   demBox = "{},{},{},{}".format(xmin,xmax,ymin,ymax)
   ```

5. Now we can calculate the slope grid:

   ```
   processing.runalg("grass7:r.slope",dem,0,False,1,0,demBox,0,slope)
   ```

6. Now we need the bounding box of the road layer:

```
ext = roadLyr.extent()
xmin = ext.xMinimum()
ymin = ext.yMinimum()
xmax = ext.xMaximum()
ymax = ext.yMaximum()
roadBox = "{},{},{},{}".format(xmin,xmax,ymin,ymax)
```

7. Now we can split the road into segments:

```
processing.runalg("grass7:v.split.length",road,500,roadBox,
                  -1,0.0001,0,segRoad)
```

8. Now we can add load the other layers we'll need for processing:

```
slopeLyr = QgsRasterLayer(slope, "Slope")
segRoadLyr = QgsVectorLayer(segRoad, "Segmented Road", "ogr")
QgsMapLayerRegistry.instance().addMapLayers([segRoadLyr,
                                             slopeLyr], False)
```

9. Then, we can add the steepness values to the road layer:

```
processing.runalg("saga:addgridvaluestoshapes",
                  segRoad,slope,0,steepness)
```

10. And then, load the gradient as a layer:

```
steepLyr = QgsVectorLayer(steepness, "Road Gradient", "ogr")
```

11. Then, we can set up the color coding for the segments:

```
roadGrade = (("Rolling Hill", 0.0, 20.0, "green"),
             ("Steep", 20.0, 40.0, "yellow"),
             ("Very Steep", 40.0, 90.0, "red"))
```

12. Now we can build the symbols for the road:

```
ranges = []
for label, lower, upper, color in roadGrade:
    sym = QgsSymbolV2.defaultSymbol(steepLyr.geometryType())
    sym.setColor(QColor(color))
    sym.setWidth(3.0)
    rng = QgsRendererRangeV2(lower, upper, sym, label)
    ranges.append(rng)
```

13. Then, we can use the symbols to create a graduated renderer:

```
field = "slopetif"
renderer = QgsGraduatedSymbolRendererV2(field, ranges)
steepLyr.setRendererV2(renderer)
```

14. Now we'll build a hillshade from the DEM as a backdrop:

```
processing.runalg("saga:analyticalhillshading",dem,0,
                158,45,4,hillshade)
```

15. Now we can add the layers to the map:

```
hs = QgsRasterLayer(hillshade, "Terrain")
QgsMapLayerRegistry.instance().addMapLayers([steepLyr, hs])
```

How it works...

For each of our 500 meter line segments, the algorithm averages the underlying slope values. This workflow is fairly simple and also provides all the building blocks you need for a more complex version. While performing calculations that involve measurements over a relatively small area, using projected data is the best option. The following image shows how the output looks:

Geolocating photos on the map

Photos taken with GPS-enabled cameras, including smartphones, store location information in the header of the file, in a format called **EXIF tags**. These tags are largely based on the same header tags used by the TIFF image standard. In this recipe, we'll use these tags to create locations on a map for some photos and provide links to open them.

Getting ready

You will need to download some sample geotagged photos from `https://github.com/GeospatialPython/qgis/blob/gh-pages/photos.zip?raw=true` and place them in a directory named `photos` in your `qgis_data` directory.

How to do it...

QGIS requires the **Python Imaging Library** (**PIL**), which should already be installed with your installation. PIL can parse EXIF tags. We will gather the filenames of the photos, parse the location information, convert it to decimal degrees, create the point vector layer, add the photo locations, and add an action link to the attributes. To do this, we need to perform the following steps:

1. In the QGIS Python console, import the libraries that we'll need, including k, for parsing image data and the `glob` module, for doing wildcard file searches:

```
import glob
import Image
from ExifTags import TAGS
```

2. Next, we'll create a function that can parse the header data:

```
def exif(img):
    exif_data = {}
    try:
        i = Image.open(img)
        tags = i._getexif()
        for tag, value in tags.items():
            decoded = TAGS.get(tag, tag)
            exif_data[decoded] = value
    except:
        pass
    return exif_data
```

3. Now, we'll create a function that can convert degrees-minute-seconds to decimal degrees, which is how coordinates are stored in JPEG images:

```
def dms2dd(d, m, s, i):
    sec = float((m * 60) + s)
    dec = float(sec / 3600)
    deg = float(d + dec)
    if i.upper() == 'W':
        deg = deg * -1
    elif i.upper() == 'S':
        deg = deg * -1
    return float(deg)
```

4. Next, we'll define a function to parse the location data from the header data:

```
def gps(exif):
    lat = None
    lon = None
    if exif['GPSInfo']:
        # Lat
        coords = exif['GPSInfo']
        i = coords[1]
        d = coords[2][0][0]
        m = coords[2][1][0]
        s = coords[2][2][0]
        lat = dms2dd(d, m ,s, i)
        # Lon
        i = coords[3]
        d = coords[4][0][0]
        m = coords[4][1][0]
        s = coords[4][2][0]
        lon = dms2dd(d, m ,s, i)
    return lat, lon
```

5. Next, we'll loop through the photos directory, get the filenames, parse the location information, and build a simple dictionary to store the information, as follows:

```
photos = {}
photo_dir = "/qgis_data/qgis_data/photos/"
files = glob.glob(photo_dir + "*.jpg")
for f in files:
    e = exif(f)
    lat, lon = gps(e)
    photos[f] = [lon, lat]
```

6. Now, we'll set up the vector layer for editing:

```
lyr_info = "Point?crs=epsg:4326&field=photo:string(75)"
vectorLyr =  QgsVectorLayer(lyr_info, "Geotagged Photos",
                            "memory")
vpr = vectorLyr.dataProvider()
```

7. We'll add the photo details to the vector layer:

```
features = []
for pth, p in photos.items():
    lon, lat = p
    pnt = QgsGeometry.fromPoint(QgsPoint(lon,lat))
    f = QgsFeature()
    f.setGeometry(pnt)
    f.setAttributes([pth])
    features.append(f)
vpr.addFeatures(features)
vectorLyr.updateExtents()
```

8. Now, we can add the layer to the map and make the active layer:

```
QgsMapLayerRegistry.instance().addMapLayer(vectorLyr)
iface.setActiveLayer(vectorLyr)
activeLyr = iface.activeLayer()
```

9. Finally, we'll add an action that allows you to click on it and open the photo:

```
actions = activeLyr.actions()
actions.addAction(QgsAction.OpenUrl, "Photos", '[% "photo"%]')
```

How it works...

Using the included PIL EXIF parser, getting location information and adding it to a vector layer is relatively straightforward. The interesting part of this recipe is the QGIS action to open the photo. This action is a default option for opening a URL. However, you can also use Python expressions as actions to perform a variety of tasks.

The following screenshot shows an example of the data visualization and photo popup:

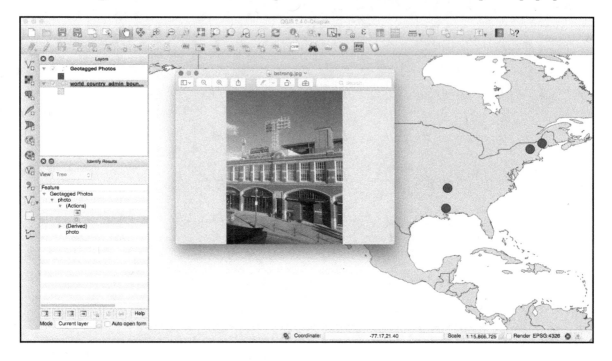

There's more...

Another plugin called Photo2Shape is available, but it requires you to install an external EXIF tag parser called **exifread**, which you can find on the Python Package Index:

`https://pypi.python.org/pypi/ExifRead`

You could also accomplish this same task using QGIS map tips as we do in the *Creating HTML labels in QGIS* recipe from `Chapter 9`, *Other Tips and Tricks*.

Image change detection

Change detection allows you to automatically highlight the differences between two images in the same area if they are properly orthorectified. In this recipe, we'll do a simple difference change detection on two images, which are several years apart, to see the differences in urban development and the natural environment.

Getting ready

You can download the two images for this recipe from
`https://github.com/GeospatialPython/qgis/blob/gh-pages/change-detection.zip?raw`
`=true` and put them in a directory named `change-detection` in the `rasters` directory of
your `qgis_data` directory. Note that the file is 55 megabytes, so it may take several
minutes to download.

How to do it...

We'll use the QGIS raster calculator to subtract the images in order to get the difference,
which will highlight significant changes. We'll also add a color ramp shader to the output in
order to visualize the changes. To do this, we need to perform the following steps:

1. First, we need to import the libraries that we need in the QGIS console:

   ```
   from PyQt4.QtGui import *
   from PyQt4.QtCore import *
   from qgis.analysis import *
   ```

2. Now, we'll set up the path names and `raster` names for our images:

   ```
   before = "/qgis_data/qgis_data/rasters/
            change-detection/before.tif"
   after = "/qgis_data/qgis_data/rasters/
            change-detection/after.tif"
   beforeName = "Before"
   afterName = "After"
   ```

3. Next, we'll establish our images as raster layers:

   ```
   beforeRaster = QgsRasterLayer(before, beforeName)
   afterRaster = QgsRasterLayer(after, afterName)
   ```

4. Then, we can build the calculator entries:

   ```
   beforeEntry = QgsRasterCalculatorEntry()
   afterEntry = QgsRasterCalculatorEntry()
   beforeEntry.raster = beforeRaster
   afterEntry.raster = afterRaster
   beforeEntry.bandNumber = 1
   afterEntry.bandNumber = 2
   beforeEntry.ref = beforeName + "@1"
   afterEntry.ref = afterName + "@2"
   entries = [afterEntry, beforeEntry]
   ```

5. Now, we'll set up the simple expression that does the math for remote sensing:

```
exp = "%s - %s" % (afterEntry.ref, beforeEntry.ref)
```

6. Then, we can set up the output file path, the raster extent, and pixel width and height:

```
output = "/qgis_data/qgis_data/rasters/
            change-detection/change.tif"
e = beforeRaster.extent()
w = beforeRaster.width()
h = beforeRaster.height()
```

7. Now, we perform the calculation:

```
change = QgsRasterCalculator(exp, output, "GTiff", e, w,
                                h, entries)
change.processCalculation()
```

8. Finally, we'll load the output as a layer, create the color ramp shader, apply it to the layer, and add it to the map, as shown here:

```
lyr = QgsRasterLayer(output, "Change")
algorithm = QgsContrastEnhancement.StretchToMinimumMaximum
limits = QgsRaster.ContrastEnhancementMinMax
lyr.setContrastEnhancement(algorithm, limits)
s = QgsRasterShader()
c = QgsColorRampShader()
c.setColorRampType(QgsColorRampShader.INTERPOLATED)
i = []
qri = QgsColorRampShader.ColorRampItem
i.append(qri(0, QColor(0,0,0,0), 'NODATA'))
i.append(qri(-101, QColor(123,50,148,255),
            'Significant Itensity Decrease'))
i.append(qri(-42.2395, QColor(194,165,207,255),
            'Minor Itensity Decrease'))
i.append(qri(16.649, QColor(247,247,247,0), 'No Change'))
i.append(qri(75.5375, QColor(166,219,160,255),
            'Minor Itensity Increase'))
i.append(qri(135, QColor(0,136,55,255),
            'Significant Itensity Increase'))
c.setColorRampItemList(i)
s.setRasterShaderFunction(c)
ps = QgsSingleBandPseudoColorRenderer(lyr.dataProvider(),
                                1, s)
lyr.setRenderer(ps)
QgsMapLayerRegistry.instance().addMapLayer(lyr)
```

How it works...

The concept is simple. We subtract the older image data from the new image data. Concentrating in urban areas tends to be highly reflective and results in higher image pixel values. If a building is added in the new image, it will be brighter than its surroundings. If a building is removed, the new image will be darker in that area. The same holds true for vegetation, to some extent.

Adjusting imprecise building footprints

Digitizing vector data from raster data is a tedious process. A common task in digitizing is to outline buildings in an image to make footprints for urban analysis. While most buildings are rectangular in shape, building footprints often end up with incongruent angles due to analysts quickly clicking points. In this recipe we'll automatically transform some non-rectangular polygons into rectangles using a simple algorithm developed by José Guerrero, which can be found at the following URL:

```
http://gis.stackexchange.com/questions/212003/how-to-modify-a-polygon-to-be-mor
e-rectangular/212325#212325
```

Getting ready

You need to download the following zipped shapefile into a directory named `shapes` in your `qgis_data` directory:

```
https://github.com/GeospatialPython/Learn/raw/master/irregular.zip
```

How to do it...

First we'll set up some reusable functions for geometry calculations. Then we'll load our footprints layer and create a memory layer for corrected footprints. Then we loop through each feature calculating the rectangles. During this loop we add the rectangles to the new layer. And finally we add the memory layer with the rectangles to the map.

1. First we create a function to calculate line slope:

```
def slope(x1, y1, x2, y2):
    return (y2 - y1) / (x2 - x1)
```

2. Next we create a function to create line intercepts:

```
def intercept(y, slope, x):
    return y - slope * x
```

3. Then we create a function to figure out the line perpendicular to another line:

```
def perpindicular(slope):
    return -1 / slope
```

4. Now we set up the path to our footprints layer in a variable:

```
pth = "/qgis_data/shapes/irregular.shp"
```

5. Next we load the layer:

```
lyr = QgsVectorLayer(pth, "Footprints", "ogr")
```

6. We need to get the CRS of the layer to make our memory layer the same:

```
epsg = lyr.crs().postgisSrid()
```

7. Now we can create the URI for the memory layer inserting the CRS:

```
uri = "Polygon?crs=epsg:{}&field=id:integer&index=yes"
        .format(epsg)
```

8. Then we create the memory layer:

```
rectangle = QgsVectorLayer(uri, 'Rectangles', 'memory')
```

9. Next we get the memory layer's data provider in order to edit it:

```
p = rectangle.dataProvider()
```

10. Now we loop through each feature and get the points:

```
for f in lyr.getFeatures():
    g = f.geometry()
    xmin, ymin, xmax, ymax = g.boundingBox().toRectF()
                                .getCoords()
    pts = f.geometry().asPolygon()[0]
```

11. Now we locate the top right point of the polygon:

```
for i in range(len(pts)-1):
    if pts[i][1] == ymax and pts[i+1][1] < pts[i][1]:
        idx = i
    if pts[i][1] == ymax and pts[i-1][1] < pts[i][1]:
        idx = i-1
```

12. Then we add the top two corner points of the polygon to the memory layer:

```
r = []
x1 = pts[idx][0]
y1 = pts[idx][1]
r.append(QgsPoint(x1,y1))
x2 = pts[idx+1][0]
y2 = pts[idx+1][1]
r.append(QgsPoint(x2,y2))
```

13. Now we get the slope of the first side that will drive the angles of the other sides:

```
s1 = slope(x1, y1, x2, y2)
```

14. Then we get the intercept of that line:

```
i1 = intercept(y1, s1, x1)
```

15. Now we can move around the polygon and calculate the other sides:

```
x3 = pts[idx+2][0]
y3 = pts[idx+2][1]
i2 = intercept(y3, s1, x3)
s3 = perpindicular(s1)
i3 = intercept(y2, s3, x2)
x4 = (i3 - i2)/(s1 - s3)y4 = s3 * x4 + i3
r.append(QgsPoint(x4, y4))
s4 = perpindicular(s1)
i4 = intercept(y1, s4, x1)
x5 = (i4 - i2)/(s1 - s4)
y5 = s4 * x5 + i4
r.extend([QgsPoint(x5, y5),QgsPoint(x1, y1)])
poly = []
poly.append(r)
g = QgsGeometry.fromPolygon(poly)
ft = QgsFeature()
ft.setAttributes([i])
ft.setGeometry(g)
p.addFeatures([ft])
```

16. And finally we can add the memory layer to the map:

```
QgsMapLayerRegistry.instance().addMapLayers([rectangle, lyr])
```

How it works...

The following image shows the adjusted rectangles as dotted lines with the original polygons as gray-filled polygons:

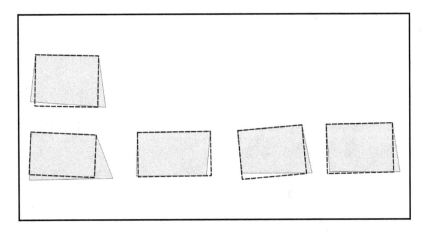

The algorithm looks at the top line and the minimum y value to build the rectangle. Because all buildings aren't prefect rectangles, this solution isn't perfect. But in most cases it will will get you much closer to reality than first-draft hand editing and you can edit further from there with less effort.

Visualizing multitemporal data

The vast majority of GIS maps are a static slice in time or summary totals of a period of time. But there are many geospatial formats capable of storing time series data. In this recipe, we'll load a dataset that has multiple time steps, and use the well-designed **TimeManager** plugin to step through the data time steps in an animation. The dataset we're using is a collection of global earthquake data from 2011 totaled by month. You can see an animation of the output of this recipe online at the following URL. The data loops through each month and renders the earthquake location and magnitude here:

```
http://geospatialpython.github.io/qgis/earthquake_loop.gif
```

Getting ready

You will need to install the QGIS Python TimeManager plugin by Anita Graser and Karolina Alexioufor this exercise. From the QGIS **Plugins** menu, select **Manage and Install Plugins...**. In the **Plugins** dialog search box, search for `TimeManager`. Select **TimeManager** plugin and click on the **Install plugin** button.

How to do it...

We will load our basemap layer, style it, then load our earthquake layer and style it. We're going to use GeoJSON files loaded from the web as our layers so you don't have to download any data. Once our map is configured, we'll set up the TimeManager plugin and start the animation.

1. First we load the `QtGui` library and import the TimeManager as a plugin:

```
from PyQt4.QtGui import *
from timemanager import *
```

2. Since we'll have a global basemap, we'll color the map background a blue color to symbolize water:

```
iface.mapCanvas().setCanvasColor(QColor(196,229,248))
iface.mapCanvas().refresh()
```

3. Now we'll set up the URL for our basemap country boundary GeoJSON layer:

```
countries = "https://raw.githubusercontent.com/"
countries += "johan/world.geo.json/master/countries.geo.json"
```

4. Next we'll set up the GeoJSON URL for our earthquakes layer:

```
quakes = "https://raw.githubusercontent.com/
         GeospatialPython/Learn/"
quakes += "master/2011_Earthquakes.geojson"
```

5. Now we can load our basemap layer:

```
basemap = QgsVectorLayer(countries, "World", "ogr")
```

6. Then we can color the countries layer a light gray color:

```
gray = {"color": "220,221,222"}
mapSym = QgsFillSymbolV2.createSimple(gray)
renderer = QgsSingleSymbolRendererV2(mapSym)
basemap.setRendererV2(renderer)
```

7. Next we add our earthquakes layer:

```
quakeLyr = QgsVectorLayer(quakes, "2011 Earthquakes", "ogr")
```

8. Since there are multiple overlapping points, we'll make the layer slightly transparent:

```
quakeLyr.setLayerTransparency(30)
```

9. Now we'll set up the properties for a graduated symbol renderer for the earthquake points. We'll have a color ramp from yellow to orange to red for smaller to larger magnitude. We'll also make the earthquake circles bigger depending on their severity:

```
magnitude = (("Light", 4.5, 4.7, "253,255,22", "2"),
             ("Moderate", 4.7, 5.0, "253,190,22", "5"),
             ("Strong", 5.0, 5.4, "253,122,22", "7.5"),
             ("Major", 5.4, 6.2, "253,99,22", "9.75"),
             ("Great", 6.2, 7.2, "253,0,22", "12"))
```

10. Now we'll set up the symbols for the earthquakes:

```
ranges = []
for label, lower, upper, color, size in magnitude:
    props = {}
    props["color"] = color
    props["size"] = size
    props["outline_width"] = "0"
    props["outline_color"] ="0,0,0,0"
    sym = QgsMarkerSymbolV2.createSimple(props)
    rng = QgsRendererRangeV2(lower, upper, sym, label)
    ranges.append(rng)
```

11. Then we can add the renderer to the layer:

```
field = "Magnitude"
renderer = QgsGraduatedSymbolRendererV2(field, ranges)
quakeLyr.setRendererV2(renderer)
```

12. We are ready to add the layers to the map and complete our map configuration:

```
QgsMapLayerRegistry.instance().addMapLayers([quakeLyr,
                                             basemap])
```

13. Now we set up the time manager specifying the field with the timestamp:

```
settings = layer_settings.LayerSettings()
settings.layer = quakeLyr
settings.startTimeAttribute = "Date"
settings.endTimeAttribute = "Date"
timeLayer = timevectorlayer.TimeVectorLayer(settings,
                                            iface=iface)
```

14. Now we need not get the plugin controller accounting for a slight difference on OSX:

```
try:
    ctrl = qgis.utils.plugins['timemanager'].getController()
except:
    # MacOS needs the capitalized name
    ctrl = qgis.utils.plugins['TimeManager'].getController()
```

15. Then we get the time layer manager from the controller:

```
tlm = ctrl.getTimeLayerManager()
```

16. Now we register the multi-temporal layer and specify the time step as months:

```
tlm.registerTimeLayer(timeLayer)
tlm.setTimeFrameType('months')
```

17. We tell the manager we want the animation to loop:

```
ctrl.setLoopAnimation(True)
```

18. Now we get the min and max time values:

```
start = time_util.str_to_datetime(timeLayer.getMinMaxValues()
                                  [0])
end = time_util.str_to_datetime(timeLayer.getMinMaxValues()[1])
```

19. We must set the start time and of course we'll use the very beginning:

```
tlm.setCurrentTimePosition(start)
```

20. We'll set the frame length of each frame to `1000` milliseconds or `1` second so it's on screen long enough to get an idea of the data:

    ```
    ctrl.setAnimationFrameLength(1000)
    ```

21. Now we can start the animation. Note that the same command will also stop it:

    ```
    ctrl.toggleAnimation()
    ```

How it works...

This plugin is very powerful. It can handle a variety of vector and raster data as well as timestamp formats. The following image shows the first frame of the animation:

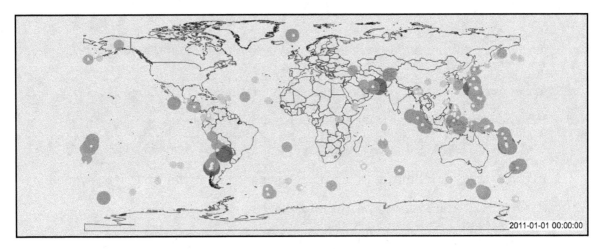

The time step appears in the lower right-hand corner. If you look at the earthquake layer before the TimeManager settings were applied, you'll see that the thousands of points were undiscernible. Breaking them up in this way and animating the data set lets you see patterns that might be otherwise difficult or impossible to see. Time series data is becoming more and more common as automated systems that generate such data become more common. Things like web server logs, traffic flow, and social media posts can all be mapped in a time series visualization.

9
Other Tips and Tricks

In this chapter, we will cover the following:

- Creating tiles from a QGIS map
- Adding a layer to geojson.io
- Rendering map layers based on rules
- Creating a layer-definition file
- Using NULL values in PyQGIS
- Using generators for layer queries
- Using alpha values to show data density
- Using the __geo_interface__ protocol
- Getting the output file names from processing algorithms
- Generating points along a line
- Using expression-based labels
- Creating dynamic forms in QGIS
- Calculating the length for all selected lines
- Using a different status bar CRS than the map
- Creating HTML labels in QGIS
- Using OpenStreetMap points of interest in QGIS
- Changing the QGIS web proxy
- Running QGIS scripts as scheduled tasks
- Visualizing data in 3D with WebGL
- Visualizing data on a globe
- Make a globe-like azimuthal orthographic projection
- Animating a layer

Introduction

This chapter provides interesting QGIS Python tricks that didn't fit within the themes of other chapters. Each recipe has a specific purpose, but in many cases, a recipe may demonstrate multiple concepts that you'll find useful in other programs. Nearly all of the recipes in this chapter are run in the QGIS Python console, except for one that is noted in this recipe. For this second edition of the book, we have added several new recipes to this chapter. The recipes include a quick way to switch web proxies if you run QGIS on a laptop and frequently move it to different network environments. Another shows you how to capture the output names of processing scripts in case you need to use that dynamically generated output in other scripts. We cover how to run QGIS scripts as scheduled tasks for truly automated processes that start themselves at set intervals. We create a 2D globe using an azimuthal orthographic projection. And finally, we've added a recipe which shows you how to create an animated movie from a layer!

Creating tiles from a QGIS map

This recipe creates Internet web map tiles from your QGIS map. What's interesting about this recipe is once the static map tiles are generated, you can serve them up from any web-accessible directory using JavaScript client-side in a browser without the need for a map server.

Getting ready

You will need to download the following zip-shape file from this URL:

`https://github.com/GeospatialPython/Learn/raw/master/countries.zip`

Unzip the file to a directory named `shapes` in your `qgis_data` directory.

You will also need to install the `QMetaTiles` plugin using QGIS Plugin Manager.

How to do it...

We will load our shapefile and randomly color each country. We'll then manipulate the `QMetaTiles` plugin using Python to generate map tiles for five zoom levels, worth of tiles.

1. First, we need to import all the necessary Python libraries, including the `QMetaTiles` plugin:

```
from PyQt4.QtCore import *
from PyQt4.QtGui import *
import QMetaTiles
import random
```

2. Now, we create a color function that can produce random colors. It accepts a mixing color, which defaults to white to change the overall tone of the color palette:

```
def randomColor(mix=(255,255,255)):
    red = random.randrange(0,256)
    green = random.randrange(0,256)
    blue = random.randrange(0,256)
    r,g,b = mix
    red = (red + r) / 2
    green = (green + g) / 2
    blue = (blue + b) / 2
    return (red, green, blue)
```

3. Next we'll create a simple callback function for notification when the tile generation is done:

```
def done():
    print "FINISHED!!"
```

4. Now, we set the path to the shapefile and the tile output direction:

```
shp = "/qgis_data/shapes/countries.shp"
dir = "/qgis_data/tilecache"
```

5. Then, we load the shapefile:

```
layer = QgsVectorLayer(shp, "Countries", "ogr")
```

6. Next, we define the field used to color the countries:

```
field = 'CNTRY_NAME'
```

7. Then, we need to get all the features, so we can loop through them:

```
features = layer.getFeatures()
```

8. We'll then build our color renderer:

```
categories = []
for feature in features:
    country = feature[field]
    sym = QgsSymbolV2.defaultSymbol(layer.geometryType())
    r,g,b = randomColor()
    sym.setColor(QColor(r,g,b,255))
    category = QgsRendererCategoryV2(country, sym, country)
    categories.append(category)
```

9. We'll set the layer renderer and add it to the map:

```
renderer = QgsCategorizedSymbolRendererV2(field, categories)
layer.setRendererV2(renderer)
QgsMapLayerRegistry.instance().addMapLayer(layer)
```

10. Now, we'll set all the properties we need for the image tiles, including the map elements and image properties:

```
canvas = iface.mapCanvas()
layers = canvas.mapSettings().layers()
extent = canvas.extent()
minZoom = 0
maxZoom = 5
width = 256
height = 256
transp = 255
quality = 70
format = "PNG"
outputPath = QFileInfo(dir)
rootDir = "countries"
antialiasing = False
tmsConvention = True
mapUrl = False
viewer = True
```

11. We are ready to generate the tiles using the efficient threading system of the `QMetaTiles` plugin. We'll create a thread object and pass it all of the tile settings from above:

```
tt = QMetaTiles.tilingthread.TilingThread(layers, extent,
                minZoom, maxZoom, width, height, transp,
                quality, format, outputPath, rootDir,
                antialiasing, tmsConvention, mapUrl,
                viewer, False, None, False, None)
```

12. Then, we can connect the finish signal to our simple callback function:

    ```
    tt.processFinished.connect(done)
    ```

13. Finally, we start the tiling process:

    ```
    tt.start()
    ```

14. Once you receive the completion message, check the output director and verify there is an HTML file named `countries.html` and a directory named countries.
15. Double-click on the `countries.html` page to open it in a browser.
16. Once the map loads, click on the plus symbol (+) in the upper-left corner twice to zoom the map.
17. Next, pan around to see the tiled version of your map load.

How it works...

You can generate up to 16 zoom levels with this plugin. After eight zoom levels, the tile-generation process takes a long time and the tile set becomes quite large on the file system, totaling hundreds of megabytes. You can see a working example of the output recipe stored in a **GitHub Pages** web directory at the following URL:

```
http://geospatialpython.github.io/qgis/tiles/countries.html
```

The following image shows the output in a browser:

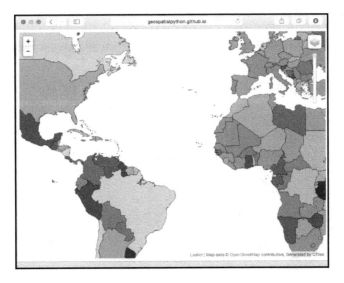

There's more...

In QGIS 2.18, you can also load these tiles in as an XYZ tiled layer. For more information, see the *Using XYZ Tiled Map Services* recipe from `Chapter 5`, *Creating Dynamic Maps*.

Adding a layer to geojson.io

Cloud services are becoming very common, and geospatial maps are no exception. This recipe demonstrates using a service named **geojson.io**, which serves vector layers online which you can upload from QGIS using Python.

Getting ready

For this recipe, you will need to install the **qgisio** plugin using the QGIS plugin manager. Note that this plugin is considered experimental, so ensure **Show also experimental plugins** is checked in you plugin manager settings.

You will also need an unprojected shapefile, such as the one from the following URL:

`https://github.com/GeospatialPython/Learn/raw/master/union.zip`

Decompress the zip file and place it in your `qgis_data` directory named `shapes`.

How to do it...

We will convert our shapefile to GeoJSON using a temporary file. We'll then use Python to call the `qgisio` plugin to upload the data for display online:

1. First, we need to import all of the relevant Python libraries:

```
from PyQt4.QtCore import *
from PyQt4.QtGui import *
from qgis.core import *
from tempfile import mkstemp
import os
from qgisio import geojsonio
```

2. Set up the layer and and get the layer name:

```
layer = QgsVectorLayer("/qgis_data/shapes/building.shp",
                       "Building", "ogr")
```

```
name = layer.name()
```

3. Next, establish a temporary file using the Python `tempfile` module for the `geojson` conversion:

```
handle, tmpfile = mkstemp(suffix='.geojson')
os.close(handle)
```

4. Then, establish the coordinate reference system needed for the conversion, which must be WGS84 geographic to work with the cloud service:

```
crs = QgsCoordinateReferenceSystem(4326,
                QgsCoordinateReferenceSystem.PostgisCrsId)
```

5. Next, write out the layer as `GeoJSON`:

```
error = QgsVectorFileWriter.writeAsVectorFormat(layer,
                     tmpfile,"utf-8", crs,
                     "GeoJSON", onlySelected=False)
```

6. We can make sure the conversion didn't have any problems:

```
if error != QgsVectorFileWriter.NoError:
    print "Unable to write geoJSON!"
```

7. Now, we can read the GeoJSON content:

```
with open(str(tmpfile), 'r') as f:
    contents = f.read()
```

8. We then need to remove the temporary file:

```
os.remove(tmpfile)
```

9. We are ready to upload our `geojson` to `geojson.io` using the `qgisio` module:

```
url = geojsonio._create_gist(contents, "Layer exported from
                             QGIS",
                     name + ".geojson")
```

10. We can then use the Qt library to open the map in a browser:

```
QDesktopServices.openUrl(QUrl(url))
```

How it works...

This recipe actually uses two cloud services. The GeoJSON data is stored on a `https://github.com/` service named **Gist**, which allows you to store code snippets such as JSON. The geojson.io service can read data from **Gist**. Note that sometimes, it can take several seconds to minutes for the generated URL to become available online.

This screenshot shows the building layer on an OSM map on geojson.io with the GeoJSON displayed next to the map:

There's more...

There are other more advanced services that can serve QGIS maps, including `http://qgiscloud.com/` and `https://carto.com/`, which can also display raster maps. Both of these services have free options and QGIS plugins. However, they are far more difficult to script from Python if you are trying to automate publishing maps to the Web as part of a workflow.

Rendering map layers based on rules

Rendering rules provide a powerful way to control how and when a layer is displayed relative to other layers or properties of the layer itself. This recipe demonstrates how to use a rule-based renderer to color code a layer based on an attribute.

Getting ready

You will need to download a zipped shapefile from the following URL:

`https://github.com/GeospatialPython/Learn/raw/master/ms_rails_mstm.zip`

Unzip it and place it in directory named `ms` in your `qgis_data` directory.

In that same directory, download and unzip the following shapefile:

`https://github.com/GeospatialPython/Learn/raw/master/Mississippi.zip`

Finally, add this shapefile to the directory as well:

`https://github.com/GeospatialPython/Learn/raw/master/jackson.zip`

How to do it...

We will set up a railroad layer; then, we'll set up our rules as Python tuples to color code it, based on frequency of use. Finally, we'll add some other layers to the map for reference.

1. First, we need the `QtGui` library to work with colors:

   ```
   from PyQt4.QtGui import *
   ```

2. Next, we'll set up our data path to avoid typing it repeatedly:

   ```
   prefix = "/Users/joellawhead/qgis_data/ms/"
   ```

3. We can then load our railroad layer:

   ```
   rails = QgsVectorLayer(prefix + "ms_rails.shp", "Railways",
                          "ogr")
   ```

4. We define our rules as a set of tuples. Each rule defines a label and expression detailing which attribute values make up that rule, a color name, and minimum/maximum map-scale values at which the described features are visible:

```
rules = (
        ('Heavily Used', '"DEN09CODE"> 3', 'red', (0, 6000000)),
        ('Moderately Used', '"DEN09CODE"< 4 AND "DEN09CODE"> 1',
         'orange', (0, 1500000)),
        ('Lightly Used', '"DEN09CODE"< 2', 'grey', (0, 250000))
        )
```

5. Next, we create a rule-based renderer and base symbol to begin applying our rules:

```
sym_rails = QgsSymbolV2.defaultSymbol(rails.geometryType())
rend_rails = QgsRuleBasedRendererV2(sym_rails)
```

6. Rules are hierarchical based on a root rule, so we must access the root first:

```
root_rule = rend_rails.rootRule()
```

7. Now, we will loop through our rules, clone the default rule, and append our custom rule to the tree:

```
for label, exp, color, scale in rules:
    # create a clone (i.e. a copy) of the default rule
    rule = root_rule.children()[0].clone()
    # set the label, exp and color
    rule.setLabel(label)
    rule.setFilterExpression(exp)
    rule.symbol().setColor(QColor(color))
    # set the scale limits if they have been specified
    if scale is not None:
        rule.setScaleMinDenom(scale[0])
        rule.setScaleMaxDenom(scale[1])
    # append the rule to the list of rules
    root_rule.appendChild(rule)
```

8. Next, we can now delete the default rule, which isn't part of our rendering scheme:

```
root_rule.removeChildAt(0)
```

9. We apply the renderer to our rails layer:

```
rails.setRendererV2(rend_rails)
```

10. We'll then establish and style a city layer that will provide a focal point to zoom into so we can easily see the scale-based rendering effect:

```
jax = QgsVectorLayer(prefix + "jackson.shp", "Jackson", "ogr")
jax_style = {}
jax_style['color'] = "#ffff00"
jax_style['name'] = 'regular_star'
jax_style['outline'] = '#000000'
jax_style['outline-width'] = '1'
jax_style['size'] = '8'
sym_jax = QgsSimpleMarkerSymbolLayerV2.create(jax_style)
jax.rendererV2().symbols()[0].changeSymbolLayer(0, sym_jax)
```

11. Then, we'll set up and style a border layer around both datasets:

```
ms = QgsVectorLayer(prefix + "mississippi.shp", "Mississippi",
                    "ogr")
ms_style = {}
ms_style['color'] = "#F7F5EB"
sym_ms = QgsSimpleFillSymbolLayerV2.create(ms_style)
ms.rendererV2().symbols()[0].changeSymbolLayer(0, sym_ms)
```

12. Finally, we'll add everything to the map:

```
QgsMapLayerRegistry.instance().addMapLayers([jax, rails, ms])
```

How it works...

Rules are hierarchical collections of symbols and expressions. Symbols themselves are collections of symbol layers. This recipe is relatively simple, but is over 50 lines of code. Rendering is one of the most complex features to code in QGIS. However, rules also have their own set of properties, separate from layers and symbols. Notice in this recipe that we are able to set labels and filters for the rules, properties that are normally relegated to layers. One way to think of rules is as separate layers. We could do the same thing by loading our railroad layer as a new layer for each rule. Rules are a more compact way to break up the rendering for a single layer.

The following image shows the rendering at a scale at which all of the rule outputs are visible:

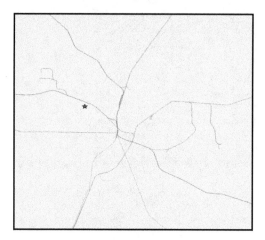

Creating a layer-definition file

Layer styling is one of the most complex aspects of the QGIS Python API. Once you've developed the style for a layer, it is often useful to save the styling to the **QGIS Markup Language (QML)** XML format.

Getting ready

You will need to download the following zipped directory, named saveqml, and decompress it to your qgis_data/rasters directory:

https://github.com/GeospatialPython/Learn/raw/master/saveqml.zip

How to do it...

We will create a color ramp for a **digital elevation model (DEM)** and then make it semi-transparent for overlay on a hillshaded tiff of the DEM. We'll save the style we create to a QML file:

1. First, we'll need the Python Qt libraries:

```
from PyQt4.QtCore import *
```

```
from PyQt4.QtGui import *
```

2. Next, we'll load up our two raster layers:

```
hs = QgsRasterLayer("/qgis_data/saveqml/hillshade.tif",
                    "Hillshade")
dem = QgsRasterLayer("/qgis_data/saveqml/dem.asc", "DEM")
```

3. Then, we'll perform a histogram stretch on our DEM for better visualization:

```
algorithm = QgsContrastEnhancement.StretchToMinimumMaximum
limits = QgsRaster.ContrastEnhancementMinMax
dem.setContrastEnhancement(algorithm, limits)
```

4. Now, we'll create a visually pleasing color ramp based on the elevation values of the DEM as a renderer and apply it to the layer:

```
s = QgsRasterShader()
c = QgsColorRampShader()
c.setColorRampType(QgsColorRampShader.INTERPOLATED)
i = []
qri = QgsColorRampShader.ColorRampItem
i.append(qri(356.334, QColor(63,159,152,255), '356.334'))
i.append(qri(649.292, QColor(96,235,155,255), '649.292'))
i.append(qri(942.25, QColor(100,246,174,255), '942.25'))
i.append(qri(1235.21, QColor(248,251,155,255), '1235.21'))
i.append(qri(1528.17, QColor(246,190,39,255), '1528.17'))
i.append(qri(1821.13, QColor(242,155,39,255), '1821.13'))
i.append(qri(2114.08, QColor(165,84,26,255), '2114.08'))
i.append(qri(2300, QColor(236,119,83,255), '2300'))
i.append(qri(2700, QColor(203,203,203,255), '2700'))
c.setColorRampItemList(i)
s.setRasterShaderFunction(c)
ps = QgsSingleBandPseudoColorRenderer(dem.dataProvider(),
                                      1, s)
ps.setOpacity(0.5)
dem.setRenderer(ps)
```

5. Add the layers to the map:

```
QgsMapLayerRegistry.instance().addMapLayers([dem, hs])
```

6. Finally, with one line, we can save the DEM styling to a reusable QML file:

```
dem.saveNamedStyle("/qgis_data/saveqml/dem.qml")
```

How it works...

The QML format is very easy to read and edit by hand. The `saveNamedStyle()` method works on vector layers the exact same way. Instead of the styling code above, you can just reference the QML file using the `loadNamedStyle()` method:

```
dem.loadNamedStyle("/qgis_data/saveqml/dem.qml")
```

When you save the QML file in the same directory as the layer and with the same name prefix, QGIS will automatically style the layer when it is loaded. You can set up complex styling as a template and then apply it easily to dynamically output layers from PyQGIS scripts. Even if you manually create the layer style and save it, you can still apply it using PyQGIS.

Using NULL values in PyQGIS

QGIS can use **NULL** values as field values. Python uses **None** objects of type None instead of NULL values, which are null memory references. The concepts are similar. You must be aware of this fact when working with Python in QGIS, which is a mixture of C++ and Python. In this recipe, we'll explore the implications of QGIS NULL values in Python.

Getting ready

In your `qgis_data/shapes` directory, download the following shapefile, which contains some NULL field values, and unzip it:

```
https://github.com/GeospatialPython/Learn/raw/master/NullExample.zip
```

How to do it...

We will load the shapefile and grab its first feature. Then, we'll access one of its NULL field values. Next, we'll run through some tests that allow you to see how the NULL values behave in Python:

1. Load the shapefile and access its first feature:

```
lyrPth = "/qgis_data/shapes/NullExample.shp"
lyr = QgsVectorLayer(lyrPth, "Null Field Example", "ogr")
features = lyr.getFeatures()
f = features.next()
```

2. Next, grab one of the NULL field values:

```
value = f["SAMPLE"]
```

3. We'll then check the NULL value's type:

```
print "Check python value type:"
print type(value)
```

4. See if the value is the Python None type:

```
print "Check if value is None:"
print value is None
```

5. Now, we'll see if it's equivalent to None:

```
print "Check if value == None:"
print value == None
```

6. See if the value matches the QGIS NULL type:

```
print "Check if value == NULL:"
print value == NULL
```

7. Then, we'll see if it is actually NULL:

```
print "Check if value is NULL:"
print value is NULL
```

8. Finally, we'll to a type match to the QGIS NULL:

```
print "Check type(value) is type(NULL):"
print type(value) is type(NULL)
```

How it works...

As you can see, the type of the NULL value is `PyQt4.QtCore.QPyNullVariant`. This class is a special type injected into the PyQt framework. It is important to note the cases where two `is` comparisons return a different value than the `==` comparison. In your code, you should be aware of the differences to avoid unexpected results. For more information on NULL values in PyQGIS, see `https://nathanw.net/2013/08/31/qgis-2-0-dealing-with-null-values-in-pyqgis/`.

Using generators for layer queries

Python generators provide an efficient way to process large datasets. A QGIS developer named Nathan Woodrow created a simple Python QGIS query engine, which uses generators to make fetching features from QGIS layers easier. We'll use this engine in this recipe to query a layer.

Getting ready

You need to install the query engine using `easy_install` or by downloading it and adding it to your QGIS Python installation. To use `easy_install`, run the following command from a console, which downloads a clone of the original code but includes a Python setup file:

```
easy_install https://github.com/GeospatialPython/qquery/archive
             /master.zip
```

You can also download the ZIP file from the following URL and copy the contents to your working directory or the site-packages directory of your QGIS Python installation:

```
https://github.com/NathanW2/qquery/archive/master.zip
```

You will also need to download the following zipped shapefile and decompress it to a directory named `ms` in your `qgis_data` directory:

```
https://github.com/GeospatialPython/Learn/raw/master/MS_UrbanAnC10.zip
```

How to do it...

We'll load a layer containing population data. Then, we'll use the query engine to do a simple query for an urban area with fewer than 50,000 people. We'll filter the results to only give us three columns: place name, population level, and land area.

1. First, we import the query engine module:

   ```
   from query import query
   ```

2. Then, we set up the path to our shapefile and load it as a vector layer:

   ```
   pth = "/Users/joellawhead/qgis_data/ms/MS_UrbanAnC10.shp"
   layer = QgsVectorLayer(pth, "Urban Areas", "ogr")
   ```

3. Following this, we can run the query that uses Python's dot notation to perform a `where` clause search and then filter using a select statement:

```
q = (query(layer).where("POP > 50000")
                 .select('NAME10', "POP", "AREALAND", "POPDEN"))
```

4. Finally, we'll use the query's generator to iterate to the first result:

```
q().next()
```

How it works...

As you can see, this module is quite handy. To perform this same query using the default PyQGIS API it would take nearly four times as much code.

Using alpha values to show data density

Thematic maps often use a color ramp based on a single color to show data density. Darker colors show higher concentration of objects, while lighter colors show lower concentrations. You can use a transparency ramp instead of a color ramp to show density as well. This technique is useful if you want to overlay the density layer on imagery or other vector layers. In this recipe, you use some bear-sighting data to show concentrations of bears over an area. We'll use alpha values to show the density. We'll use an unusual hexagon grid to divide the area and a rule-based renderer to build the display.

Getting ready

You will need to install the MMQGIS plugin used to build the hexagon grid using the QGIS plugin manager.

You also need to download the bear data from the following URL, unzip the shapefile, and put it in the ms directory of your qgis_data directory:

https://github.com/GeospatialPython/Learn/raw/master/bear-data.zip

How to do it...

We will load the bear data. Then, we will use the MMQGIS plugin to generate the hexagon grid. We'll use the Processing Toolbox to clip the hexagon to the bear shapefile and join the shapefile attribute data to the hexagon grid. Finally, we'll use a rule-based renderer to apply alpha-values based on bear-sighting density and add the result to the map.

1. First, we import all the libraries we'll need, including the processing engine, the PyQt GUI library for color management, and the MMQGIS plugin:

   ```
   import processing
   from PyQt4.QtGui import *
   from mmqgis import mmqgis_library as mmqgis
   ```

2. Next, we'll set up the paths for all of our input and output shapefiles:

   ```
   dir = "/qgis_data/ms/"
   source = dir + "bear-data.shp"
   grid = dir + "grid.shp"
   clipped_grid = dir + "clipped_grid.shp"
   output = dir + "ms-bear-sightings.shp"
   ```

3. We can set up the input shapefile as a layer:

   ```
   layer = QgsVectorLayer(source, "bear data", "ogr")
   ```

4. We'll need the extent of the shapefile to create the grid as well as the width and height in map units:

   ```
   e = layer.extent()
   minx = e.xMinimum()
   miny = e.yMinimum()
   maxx = e.xMaximum()
   maxy = e.yMaximum()
   w = e.width()
   h = e.height()
   ```

5. Then, we need to obtain the CRS of the layer:

   ```
   crs = layer.crs()
   ```

6. Now, we can use the MMQGIS plugin to generate the grid over the entire shapefile extent. We'll use a grid cell size of 1/10 of a degree (approximately, six miles):

   ```
   mmqgis.mmqgis_grid(iface, "Hexagons", crs, .1, .1, minx, miny,
   ```

```
                     maxx, maxy, "Hexagon (polygon)",
                     grid, False)
```

7. We can then clip the grid to the shape of our source data using the Processing Toolbox:

```
processing.runalg("qgis:clip",grid,source,clipped_grid)
```

8. Next, we need to do a spatial join to match the source data attributes, based on counties, to each grid cell:

```
processing.runalg("qgis:joinattributesbylocation",
                  clipped_grid,source,'intersects'],0,0,
                  "sum,mean,min,max,median",0,output)
```

9. Add that output as a layer:

```
bears = QgsVectorLayer(output, "Bear Sightings", "ogr")
```

10. Next, we create our rendering rule set as Python tuples specifying a label, value expression, color, and alpha level for the symbol between 0 and 1:

```
rules = (('RARE', '"BEARS"<= 5', (227,26,28,255), .2),
         ('UNCOMMON', '"BEARS"> 5 AND "BEARS"<= 15',
           (227,26,28,255), .4),
         ('OCCASIONAL', '"BEARS"> 15 AND "BEARS"<= 50',
           (227,26,28,255), .6),
         ('FREQUENT', '"BEARS"> 50', (227,26,28,255), 1),
)
```

11. Create the default symbol, the rule renderer, and add the rules to the renderer:

```
sym_bears = QgsFillSymbolV2.createSimple({"outline_color":
                        "white","outline_width":".26"})
rend_bears = QgsRuleBasedRendererV2(sym_bears)
root_rule = rend_bears.rootRule()
for label, exp, color, alpha in rules:
    # create a clone (i.e. a copy) of the default rule
    rule = root_rule.children()[0].clone()
    # set the label, exp and color
    rule.setLabel(label)
    rule.setFilterExpression(exp)
    r,g,b,a = color
    rule.symbol().setColor(QColor(r,g,b,a))
    # set the transparency level
    rule.symbol().setAlpha(alpha)
    # append the rule to the list of rules
```

```
root_rule.appendChild(rule)
```

12. We remove the default rule:

```
root_rule.removeChildAt(0)
```

13. We apply the renderer to the layer:

```
bears.setRendererV2(rend_bears)
```

14. Finally, we add the finished density layer to the map:

```
QgsMapLayerRegistry.instance().addMapLayer(bears)
```

How it works...

The rule-based renderer is the core of this recipe. However, the hexagon grid provides a more interesting way to visualize statistical data. Like a dot-based density map, the hexagons are not entirely spatially accurate or precise but make it very easy to understand the overall trends of the data. They also provide an advantage over rectangular grids when binning linear features.

The following image shows what the resulting map looks like:

Using the __geo_interface__ protocol

The **__geo_interface__** is a newer protocol, created by Sean Gillies and targeted mainly at Python, to provide a string representation of geographical data following Python's built-ins protocol. The string representation for geographical data is basically GeoJSON. You can read more about this protocol here:

```
https://gist.github.com/sgillies/2217756
```

Two developers, Nathan Woodrow and Martin Laloux, refined a version of this protocol for QGIS Python data objects. This recipe borrows from their examples to provide a code snippet, which you can put at the beginning of your Python scripts to retrofit QGIS feature and geometry objects with a __geo_interface__ method.

Getting ready

This recipe requires no preparation.

How to do it...

We will create two functions: one for features and one for geometry. We'll then use Python's dynamic capability to patch the QGIS objects with a __geo_interface__ built-in method.

1. First, we'll need the Python `json` module:

   ```
   import json
   ```

2. Next, we'll create our function for features, which takes a feature as input and returns a geojson-like object:

   ```
   def mapping_feature(feature):
       geom = feature.geometry()
       properties = {}
       fields = [field.name() for field in feature.fields()]
       properties = dict(zip(fields, feature.attributes()))
       return { 'type' : 'Feature',
                'properties' : properties,
                'geometry' : geom.__geo_interface__}
   ```

3. Create the geometry function:

   ```
   def mapping_geometry(geometry):
   ```

```
geo = geometry.exportToGeoJSON()
return json.loads(geo)
```

4. Finally, we'll patch the QGIS feature and geometry objects with our custom built-in to call our functions when the built-in is accessed:

```
QgsFeature.__geo_interface__ = property(lambda self:
                                   mapping_feature(self))
QgsGeometry.__geo_interface__ = property(lambda self:
                                   mapping_geometry(self))
```

How it works...

This recipe is almost surprisingly simple, but exploits some of Python's most interesting features. First, note that the feature function actually calls the geometry function as part of its output. Also, note that adding the `__geo_interface__` built-in function is as simple as using the double-underscore naming convention and using Python's built-in property method to declare lambda functions as internal to the objects. Another interesting Python feature is that QGIS objects are able to pass themselves to our custom functions using the `self` keyword.

Getting the output file names from processing algorithms

Sometimes, you need to know the variable name a QGIS processing algorithm uses to hold the location of temporary output files. Of course you can set the output file name for most algorithms, but if you are chaining several processes together, you can take advantage of the automatic cleanup for temporary files provided by QGIS when it exits if you use the temporary file. While the processing framework is mostly very consistent, the names of output variables vary. In this recipe, we'll use PyQGIS to programmatically get the output variable name.

Getting ready

Open the QGIS Python Console by going to the **Plugins** menu and selecting **Python Console**.

How to do it...

We'll import the processing module and create a function to access algorithm output names. Then, we'll test out a couple of algorithms to see if the function works as expected:

1. First, we import the processing module:

```
import processing
```

2. Next, we'll create a function that makes it easy to get the output variable name:

```
def proc_output(algorithm):
    for output in processing.Processing.getAlgorithm(algorithm)
                                                        .outputs:
        return output.name
```

3. Test the GRASS aspect algorithm expecting the output name `aspect`:

```
proc_output("grass7:r.aspect")
```

4. Finally, we'll test the **QGIS Join Attributes by Location** algorithm, expecting the generic name OUTPUT:

```
proc_output("qgis:joinattributesbylocation")
```

How it works...

This recipe takes advantage of Python's powerful introspection capability. We can peek into a module to see how it works. Then, we can programmatically and dynamically get the information we need to perform additional operations.

Generating points along a line

You can generate points within a polygon fairly simply using a point in polygon method. But sometimes, you may want to generate points along a line. You can randomly place points inside the polygon's extent, which is essentially just a rectangular polygon, or you can place points at random locations along the line as random distances. In this recipe, we'll demonstrate both of these methods.

Getting ready

You will need to download the following zipped shapefile and place it in a directory named `shapes` in your `qgis_data` directory:

`https://github.com/GeospatialPython/Learn/raw/master/path.zip`

How to do it...

First, we will generate random points along a line using a grass function in the Processing Toolbox. We'll then generate points within the line's extent using a native QGIS processing function:

1. First, we need to import the processing module:

   ```
   import processing
   ```

2. Then, we'll load the line layer onto the map:

   ```
   line = QgsVectorLayer("/qgis_data/shapes/path.shp", "Line",
                         "ogr")
   QgsMapLayerRegistry.instance().addMapLayer(line)
   ```

3. Next, we'll generate points along the line, specifying the path to the shapefile, a maximum distance between points in map units (meters), which type of feature we want to output (vertices), the extent, the snap tolerance option, the minimum distance between points, the output type, and the output name. We won't specify the name and tell QGIS to load the output automatically:

   ```
   processing.runandload("grass7:v.to.points",line,"100",1,False,
                         "435727.015026,458285.819185,
                          5566442.32879,5591754.78979",
                         -1,0.0001,0,None)
   ```

4. Finally, we'll create some points within the line's extent and load them as well:

   ```
   processing.runandload("qgis:randompointsinextent",
                         "435727.015026,458285.819185,
                          5566442.32879,5591754.78979",
                         100,100,None)
   ```

How it works...

The first algorithm puts the points on the line. The second places them within the vicinity. Both approaches have different use cases. The following screenshot shows what the output looks like with the random points at 50% transparency for separation:

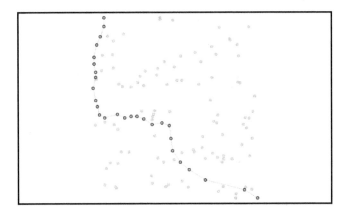

There's more...

A third option would be to create a buffer around the line at a specified distance and clip the output of the second algorithm so the points aren't near the corners of the line extent.

Using expression-based labels

Expressions are a kind of mini-programming language or SQL-like language found throughout different QGIS functions to selected features. One important use of expressions is controlling labels. Maps easily become cluttered if you label every single feature. Expressions make it easy to limit labels to important features. You can filter labels using expressions from within Python, as we will do in this recipe.

Getting ready

You will need to download the following zipped shapefile and decompress it to a directory named ms in your qgis_data directory:

https://github.com/GeospatialPython/Learn/raw/master/MS_UrbanAnC10.zip.

How to do it...

We'll use the QGIS PAL labeling engine to filter labels based on a field name. After loading the layer, we'll create our **PAL** settings and write it to the layer. Finally, we'll add the layer to the map.

1. First, we'll set up the path to our shapefile:

   ```
   pth = "/Users/joellawhead/qgis_data/ms/MS_UrbanAnC10.shp"
   ```

2. Next, we'll load our layer:

   ```
   lyr = QgsVectorLayer(pth, "Urban Areas", "ogr")
   ```

3. Then, create a labeling object and read the layer's current labeling settings:

   ```
   palyr = QgsPalLayerSettings()
   palyr.readFromLayer(lyr)
   ```

4. Now, we create our expression to only label features whose population field is greater than 50,000:

   ```
   palyr.fieldName = 'CASE WHEN "POP"> 50000 THEN NAME10 END'
   ```

5. Then, we enable these settings:

   ```
   palyr.enabled = True
   ```

6. Finally, we apply the labeling filter to the layer and add it to the map:

   ```
   palyr.writeToLayer(lyr)
   QgsMapLayerRegistry.instance().addMapLayer(lyr)
   ```

How it works...

While the labels are a function of the layer, the settings for the labeling engine are controlled by an outside object and then applied to the layer. The following screenshot shows what the output looks like:

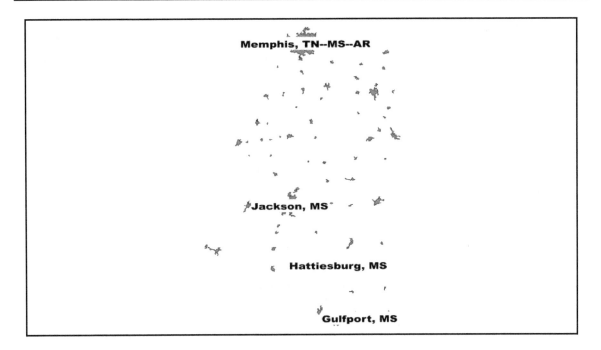

Creating dynamic forms in QGIS

When you edit the fields of a layer in QGIS, you have the option of using a spreadsheet-like table view or a database-style form view. Forms are useful because you can change the design of the form, and you can add interactive features which react to user input to better control data editing. In this recipe, we'll add some custom validation to a form that checks user input for valid values.

Getting ready

You will need to download the following zipped shapefile and decompress it to a directory named ms in your qgis_data directory:

https://github.com/GeospatialPython/Learn/raw/master/MS_UrbanAnC10.zip

You'll also need to create a blank Python file called validate.py, which you'll edit with the following steps. Put the validate.py in the ms directory of your qgis_data directory with the shapefile.

How to do it...

We'll create the two functions we need for our validation engine. Then, we'll use the QGIS interface to attach the action to the layer. Make sure you add the following code to the `validate.py` file in the same directory as the shapefile:

1. First, we'll import the the Qt libraries:

```
from PyQt4.QtCore import *
from PyQt4.QtGui import *
```

2. Next, we'll create some global variables for the attribute we'll be validating and the form dialog:

```
popFld = None
dynamicDialog = None
```

3. Now, we'll begin building the function that changes the behavior of the dialog and create variables for the field we want to validate and the submit button:

```
def dynamicForm(dialog, lyrId, featId):
    global dynamicDialog
    dynamicDialog = dialog
    global popFld
    popFld = dialog.findChild(QLineEdit, "POP")
    buttonBox =dialog.findChild(QDialogButtonBox, "buttonBox")
```

4. Disconnect the dialog form the action that controls the form acceptance:

```
buttonBox.accepted.disconnect(dynamicDialog.accept)
```

5. Reconnect the dialog's actions to our custom actions:

```
buttonBox.accepted.connect(validate)
buttonBox.rejected.connect(dynamicDialog.reject)
```

6. Now, we'll create the validation function that will reject the form if the population field has a value less than 1:

```
def validate():
    if not float(popFld.text()) > 0:
        msg = QMessageBox(f)
        msg.setText("Population must be greater than zero.")
        msg.exec_()
    else:
        dynamicDialog.accept()
```

7. Next open QGIS and drag and drop the shapefile from your file system onto the map canvas.
8. Save the script and give it a name in the same directory as the `validate.py` file.
9. In the QGIS legend, double-click on the layer name.
10. Choose the **Fields** tab on the left side of the **Layer Properties** dialog.
11. In the **Fields** tab on the top-right corner, select **Load from external file** from the pull-down menu.
12. In the input boxes that appear below that, enter `dynamicForm` for the **Function name**, and browse to the `validate.py` file in the **External file** input box.
13. Click on the **OK** button in the bottom right of the **Layer Properties** dialog.
14. Now, use the identify tool to select a feature.
15. In the feature properties dialog, click on the form icon on the top-left corner of the image.
16. Once the feature form is open, switch back to the QGIS legend, right-click on the layer name, and choose **Toggle Editing**.
17. Switch back to the feature form, scroll down to the **POP** field, and change the value to 0.
18. Now, click on the **OK** button and verify you receive the warning dialog requiring the value to be greater than 0.

How it works...

The `validate.py` file must be in your Python path. Putting this file in the same directory as a project makes the functions available. Validation is one of the simplest functions you can implement.

This screenshot shows the rejection message when the population is set to 0:

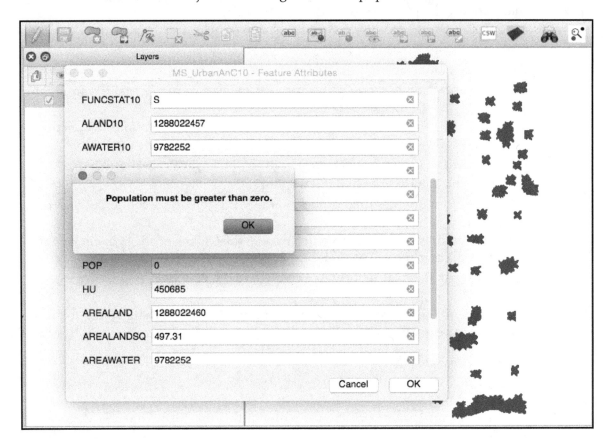

There's more...

If you want to implement more advanced input validation, you can use the QValidator object. QValidator can use regular expressions to help validate text input and also works with Qt forms. For more information on this class, see:

```
https://snorfalorpagus.net/blog/2014/08/09/validating-user-input-in-pyqt4-using
-qvalidator/
```

Calculating length for all selected lines

If you need to calculate the total of a given dataset property such as length, the easiest thing to do is just use Python. In this recipe, we'll total the length of all of the railways in a dataset.

Getting ready

You will need to download a zipped shapefile from the following URL:

`https://github.com/GeospatialPython/Learn/raw/master/ms_rails_mstm.zip`

Unzip it and place it in directory named `ms` in your `qgis_data` directory.

How to do it...

We will load the layer, loop through the features while keeping a running total of line lengths, and finally, convert the result to kilometers:

1. First, we'll set up the path to our shapefile:

   ```
   pth = "/Users/joellawhead/qgis_data/ms/ms_rails_mstm.shp"
   ```

2. Then, we'll load the layer:

   ```
   lyr = QgsVectorLayer(pth, "Railroads", "ogr")
   ```

3. Next, we need a variable to `total` the line lengths:

   ```
   total = 0
   ```

4. Now, we loop through the layer getting the length of each line:

   ```
   for f in lyr.getFeatures():
       geom = f.geometry()
       total += geom.length()
   ```

5. Finally, we print the total converted to kilometers:

   ```
   print "{0:.2f} total kilometers of rails.".format(total / 1000)
   ```

How it works...

This function is simple, but it's not available directly in the QGIS API. However, because PyQGIS is fully integrated with Python, we can easily manipulate any data we can access in QGIS. You could modify this example to calculate the length for certain categories, for example, road types.

Using a different status bar CRS than the map

Sometimes, you want to display a different coordinate system for the mouse coordinates in the status bar than what the source data is. With this recipe, you can set a different coordinate system without changing the data.

Getting ready

Download the following zipped shapefile and unzip it to your `qgis_data/ms` directory:

`https://github.com/GeospatialPython/Learn/raw/master/MSCities_Geo.zip`

Also, in your project settings, verify the **Enable on the fly projection** checkbox is checked.

How to do it...

We will load our layer and then change the destination coordinate system of the map canvas:

1. First, we will set up the path to the shapefile and load it as a layer:

   ```
   pth = "/qgis_data/ms/MSCities_Geo_Pts.shp"
   lyr = QgsVectorLayer(pth, "Cities", "ogr")
   ```

2. Then, we add the layer to the map:

   ```
   QgsMapLayerRegistry.instance().addMapLayer(lyr)
   ```

3. Finally, we change the display coordinate system to a different CRS:

   ```
   iface.mapCanvas().setDestinationCrs
                 (QgsCoordinateReferenceSystem("EPSG:3815"))
   ```

How it works...

The coordinate transformation engine in QGIS is very fast. Normally, QGIS tries to transform everything to WGS84 geographic, but sometimes you need to view coordinates in a different reference system.

Creating HTML labels in QGIS

QGIS map tips allow you to hover the mouse cursor over a feature to create a popup that displays information. This information is normally a data field, but you can also display other types of information using a subset of HTML tags. In this recipe, we'll create an HTML map tip that displays a Google Street View image at the feature's location.

Getting ready

In your `qgis_data` directory, create a directory named `tmp`.

You will also need to download the following zipped shapefile and place it in your `qgis_data/nyc` directory:

`https://github.com/GeospatialPython/Learn/raw/master/NYC_MUSEUMS_GEO.zip`

How to do it...

We will create a function to process the Google data and register it as a QGIS function. Then, we'll load the layer and set its map-tip display field:

1. First, we need to import the Python libraries we'll need:

    ```
    from qgis.utils import qgsfunction
    from qgis.core import QGis
    import urllib
    import os
    ```

2. Next, we'll set a special QGIS Python decorator that registers our function as a QGIS function:

    ```
    @qgsfunction(0, "Python")
    ```

3. Create a function that accepts a feature and uses its geometry to pull down a Google Street View image. We must cache the images locally because the Qt widget that displays the map tips only allows you to use local images:

```
def googleStreetView(values, feature, parent):
    x,y = feature.geometry().asPoint()
    baseurl = "https://maps.googleapis.com/maps
              /api/streetview?"
    w = 150
    h = 150
    fov = 90
    heading = 235
    pitch = 10
    params = "size={w}x{h}&".format(w,h)
    params += "location={y},{x}&".format(y,x)
    params += "fov={}&heading={}&pitch={}"
              .format(fov, heading, pitch)
    url = baseurl + params
    tmpdir = "/qgis_data/tmp/"
    img = tmpdir + str(feature.id()) + ".jpg"
    if not os.path.isfile(img):
      urllib.urlretrieve(url, img)
    uri = "file://" + img
    return uri
```

4. Now, we can load the layer:

```
pth = "/qgis_data/nyc/nyc_museums_geo.shp"
lyr = QgsVectorLayer(pth, "New York City Museums", "ogr")
```

5. Next, we can set the display field using a special QGIS tag with the name of our function:

```
lyr.setDisplayField('<imgsrc="[%googleStreetView()%]"/>')
```

6. Finally, we add it to the map:

```
QgsMapLayerRegistry.instance().addMapLayer(lyr)
```

7. Select the **Map Tips** tool and hover over the different points to see the Google Street View images.

How it works...

The key to this recipe is the `@qgsfunctiondecorator`. When you register the function this way, it shows up in the menus for Python functions in expressions. The function must also have the `parent` and `value` parameters, but we didn't need them in this case.

The following screenshot shows a Google Street View Map Tip:

Note that your layer must be in WGS84; otherwise, you'd need to reproject it to be compatible with Google Street View.

There's more...

If you don't need the function anymore, you must unregister it for the function to go away. The unregister command uses the following convention, referencing the function name with a dollar sign:

```
QgsExpression.unregisterFunction("$googleStreetView")
```

Using OpenStreetMap points of interest in QGIS

OpenStreetMap has an API called Overpass that lets you access OSM data dynamically. In this recipe, we'll add some OSM tourism points of interest to a map.

Getting ready

You will need to use the QGIS plugin manager to install the **QuickOSM** plugin.

You will also need to download the following shapefile and unzip it to your `qgis_data/ms` directory:

`https://github.com/GeospatialPython/Learn/raw/master/MSCoast_geo.zip`

How to do it...

We will load our base layer that defines the area of interest. Then, we'll use the Processing Toolbox to build a query for OSM, download the data, and add it to the map:

1. First, we need to import the `processing` module:

   ```
   import processing
   ```

2. Next, we need to load the base layer:

   ```
   lyr = QgsVectorLayer("/qgis_data/ms/MSCoast_geo.shp",
                        "MS Coast", "ogr")
   ```

3. Then, we'll need the layer extent for the processing algorithms:

   ```
   ext = lyr.extent()
   w =   ext.xMinimum()
   s =   ext.yMinimum()
   e =   ext.xMaximum()
   n =   ext.yMaximum()
   ```

4. We'll create a variable for our bounding box:

   ```
   bbox = "%s,%s,%s,%s".format(w,e,s,n)
   ```

5. Next, we create the query:

```
factory = processing.runalg("quickosm:queryfactory","tourism",
                            "",True,"",25)
q = factory["OUTPUT_QUERY"]
```

6. Now, we download the OSM data using our query:

```
results = processing.runalg("quickosm:
                            queryoverpassapiwithastring",
                            "http://overpass-api.de/api/",
                            q,bbox,"",None)
osm = results["OUTPUT_FILE"]
```

7. Define the names of the shapefiles we will create from the OSM output:

```
poly = "/qgis_data/ms/tourism_poly.shp"
multiline = "/qgis_data/ms/tourism_multil.shp"
line = "/qgis_data/ms/tourism_lines.shp"
points = "/qgis_data/ms/tourism_points.shp"
```

8. Now, we convert the OSM data to shapefiles:

```
processing.runalg("quickosm:ogrdefault",osm,"",
                  "","","",poly,multiline,line,points)
```

9. Pull the points in as a layer:

```
tourism_points = QgsVectorLayer(points, "Points of Interest",
                                "ogr")
```

10. Finally, we can add them to a map:

```
QgsMapLayerRegistry.instance().addMapLayers([tourism_points,
                                            lyr]
```

How it works...

The QuickOSM plugin manages the Overpass API. What's interesting about this plugin is that it provides processing algorithms in addition to a GUI interface. The processing algorithm creates the query. The API returns an OSM XML file that we must convert to shapefiles for use in QGIS.

Changing the QGIS web proxy

QGIS, conveniently, has settings for changing the web proxy it uses to access the Internet. If you are running QGIS on a laptop, you may find yourself changing these settings frequently when you change locations, for example, between work and home or maybe a coffee shop. In this recipe, we'll use PyQGIS to change these settings based on pre-configured options. You can then set a variable name to one of those options, and PyQGIS will change the multiple values needed to alter the proxy.

Getting ready

Open the QGIS Python console by going to the **Plugins** menu and selecting **Python Console**.

How to do it...

We will build some dictionary variables for each proxy we want to access. Then, we'll create a variable naming the proxy we want to use. Change the QGIS archived settings, which are accessed when QGIS first launches. Finally, we'll change the settings for the current instance of QGIS so the changes take effect immediately:

1. First, we import the libraries we need to change the settings:

   ```
   from qgis.core import *
   from PyQt4.QtCore import *
   from PyQt4.QtNetwork import QNetworkRequest, QNetworkProxy
   ```

2. Then, we build a dictionary mapping readable names to the setting names:

   ```
   settings={"Proxy enabled": u'proxy/proxyEnabled',
             "Proxy Host ": u'proxy/proxyHost',
             "Proxy Port": u'proxy/proxyPort'}
   ```

3. Build the dictionaries with settings for each proxy we want to use:

   ```
   home={"Proxy enabled": True, "Proxy Host": "localhost",
         "Proxy Port": 8888}
   office={"Proxy enabled": True, "Proxy Host": "192.168.168.165",
           "Proxy Port": 8080}
   cafe={"Proxy enabled": False, "Proxy Host ": "192.168.168.107",
         "Proxy Port": 8080}
   ```

4. Now, we create a variable naming which proxy we want to use:

```
current=home
```

5. Then, we need to access the QGIS settings object:

```
s = QSettings()
```

6. Next, we loop through the proxy settings and assign them to the QGIS stored settings:

```
for key, val in settings.iteritems():
    settings_key=key
    for key2, val2 in current.iteritems():
        if key2==settings_key:
            settings_val=val2
    current_setting = s.value(str(val).decode
                                ('unicode-escape'))
    s.setValue(unicode(str(val)), settings_val)
```

7. To save the settings, we need to sync them to disk:

```
s.sync()
```

8. Finally, we can alter the live settings of QGIS:

```
proxyEnabled = s.value("proxy/proxyEnabled", "")
proxyType = s.value("proxy/proxyType", "")
proxyHost = s.value("proxy/proxyHost", "")
proxyPort = s.value("proxy/proxyPort", "")
proxyUser = s.value("proxy/proxyUser", "")
proxyPassword = s.value("proxy/proxyPassword", "" )
proxy = QNetworkProxy()
proxy.setType(QNetworkProxy.HttpProxy)
proxy.setHostName(proxyHost)
proxy.setPort(int(proxyPort))
proxy.setUser(proxyUser)
proxy.setPassword(proxyPassword)
QNetworkProxy.setApplicationProxy(proxy)
net_man=QgsNetworkAccessManager.instance()
stringlist= ""
net_man.setupDefaultProxyAndCache()
net_man.setFallbackProxyAndExcludes(proxy, stringlist)
```

How it works...

The key here is you must change the settings in two places. If we only change the stored settings, there is no way to make QGIS refresh those settings for the proxy. If we only changed the live settings, then the changes would be lost the next time we started QGIS.

There's more...

You can easily run this script in the Python Console. A better option would be to set it up in the Script Runner plugin to save time. It would be better to build your own plugin as demonstrated in the *Creating a QGIS Plugin* recipe in Chapter 1, *Automating QGIS* to make changing a proxy a simple menu choice, with a dialog to add, edit, and delete proxies.

Running QGIS scripts as scheduled tasks

The theme of this book is using PyQGIS to automate QGIS to transform it from a desktop application into a framework. Most of the time, when you are automating a process, you do so because you want to repeat that workflow over and over again. If the workflow is fairly static, with only a few simple variables, you can even automate running that task on a schedule. In this recipe, we'll automate downloading some precipitation data, and clipping it to a political boundary. Then, we'll set up that process to run automatically on a periodic basis.

Getting ready

We'll be creating a standalone QGIS script. So, you'll need to create a Python file and open it in a text editor. You will also need to install the Python pytz and schedule modules, both available on PyPI. Finally, you'll need to download the following zipped shapefile and extract it to a directory named ms in you qgis_data directory:

https://github.com/GeospatialPython/Learn/raw/master/Mississippi.zip

How to do it...

We will download a 60-day total of precipitation for the United States provided by the **National Oceanic and Atmospheric Administration (NOAA)**. This data is available as 1-day totals, which would be a more likely use case, but to ensure that we have a file with some data in it, we'll use a broader time range. Once the tar and zip-compressed file is downloaded based on the date, we'll extract the shapefiles. Then, we'll use another polygon shapefile to subset that nationwide shapefile to the state of Mississippi, all inside of a single function. Finally, we'll schedule that function to run at intervals:

1. First, we need to import the large number of libraries we'll need:

```
import urllib
import datetime
import pytz
import tarfile
import sys
import os
import time
import schedule
```

2. Now, we'll need to point to the location of the processing framework and plugins directory for our system and add that to the Python path. This example shows the path for OSX. These directories will be in the QGIS program directory for your platform:

```
sys.path.append('/Applications/QGIS.app/Contents
                /Resources/python')
sys.path.append("/Applications/QGIS.app/Contents
                /Resources/python/plugins/")
```

3. Once the Python path is updated, we can import the QGIS and Qt core libraries:

```
from qgis.core import *
from PyQt4.QtGui import *
```

4. Now, we can build the function that downloads, extracts, and clips the shapefile. This first portion downloads and extracts it:

```
def clip():
    # NOAA NEXRAD daily precip shapefile base URL
    url = "http://water.weather.gov/precip/p_download_new"
    # Get the current date
    c = pytz.timezone("US/Central")
    d = c.localize(datetime.datetime.today())
    # Convert the current date values to strings
```

```
        padded with zeros
year, month, day = d.year, str(d.month).zfill(2),
                     str(d.day).zfill(2)
# Format the date values for the URL
y_m_d = "{}/{}/{}".format(year, month, day)
# Base filename for the download and shapefile
base = "nws_precip_last60days_observed"
# Date string for file names
ymd = "{}{}{}".format(year, month, day)
# Tar'd/zipped download name
targz = "{}_shape_{}.tar.gz".format(base, ymd)
# Full precipitation data download URL
download = "{}/{}/{}".format(url, y_m_d, targz)
if not os.path.isfile(targz):
    # Download the tar-zipped shapefile
    urllib.urlretrieve(download, targz)
    # Extract the shapefile
    with tarfile.open(targz, "r:gz") as tfile:
        tfile.extractall(".")
# precipitation shapefile name
shp = "{}_{}.shp".format(base, ymd)
shx = "{}_{}.shx".format(base, ymd)
prj = "{}_{}.prj".format(base, ymd)
dbf = "{}_{}.dbf".format(base, ymd)
```

5. Then, set up the paths for the input shapefiles and the output shapefile:

```
# Shapefile to clip
in_shp = os.path.join(os.getcwd(), shp)
# Shapefile we will use to clip
clip = "/qgis_data/ms/mississippi.shp"
# Output clipped shapefile
clipped = "/qgis_data/ms/60_day_rainfall_{}.shp".format(ymd)
```

6. Next, we can set up the QGIS application object that will let us run this script standalone:

```
app = QgsApplication([],True)
QgsApplication.setPrefixPath(r"/Applications/QGIS.app
                     /Contents/Plugins", True)
QgsApplication.initQgis()
from processing.core.Processing import Processing
from processing.tools import general
Processing.initialize()
```

7. Now, we can run the clip algorithm on our shapefiles and clean up the downloads:

```
# Clip the shapefile
general.runalg("qgis:clip", in_shp, clip, clipped)
if os.path.isfile(targz):
    os.remove(targz)
    os.remove(shp)
    os.remove(shx)
    os.remove(prj)
    os.remove(dbf)
    QgsApplication.exitQgis()
```

8. Then, we set up the schedule for our clip function to run every 30 seconds. Obviously, this schedule is too frequent, and you would normally set this task to run once a day, but we want to see it right away. So, this schedule ensures that we only have to wait 30 seconds or less to see the result:

```
schedule.every(30).seconds.do(clip)
```

9. Finally, we set up a while loop to check the schedule every second:

```
while True:
    schedule.run_pending()
    time.sleep(1)
```

How it works...

In this example, we use QGIS as just a library, which really gives you an idea of the power of QGIS beyond a GUI user application. We put the geoprocessing task in a function because that's what the `schedule` module needs to run. But, you could also write it without the function and use Windows Task Scheduler, Linux cron, or OSX Automator (or cron) to run the script on a schedule. The nice part about the schedule module is it is completely pure Python and therefore cross platform.

Visualizing data in 3D with WebGL

QGIS displays data in a two dimensions even if the data is three dimensional. However, most modern browsers can display 3D data using the WebGL standard. In this recipe, we'll use the `Qgis2threejs` plugin to display QGIS data in 3D in a browser.

Getting ready

You will need to download some raster elevation data in the following zipped directory and place it in your `qgis_data` directory:

`https://github.com/GeospatialPython/Learn/raw/master/saveqml.zip`

You will also need to install the `Qgis2threejs` plugin using the QGIS plugin manager.

How to do it...

We will set up a color ramp for a DEM draped over a hillshade image and use the plugin to create a WebGL page to display the data:

1. First, we will need to import the relevant libraries and the plugin:

```
from PyQt4.QtCore import QSize
from qgis.core import QgsCoordinateReferenceSystem,
                      QgsCoordinateTransform, QgsPoint
from Qgis2threejs.api import Exporter
```

2. Next, we'll disable the QGIS automatic reprojection to keep the data display in meters:

```
iface.mapCanvas().setCrsTransformEnabled(False)
iface.mapCanvas().setMapUnits(0)
```

3. Now, we can load our raster layers:

```
demPth = "/qgis_data/rasters/dem.asc"
hillshadePth = "/qgis_data/rasters/hillshade.tif"
dem = QgsRasterLayer(demPth, "DEM")
hillshade = QgsRasterLayer(hillshadePth, "Hillshade")
```

4. Then, we can create the color ramp renderer for the DEM layer:

```
algorithm = QgsContrastEnhancement.StretchToMinimumMaximum
limits = QgsRaster.ContrastEnhancementMinMax
dem.setContrastEnhancement(algorithm, limits)
s = QgsRasterShader()
c = QgsColorRampShader()
c.setColorRampType(QgsColorRampShader.INTERPOLATED)
i = []
qri = QgsColorRampShader.ColorRampItem
i.append(qri(356.334, QColor(63,159,152,255), '356.334'))
```

```
i.append(qri(649.292, QColor(96,235,155,255), '649.292'))
i.append(qri(942.25, QColor(100,246,174,255), '942.25'))
i.append(qri(1235.21, QColor(248,251,155,255), '1235.21'))
i.append(qri(1528.17, QColor(246,190,39,255), '1528.17'))
i.append(qri(1821.13, QColor(242,155,39,255), '1821.13'))
i.append(qri(2114.08, QColor(165,84,26,255), '2114.08'))
i.append(qri(2300, QColor(236,119,83,255), '2300'))
i.append(qri(2700, QColor(203,203,203,255), '2700'))
c.setColorRampItemList(i)
s.setRasterShaderFunction(c)
ps = QgsSingleBandPseudoColorRenderer(dem.dataProvider(), 1, s)
ps.setOpacity(0.5)
dem.setRenderer(ps)
```

5. Now, we're ready to add the layers to the map:

```
QgsMapLayerRegistry.instance().addMapLayers([dem, hillshade])
```

6. We need to set up the output path for the 3D web app:

```
outputPath = "/qgis_data/3D/3d.html"
```

7. Next, we must create a dictionary of properties needed by the plugin. The most important one is the layer ID of the DEM layer:

```
props = {
    "DEM": {
        "checkBox_Clip": False,
        "checkBox_Frame": False,
        "checkBox_Shading": True,
        "checkBox_Sides": True,
        "checkBox_Surroundings": False,
        "checkBox_TransparentBackground": False,
        "comboBox_ClipLayer": None,
        "comboBox_DEMLayer": dem.id(),
        "comboBox_TextureSize": 100,
        "horizontalSlider_DEMSize": 2,
        "lineEdit_Color": "",
        "lineEdit_ImageFile": "",
        "lineEdit_centerX": "",
        "lineEdit_centerY": "",
        "lineEdit_rectHeight": "",
        "lineEdit_rectWidth": "",
        "radioButton_MapCanvas": True,
        "radioButton_Simple": True,
        "spinBox_Height": 4,
        "spinBox_Roughening": 4,
        "spinBox_Size": 5,
```

```
                    "spinBox_demtransp": 0,
                    "visible": True
                },
                "OutputFilename": outputPath,
                "PluginVersion": "1.4.2",
                "Template": "3DViewer(dat-gui).html"
            }
```

8. Now, we create the Exporter object, which creates the HTML and JavaScript files:

```
e = Exporter(iface)
```

9. Then, we add the properties and configure the Exporter:

```
e.settings.loadSettings(props)
canvas = iface.mapCanvas()
e.setMapSettings(canvas.mapSettings())
```

10. Finally, we export the files:

```
e.export(outputPath, openBrowser=True)
```

11. On your filesystem, navigate to the HTML output page and open it in a browser.
12. Follow the help instructions to move the 3D elevation display around.

How it works...

This plugin is absolutely not designed for script-level access. However, Python is so flexible that we can even script the plugin at the GUI level and avoid displaying the GUI so it is seamless to the user. The only glitch in this approach is that the save method overwrites the properties we set, so we must insert a dummy function, which prevents this overwrite.

The following image shows the WebGL viewer in action:

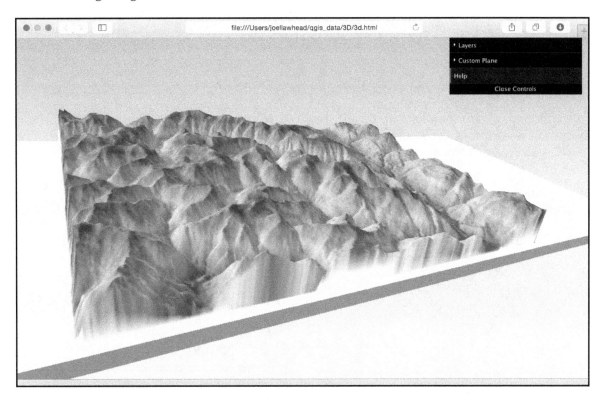

Visualizing data on a globe

Ever since the release of **Google Earth**, *spinning globe* applications are a useful and popular method of geographical exploration. QGIS has an experimental plugin called **QGIS Globe** that is similar to Google Earth; however, it is extremely unstable. In this recipe, we'll display a layer in Google Earth.

Getting ready

You will need to use the QGIS plugin manager to install the mmqgis plugin.

Make sure you have Google Earth installed from https://www.google.com/earth/.

You will also need the following dataset from a previous recipe. It is a zipped directory called `ufo`, which you should uncompress to your `qgis_data` directory:

`https://github.com/GeospatialPython/Learn/raw/master/ufo.zip`

How to do it...

We will load our layer and set up the attribute we want to use for the Google Earth KML output as descriptors. We'll use the `mmqgis` plugin to output our layer to KML. Finally, we'll use a cross-platform technique to open the file, which will trigger it to open in Google Earth:

1. First, we will import the relevant Qt and Python libraries, including the plugin:

```
from PyQt4.QtCore import *
from PyQt4.QtGui import *
from mmqgis import mmqgis_library as mmqgis
import platform
import os
```

2. Now, we'll load the layer:

```
pth = "/Users/joellawhead/qgis_data/continental-us"
lyrName = "continental-us"
lyr = QgsVectorLayer(pth, lyrName, "ogr")
```

3. Next, we'll set the output path for the KML:

```
output = "/Users/joellawhead/qgis_data/us.kml"
```

4. We'll then set up the variables which the plugin will use to make up the layer identifier in the KML. This identifier will pop up a descriptive text box in Google Earth when the user clicks on the layer:

```
nameAttr = "FIPS_CNTRY"
desc = "{{CNTRY_NAME}}"
```

5. Now, we can use the plugin to create the KML:

```
mmqgis.mmqgis_kml_export(iface, lyrName, nameAttr, desc,
                         True, output, False)
```

6. Finally, we'll use the cross-platform `QDesktopServices` object to open the KML file, which will default to opening in Google Earth:

```
qds = QDesktopServices()
url = QUrl.fromLocalFile(output)
qds.openUrl(url)
```

How it works...

The `mmqgis` plugin does a good job with custom scripts and has easy-to-use functions. While our method for automatically launching Google Earth may not work in every possible case, it is almost perfect. The following image shows the output:

Make a globe-like azimuthal orthographic projection

Sometimes, you want to provide a globe-like view on a static GIS map. Azimuthal orthographic projections can warp a layer containing countries to represent a round globe. In this recipe, we'll present data in one of these projections, named **Sphere Azimuthal Equidistant**.

Getting ready

You will need the **Clip to Hemisphere** plugin. Use the QGIS plugin manager to install it. The plugin will appear in the Processing Toolbox. You will also need to download the following zipped shapefile and extract it to your `qgis_data` directory:

```
https://github.com/GeospatialPython/Learn/raw/master/countries.zip
```

How to do it...

We are going to load the countries shapefile and clip it by centering the map on Africa and then removing the portions of the map that would be out of view on a globe. Then, we'll reproject the map to achieve the globe affect:

1. First, we import the Processing Toolbox:

   ```
   import processing
   ```

2. Next, we'll establish the path to our shapefile:

   ```
   pth = "/qgis_data/countries.shp"
   ```

3. Now, we set up variables for the paths for the clipped shapefile and the final output:

   ```
   clipped = "/qgis_data/clipped_countries.shp"
   warped = "/qgis_data/sphere.shp"
   ```

4. We then provide the latitude and longitude for the center point of the map:

   ```
   x = 22
   y = 36
   ```

5. Now, we can run the clipping algorithm to clip the shapefile providing the center point:

   ```
   processing.runalg("cliptohemisphere:clipavectorlayertothe
                   hemispherecentredonauserspecifiedpoint",
               pth,y,x,500,clipped, progress=None)
   ```

6. Finally, we can run the reprojection algorithm with the EPSG code for the Sphere Azimuthal Equidistant projection:

```
processing.runandload("qgis:reprojectlayer",clipped,
                    "EPSG:53032",warped)
```

7. Verify your map looks similar to the following image:

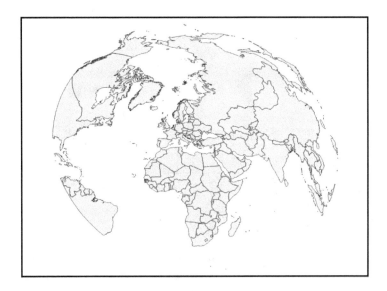

How it works...

When you are looking at a globe, a certain portion of the Earth is out of view. In order to replicate the view, we must get rid of the data that wouldn't be visible; otherwise, there will be strange artifacts, as the data would be stretched to both edges of the map. The Clip to Hemisphere plugin takes care of that problem when you give it a center point for orientation.

The following image shows the how the clipped data looks. The dark portion is the part we removed:

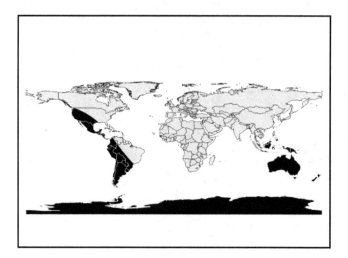

Animating a layer

QGIS increasingly supports cartographic visualizations that go beyond GIS analysis. Many of these visualizations are provided by plugins, such as the animation feature of the mmqgis plugin. You can animate lines and points to bring your thematic map to life. In this example, we'll animate hub lines generated from the nearest neighbor analysis of UFO sightings in major cities. This data is the output from the Chapter 8, *QGIS Workflows, Performing nearest neighbor analysis* recipe.

Getting ready

You will need to make sure you have the mmqgis plugin installed via the QGIS plugin manager. Once installed, the plugin will show up as its own menu.

Unzip the following two zipped datasets and extract them to a directory named ufo in your qgis_data directory:

https://github.com/GeospatialPython/Learn/raw/master/ufo.zip

You can download the second dataset here:

https://github.com/GeospatialPython/Learn/raw/master/alien_invasion.zip

You will need to create a directory named `video` in the `ufo` directory in your `qgis_data` directory.

Finally, the animation works in edit mode, so we'll need to turn off vertex markers so they don't distract from the animation. Go to the **Settings** menu and select **Options...**. In the **Options** dialog, choose the **Digitizing** tab. On the **Digitizing** tab, in the **Vertex Markers** panel, change **Marker Style** to **None**.

How to do it...

We will load a boundary layer for the United States and our line layer, which is a series of lines that radiate from points throughout the country. Once loaded, we'll be able to use the `mmqgis` animate function to create image frames in the output directory. Then, we'll be able to upload those images to a website that converts them to an animated GIF. You can see what the final product looks like here:

```
http://geospatialpython.github.io/qgis/hub_lines.gif
```

1. First, we import the `mmqgis` module:

   ```
   from mmqgis import mmqgis_library as mmqgis
   ```

2. Next, we set variables for the dataset paths:

   ```
   ufo_shp = "/qgis_data/ufo/alien_invasion.shp"
   us_shp = "/qgis_data/ufo/continental-us.shp"
   ```

3. Then, we can load the layers and add them to the map:

   ```
   ufo = QgsVectorLayer(ufo_shp, "UFOs", "ogr")
   us = QgsVectorLayer(us_shp, "US", "ogr")
   QgsMapLayerRegistry.instance().addMapLayers([ufo, us])
   ```

4. Now, we'll animate the line layer, specifying 50 frames. The more frames you have, the slower the video will run. You'll see the progress of the output in the status bar:

   ```
   mmqgis.mmqgis_animate_lines(iface, "UFOs", False, 50,
                         "/qgis_data/ufo/video")
   ```

5. Next, in a browser, go to `http://gifcreator.me`.
6. Click on the **Upload Images** button and select only the **PNG** files in the video directory.

7. Change the animation speed to `50 milliseconds`.
8. Then, click on the **Create Animation** button at the bottom of the page.
9. Finally, click on the link that says **View GIF**.
10. Your animation will appear in a new browser window similar to this image:

Index

adding, to map 263, 266

D

data density
  viewing, alpha values used 389, 390
data
  removing, from vector layer 97
  visualizing, in 3D with WebGL 415, 416, 419
  visualizing, on globe 419, 420
Debian package manager
  used, for installing PyQGIS 11
Debug Perspective 29
Digital Elevation Model (DEM)
  about 129, 338, 343, 384
  creating, from LIDAR 343, 345, 347
  elevation data, adding to line vertices 138
Dijkstra Algorithm
  reference link 328
dock widget
  creating 298, 299
dot density map
  creating 350, 352
dynamic forms
  creating, in QGIS 399, 400, 402

E

ElementTree library 79
elevation data
  adding, to line vertices with DEM 138
  used, for computing road slope 355, 356, 358
  vector contours, creating 131
elevation hillshade
  creating 129
EmittingPoint 232
error dialog
  creating 283
Esri ArcGIS 129
Esri ArcGIS services
  ArcGIS feature services 215
  ArcGIS map services 215
  using 215
Esri's ArcGIS ArcToolbox 128
EXIF tags 359
exifread
  about 362

reference link 362
expression-based labels
  using 397

F

feature
  buffering 62
  color, setting column used in CSV file 181
  labeling 218
field data
  collecting 352, 355
  reference link 353
field
  adding, to vector layer 90
file input dialog
  creating 289
  reference link 291
filled marker symbols
  about 176
  using 176
font markers
  outline, using for 187

G

GDAL
  about 116
  reference link 131
General Public License (GPL) 39
generators
  using, for layer queries 388
geocoding 318
GeoCoding plugin
  used, for geocoding addresses 318
geojson.io
  about 378
  adding, layer 378
GeoJSON
  about 100
  reference link 353
  shapefile, converting 100
geometry
  layer, filtering 57, 60
GeoPackage format
  about 112
  layer, exporting 112

Python's Script Runner plugin
   using 16, 19

Q

QGIS 2.18
   environment variables, setting 11
   environment variables, setting on Linux 12
   environment variables, setting on Windows 11
   installing, for development 10
   PyQGIS path, finding on Windows 12
   PyQGIS, installing Debian package manager
      used 11
   PyQGIS, installing RPM package manager used
      11
   Python modules, installing 10
   QGIS Python installation, location finding on other
      platforms 13
   URL, for installing 10
QGIS Cloud
   about 52
   reference link 52
QGIS Globe 419
QGIS IDE
   environment variables, adding 25
   PyQGIS API, adding 24
   PyQGIS module paths, adding to interpreter 22
   Python interpreter, adding to Windows 20
   setting up 19
QGIS Join Attributes by Location algorithm 395
QGIS map
   references 380
   tiles, creating 374, 375, 376
QGIS Markup Language (QML) 384
QGIS plugin
   distributing 39
   references 35
QGIS Python scripts
   debugger, testing 29
   debugging 26
   Eclipse, configuring 27
   QGIS, configuring 26
QGIS
   dynamic forms, creating 399, 400, 402
   HTML labels, creating 405, 406, 407
   OpenStreetMap point of interest, using 408, 409

Python console, using for interactive control 14
   reference link 30, 47, 354
   scripts, executing as scheduled tasks 412, 413,
      415
   web proxy, modifying 410
qgisio plugin 378
QgsVector
   reference link 51
QgsVectorLayer 82
Qt Creator
   about 36
   reference link 36
Qt
   about 278
   reference link 278
QuickOSM plugin 408
QUrl class
   reference link 76
QValidator
   reference link 402

R

radio buttons
   creating 292, 294
raster dataset
   sampling, with regular grid 134
raster layer
   cell size, obtaining 121
   loading 117
raster renderers
   reference link 125
raster
   bands, counting 123
   bands, swapping 124
   classifying 158
   clipping, with shapefile 164
   common extent, creating 141
   converting, to vector 160
   data value, querying at specified point 125
   footprints, creating 320, 323, 324
   georeferencing, from control points 162
   height, obtaining 122
   KML image overlay, creating 154
   mosaicing 147
   pyramids, creating 149

www.ingramcontent.com/pod-product-compliance
Lightning Source LLC
LaVergne TN
LVHW081328050326
832903LV00024B/1065